Straight Talk
about Stock
Investing

Other *Straight Talk* Books from McGraw-Hill

Vujovich
STRAIGHT TALK ABOUT MUTUAL FUNDS

Straight Talk about Stock Investing

John Slatter, CFA

McGraw-Hill, Inc.

New York San Francisco Washington, D.C. Auckland Bogotá
Caracas Lisbon London Madrid Mexico City Milan
Montreal New Delhi San Juan Singapore
Sydney Tokyo Toronto

Library of Congress Cataloging-in-Publication Data

Slatter, John.
    Straight talk about stock investing / John Slatter.
        p.   cm.
    Includes index.
    ISBN 0-07-058142-8 (pbk.)
    1. Stocks.   2. Investments.   I. Title.
    HG6041.S58   1995
    332.63'22—dc20   94-32872
                                             CIP

1 2 3 4 5 6 7 8 9 0   DOC/DOC   9 0 9 8 7 6 5 4 (PBK)

ISBN 0-07-058142-8 (PBK)

The sponsoring editor for this book was David Conti, the editing supervisor was Jane Palmieri, and the production supervisor was Donald Schmidt. It was set in Palatino by McGraw-Hill's Professional Book Group composition unit.

Printed and bound by R. R. Donnelley & Sons Company.

This publication is designed to provide accurate and authoritative information in regard to the subject matter covered. It is sold with the understanding that the publisher is not engaged in rendering legal, accounting, or other professional service. If legal advice or other expert assistance is required, the services of a competent professional person should be sought.

        —from a declaration of principles jointly adopted by a committee
          of the American Bar Association and a committee of publishers

 This book is printed on recycled, acid-free paper containing a minimum of 50% recycled de-inked fiber.

To the women I love: Beverly, Carol, Sarah, and Melanie

Contents

Preface   xiii
Acknowledgments   xv

Introduction   1

If you are looking for a book that introduces you to the world of
common stocks, you will find *Straight Talk about Stock Investing*
extremely helpful regardless of whether you are a novice investor
or one with more experience. You will learn the language of Wall Street
and the techniques of stock selection that have proven to be effective
in past decades. What's more, this book will convince you that the road
to financial security and wealth can be achieved by investing in
common stocks. It will show you how to diversify, how to avoid the
pitfalls, and why you should not be trapped into thinking mutual
funds or certificates of deposit (CDs) are the best investments. Finally,
you will learn how to select stocks that will enable you to build a
portfolio that will perform better than the general market—and better
than most professionals.

1. Setting Goals   12

If you plan to have enough money for education or retirement, it
is imperative that you save regularly and systematically. Both of these
goals are important, and both are expensive. Time is on your side if
you begin early—and if you invest in common stocks. Perhaps the most
important goal is providing for retirement. Increasingly, however,
companies are dropping their retirement plans, and some are canceling
their pledges to pay for health care after retirement. In short, it is *you*
and you alone who must make plans for a long and secure retirement

that could easily last 15 or 20 years—a long time to live from hand to mouth.

2. Where to Find Information   23

There is no need to grope in the dark when you are considering the purchase of a common stock. This chapter tells you about company annual reports as well as important periodicals, such as *The Wall Street Journal, Barron's, Financial World, Fortune, Business Week*, and *Forbes*. It also covers such important services as the *Standard & Poor's Stock Guide* and *Value Line Survey*, both crucial to making informed decisions.

3. Why Common Stocks Are Your Best Investment   40

I am constantly amazed at the number of successful people who are blithely ignorant of common stocks. Even though they can easily afford to invest, they mistakenly think that stocks are beyond the realm of understanding—and so speculative that only a reckless plunger would dare indulge. Nonsense. Not only are common stocks the real road to wealth, they are not that hard to understand. There are methods of stock selection, moreover, that will enable you to build a portfolio virtually blindfolded.

4. The Glossary   47

Nearly every glossary you have ever seen is stuck at the back of the book—where you won't notice it or use it. By placing the glossary up front, I give you a bird's-eye view of the terminology and philosophy of investing. This glossary alone is worth the price of the book. If you read it first, you will have less trouble understanding the chapters that follow.

5. Diversification and Asset Allocation   64

If you invest long enough, you will occasionally lose money. But you will also *make* money if you spread the risk of investing through diversification. This means buying 10, 15, or 20 different stocks, being careful not to concentrate your assets in any two or three industries. What's more, diversification can also mean investing in foreign stocks because these offshore markets march to a different drummer than domestic stocks. Asset allocation involves balancing your investments among common stocks, money-market funds, and bonds. If done properly—and this book shows you how—you have nothing to fear but your own timidity.

6. A Simple Way to Play the Stock Market   82

Investors often want capital gains as well as liberal dividend yields. This chapter shows you how these seemingly contradictory goals can be reached with relative ease. The 30 stocks that make up the Dow

Jones Industrial Average are all you need—plus a good calculator. This chapter also instructs you on how to calculate the standard deviation, a valuable statistical tool.

7. Some Thoughts on Analyzing Stocks   99

One of the best tools for analyzing stocks is *Value Line Survey*. Each issue contains reports on half a dozen different industries. An industry may be made up of a dozen or more companies. Unless you know what to look for, this mass of figures and tables will be meaningless. This chapter shows you how to evaluate growth, financial strength, and value, the three key ingredients in analysis.

8. The Logic of Foreign Investing   112

In years past, most Americans focused exclusively on domestic stocks, often those listed on a major exchange. Today, our horizon is much broader, largely because of advances in communications. Prudent investors now include three or four foreign stocks in their portfolios. Such stocks as Royal Dutch Petroleum; Unilever, N.V.; Schlumberger; and Reuters no longer sound so odd. This chapter offers some thoughts on how to spice up your portfolio with stocks from abroad.

9. A Detective Story   124

In this chapter, I resort to a story to explain an interesting way of constructing a portfolio. I have invented a detective on the Cleveland police force. Dan Pomodoro tells me something about police work, and I indoctrinate him in the ways of Wall Street. Don't worry about being shot. Dan keeps his six-shooter firmly in the holster till the very end.

10. How to Build a Portfolio for Growth and Income   136

Throughout this book, I harp on a few simple truths. One is that you can easily combine growth and income in one portfolio. In this chapter, I demonstrate a simple way to select stocks, using just two factors: the dividend yield and the number of institutional owners. Institutions (such as banks, mutual funds, and pension plans)—as I will repeat time and time again—are often wrong when they invest heavily in such stocks as IBM, Merck, and Philip Morris.

11. How to Reduce Risk   146

If you invest in common stocks, you must be prepared to accept a certain amount of risk. It goes with the territory. Most stocks fluctuate every day, sometimes a point or more. Every once in a while, a stock will rise or fall four or five points. In order to mitigate this risk, there are a dozen or more strategies that you should know about. They're all in Chapter 11.

12. An Interview with a Middle-Aged Couple   157

On a recent trip to London, I met Mr. and Mrs. Bryce Wicker, a farmer and his wife, who were staying at our hotel in Hampstead. While the ladies rested up before dinner, "Wick" and I hashed over an idea on how to pick stocks. I was determined to explain it fully, but he kept insisting it was time to "put on the feed bag." It took a little doing, but I finally finished my presentation—just as he collapsed on the floor from lack of food. A pity.

13. How to Combine Quality, Income, and Growth in One Portfolio   172

Here is still another method of building a portfolio. It combines two disparate elements: a group of high-quality stocks coupled with a group of high-yield stocks. In any given year, one group will do well; the other may not. By combining the two groups you will have consistently good results every year—or nearly every year.

14. An Interview with a Widow from Vermont   189

Here is yet another drama in real life. I met Olivia Terpsichorean, a retired widow from Vermont. She and I were both visiting Natchez, Mississippi, on a hot day in August. Her husband, a physician, had left her a portfolio with too many pharmaceutical stocks, most of which had seen better days. Here I show her how to achieve better diversification using the 30 stocks in the Dow Jones Industrial Average.

15. How to Achieve Income and Growth in One Portfolio   202

You may get the idea that some of my chapters have similar titles. To be sure, there is some repetition. But that's not all bad. Because these ideas are new to you, it often pays to explain them more than once. In this instance, however, I add a new wrinkle to the equation. I show you how to combine the dividend payout ratio with the yield to construct a balanced portfolio.

16. When to Sell   213

Investors tend to be worriers. The day after they buy a stock, they sit back and begin to stew about the best time to sell. If the stock goes up five points, they are sure it is only temporary. Better call a broker and see whether it's time to bail out. After all, you can't lose money by making a profit. That happens to be one of the biggest lies you'll ever hear. Long-term investing is the way to riches. Still, there are times when you should consider selling. It's all here in Chapter 16.

17. The Ultimate Road to Wealth   220

This is the chapter you've been waiting for. The method for selecting
stocks is a bit more complicated—that's why I have saved it for now. If
you have gotten this far in the book, you have proved your mettle.
You are made of sterner stuff. This method of stock selection uses four
factors: the price/earnings (P/E) ratio, the normalized P/E ratio, the
payout ratio, and the normalized payout ratio. This may all sound like
Greek, but it is really quite simple, once you read this chapter. One
word of warning. This is a growth-stock formula, so don't expect
fat dividends.

18. How to Restructure a Growth Portfolio   237

Now that you know the basics, you are ready for the heavy stuff. If you
have been investing for several years, your portfolio is probably in
dire need of some restructuring. Assuming you are a growth investor,
this chapter explains how to put your house in order.

19. How to Restructure an Income Portfolio   246

If you are more interested in income, as most investors are, then this
chapter will help you patch up your portfolio. But first you must
read Chapter 18 because it gives you the feel of the restructuring
process. Then, return to this chapter and dive right in.

20. Some Maxims on How to Keep on the Straight and Narrow   252

As a grand summary to my book, I give you a wealth of pithy maxims—
mostly dos and don'ts. It's a chapter you may want to read once a
month until you get these ideas emblazoned into your consciousness.
You may come to believe that this chapter has more good horse
sense than the rest of the book put together.

Index   263

Preface

Three or four years ago, I read several books on how to write a novel—none of which was able to transform me into another Dick Francis.

For some strange reason, the advice of one author lingers in my consciousness: "*Never, never, never* hold back anything from the book you're working on, expecting to use it in a future work. The book you're writing *now* is the one to concentrate on. Use every scrap of information, imagery, and rhetoric to make *this book* as good as you possibly can—don't worry about the next book until you get to it."

Rest assured, I have taken this suggestion into account in writing *Straight Talk about Stock Investing*. The ideas I have developed over the last 33 years are all packed between the covers of this book—at least the ones that were worth preserving. Nothing important has been left out. No secrets are being denied to my readers.

What's more, my innovative methods of stock selection are entirely my own and have not been purloined from another portfolio strategist. As a consequence, this book should be worthwhile reading for veteran investors.

On the other hand, I am assuming many of my readers are new to the world of Wall Street and may not be familiar with the jargon of the investment world. To bridge this gap, I have devoted a chapter to terms and concepts that you will need if you are to become an effective investor.

But don't stop here. Once you know the lingo, you will want to know where to find additional information such as newspapers, magazines, and advisory services.

Having written two novels, I believe that I have improved my writing skills, which should make this book easier to grasp. Three chapters, moreover, are presented in a narrative form. To do this, I have created fictional characters and put them into make-believe dramas. Those who read *Safe Investing* have told me that these animated chapters were fun to read.

Incidentally, if you have any questions as you read this book, feel free to call me at (216) 781-5600.

John Slatter, CFA
Senior Portfolio Strategist
Hickory Investment Advisors
Cleveland, Ohio

Acknowledgments

As most investors are aware, the investment scene is vast and complex—and getting more tangled, involved, and confusing every day. For that reason, I felt it imperative that I submit every chapter to my "board of directors."

But before I tell you about this "brain trust," let me pay tribute to two grand and lovely ladies who work with me at Hickory Investment Advisors. Both have been of inestimable help in figuring out the labyrinths of WordPerfect, a premier word processing system.

WordPerfect, like French, is a second language for me. When I first began to compose on a computer, I learned another system and was quite happy with it. Through no fault of my own, the rug was pulled out from under me, and I was forced at gunpoint to learn WordPerfect—I was told in no uncertain terms that WordPerfect was better and that everyone with an ounce of sense was using it. Which, of course, is entirely true. Once you know WordPerfect, it is a delight to behold.

This was some three years ago, and I am still stumbling around in the dark trying to dope out its many secrets. (The four books I purchased were all written in Greek rather than French, my second language.) Only through the patience and diligence of Susan A. Svenson and Shirley Jeung have I been able to survive this ordeal. Never at any time—when I was hopelessly mired in confusion—have these two kindhearted damsels failed to rescue me from an agonizing demise. They are consummate masters of WordPerfect, and I thank them for their perseverance through my hours of travail.

Happily, all this computer work takes place in my elegant office in the basement of my home in Chagrin Falls. This cherry-paneled office was built by my creative and talented son, Stephen W. Slatter, who also swings a lethal tennis racket and who has no compunctions about beating his old man.

And, now, back to the "board of directors."

Each is someone I know well and respect. More important, each (except for Dave Loyd) is a veteran stockbroker. Finally, each is a keen judge of investment products and a fount of wisdom. As a group, this editorial team has saved me from committing some egregious boners.

I pondered how to arrange their names and decided that, so as not to bruise any egos, I would name them alphabetically:

Paul R. Abbey, president of Hickory Investment Advisors, is a man of many talents. He is recognized as a superb athlete and is a leading golfer. Professionally, he has an exceptional background, having learned the rudiments of the business working for a bank trust department, followed by 12 years as a stockbroker before creating his own firm over six years ago.

Of all the people I have ever worked for, Paul stands alone as a man of dedication to his trade and an exemplary human being as well. My job at Hickory is to analyze portfolios and report my findings to Paul. He handles the bond purchases but also shows penetrating insight into stocks. His contributions to this book have been invaluable.

Max Lammers, a long-time broker with Prescott, Ball & Turben (now Kemper Securities), has recently been named an executive vice president with A.T. Brod in Cleveland. Max has a keen eye for the printed word and has been one of my editors on all four of my books. From what I have heard, his clients would follow him to the end of the world never doubting his leadership. Max is also an authority on horses and can ride bareback on a steed while sitting backwards.

Steve Lazarides (pronounced *Laz ar ee deez*) is a senior financial consultant with Merrill Lynch in Canton, Ohio. I have known Steve for many years since he started in the business when both of us were at Prescott, Ball & Turben. He is revered by his clients because of his sincerity and integrity. His charm and warmth make him the ideal luncheon companion.

Dr. David P. Loyd is a retired college professor who lives in Ashland, Ohio. After everyone else has read and commented on my chapters, the finished product was sent to Dave. That rascal found all sorts of things wrong. You can't hate a man for being thorough. I expect he will be my editor in chief when I write my next book, *The Age of Caesar and Cicero*. Dave is not only a great editor, he is a solid friend.

Denny Mardas is a senior vice president with Kemper Securities in Columbus, Ohio, and has a devout following of clients—largely because of his ability to pick stocks that are undervalued. Denny has an incisive mind and is a joy to do business with.

George G. Morris, CFA, is a senior vice president with Kemper Securities in Cleveland. George spent many years as a securities analyst before switching to the sales side. He happens to be my personal broker. Not only does George have an in-depth knowledge of the stock market, he is also eager to provide his clients with superior service. His only fault is his lack of concern and sympathy when he whips me on the tennis court.

Dick Niemiec (pronouced *Neemick*), a branch manager at Kemper Securities in Wooster, Ohio, is a graduate engineer and one of the best stock pickers I have ever known. He is also down to earth, easy to know, and a broker with impeccable credentials. Dick has a huge following of clients who have the utmost confidence in his approach to portfolio management.

My many thanks to these busy men and women for their help in perfecting this book.

Introduction

Although *Straight Talk about Stock Investing* gives you all the basics you'll ever need, it jumps headlong into the real meat—my simple yet effective methods for picking stocks and building a portfolio. It is here that I think you'll find this book a unique and valuable tool.

To be sure, money can be made in stocks even if you pick them blindfolded—or by throwing darts. But if you use my simple strategies, your results should be distinctly better than random selection.

In fact, each idea presented has been back-tested (verified) for its validity in past markets. Admittedly, this does not guarantee that it will work equally well year in and year out. However, bear in mind that I have made money for my clients—and for myself—for more than three decades.

If you are just getting acquainted with the world of investing, *Straight Talk about Stock Investing* explains:

- How to read and understand *The Wall Street Journal*
- What to look for when you read an annual report
- How to fathom the handy monthly reference manual, the *Standard & Poor's Stock Guide*
- How to use *Value Line Survey* for fun and profit.

In fact, I have devoted a whole chapter to explaining the secrets of reading and understanding these informative, important, and interesting publications: what to concentrate on; what to ignore.

Most important, you will find *Straight Talk about Stock Investing* easy to read, without the jargon that many professionals spew forth. If I use a term that I think may not be familiar, I will explain it. In addition, I have included a helpful glossary at the beginning—rather than at the end—of the book (see Chapter 4).

What about Mutual Funds?

Straight Talk about Stock Investing also tells you how mutual funds work and outlines their advantages and disadvantages. Unfortunately, most books and articles don't stress the key *disadvantages* inherent in mutual fund investing. I think that once you understand the shortcomings of these investments you may find my methods of stock selection to be far superior.

For instance, were you aware that mutual funds are *costly* to buy? This is because they deduct a management and expense fee from your dividends that is typically about 1.45 percent—and sometimes as high as 2 or 3 percent.

As a consequence, if the underlying dividend yield of the stocks they own is 3 percent, you actually receive only 1.55 percent. This applies to so-called no-load funds as well as those that have a load, or commission. When you consider that the average mutual fund does *not* perform even as well as the general market—or such indices as the Dow Jones Industrial Average or the Standard & Poor's 500—you might wonder why people buy them.

Nearly half of the mutual funds available today are temporarily waiving some or all of their expenses. The majority are bond and money-market mutual funds, where yields have declined because of lower interest rates. In 1992, 63% of all money-market funds waived a portion of their fee, up from 44% in 1988, according to Lipper Analytical Services. Doing this enables a fund to distinguish itself from a pack of similar funds investing in the same, low-yielding securities. In addition, fee waivers give small, new funds a "tailwind" over competitors, says Don Phillips, vice president at Morningstar, a mutual-fund rating service. "An extra 150 basis points (1.5%) can move you up an awful long way" in the rankings, he explains.

But he warned: Like banks that promise low introductory interest rates on adjustable-rate mortgages, fund companies absorb fees as a carrot to attract investors but offer no apologies when it is taken away. Once fees are reinstated, the yield inevitably goes down.

SOURCE: Amey Stone in "Smart Money," *Business Week*, July 12, 1993.

A good reason to buy a mutual fund, of course, is to achieve broad diversification. All stocks have risk, but by spreading this risk, you can reduce it to manageable proportions. If you are a small investor, this diversification can best be achieved by investing in an investment company, such as a mutual fund.

The Importance of Diversification

On the other hand, you can achieve diversification by following the concepts outlined in *Straight Talk about Stock Investing*. Although it would be ideal to own 15 or 20 stocks, adequate diversification can be achieved with as few as 10 stocks. On the other hand, it is conceivable that you would *not* be properly diversified even if you owned 30 or 40 stocks.

This is because many of the stocks in some poorly diversified portfolios are invested in the same industry. It is not uncommon, for instance, for an investor to have the bulk of assets invested in three industries, typically, utilities, oils, and banks.

This may seem strange when you realize that there are at least 80 different industries to choose from including some very obvious ones, such as food, packaging, transportation, drugs, autos, electrical equipment, insurance, automobile parts, supermarket chains, department store chains, and many more.

This book tells you precisely how to diversify your holdings so as to protect yourself from undue risk and, at the same time, achieve above-average growth of capital—including a steady stream of increasing dividends.

Asset Allocation

Tied in with diversification is asset allocation. There are at least three types of assets:

- Common stocks
- Bonds
- Money-market funds

It is important to invest the proper percentage in each of these sectors. Many people with substantial amounts of money never get beyond the most conservative of these sectors: certificates of deposit (CDs). As this book is being written, these CDs have reduced their return to a historically low level. Investors who thought they were being prudent by investing in CDs have found that their ultraconservative approach to investing is leading to financial disaster.

Why You Should Invest in Common Stocks

In this book, you will learn why common stocks are the path to achieving financial independence. To be sure, there are some risks, but you will learn how to deal with them. You will discover how much should be allocated to each of the three sectors depending on your age and temperament.

Mistakes Investors Make

In my 30-plus years in the investment business, I have analyzed hundreds of portfolios and have talked with scores of investors, both large and small. Thus, I know firsthand what mistakes they are making. Very briefly, here are a few:

- An obsession with high yield, particularly electric utility stocks. This obsession has meant near poverty for thousands, perhaps millions, of investors who bought a dozen of the highest-yielding electric utilities. More than 30 of these companies ultimately cut or eliminated their dividends. They include such well-known names as Commonwealth Edison, Pacific Gas & Electric, Middle South Utilities (now Entergy), Ohio Edison, Niagara Mohawk, Illinois Power, Consumers Power (now CMS Energy), Centerior Energy, PacifiCorp, Public Service of New Mexico, and Long Island Lighting. As you can see, the scourge of dividend bashing was not confined to small companies. On the contrary, it was the large companies that were most often the casualties.

- Failure to examine a stock before buying it. Many people buy a stock simply because they hear about it from a friend, stockbroker, or an analyst being interviewed on TV. Or perhaps they have read about it in a financial publication. *They fail to look further.* Instead, they invest $5000, $10,000, or $20,000 in something that they know practically nothing about. If you read this book, you will learn how to understand companies and where to find information that is authoritative.

- Buying the stocks of companies that are financially weak. A strong balance sheet is the key. I will outline the best way to find how much debt a company has and how to determine when a stock is too highly leveraged—a company with too much debt.

- Buying stocks that have poor records of dividend increases. Investors often buy a stock because it has a higher yield than another one in the same industry. They don't go beyond the yield. If they did, they might find a company that has not raised its payout in five years. This is the kind of stodgy company that should be avoided.

- Having a sentimental attachment to a stock simply because your father, husband, aunt, or some other member of the family worked there or gave you a block of it. I see no harm in owning such a stock as long as the amount is not too large. Quite often, these shares constitute one-third or one-half of the portfolio. Because all stocks are risky, this emotional approach can turn into a nightmare. Even blue-chip stocks fall on hard times or can be shunned by the market, including IBM, Eastman Kodak, Borden, Westinghouse Electric, Merck, Philip Morris, Manville, J.M. Smucker, U.S. Surgical, Syntex, Delta Air Lines, Baxter International, Woolworth, Dow Jones & Company, American Brands, and Navistar—and there are plenty more.

This is just a brief sample of some of the mistakes investors make. In Chapter 20, I will deal with this topic in much greater detail.

The Essence of Foreign Investing

An important advantage of *Straight Talk about Stock Investing* is that it tells you how to invest in foreign stocks. Many of the world's finest companies are situated in other countries—such as Royal Dutch Petroleum (the Netherlands); Alcatel (France); Repsol (Spain); Grand Metropolitan (United Kingdom); Ericsson Telecomm (Sweden); Elf Aquitaine (France); British Telecomm; ENDESA (Spain); Reuters (Britain); Unilever, N.V. (the Netherlands); and Hong Kong Tel (Hong Kong)—but they are available here as American Depositary Receipts (ADRs) and can be purchased in exactly the same way that General Electric, Exxon, and AT&T are purchased.

Quite often, foreign stocks are more reasonably priced and have more attractive dividend yields. What's more, foreign stocks can make your portfolio less volatile.

Systematic Methods of Picking Stocks

One reason that investors are intimidated by investments is the staggering number of alternatives to choose from. There are thousands of stocks available for consideration. On the New York Stock Exchange alone some 2600 large companies are listed. How do you know which ones to buy and which ones to shun?

This book outlines several different easy-to-use methods to sort the wheat from the chaff. These quantitative methods do not let emotion sway you from proper action. I back up my systematic approach to investing with historical verification. In other words, my methods have worked in the past—and they do not require excessive reading, luck, knowledge of industries and economics, or making judgments on the quality of a company or its stock. Most important, they do not require forecasting of any kind.

Investment Terminology— The Language of Wall Street

The typical novice investor may avoid reading such publications as *The Wall Street Journal, Forbes, Barron's, Financial World,* or *Business Week.* One reason is the inability to understand the terminology. To overcome this problem, I will explain in understandable English what these frequently used terms and expressions mean:

- Price/earnings (P/E) ratio
- Dividend yield
- Short selling
- Leverage
- Compound interest
- Indicated yield
- Dividend payout ratio
- Preferred stock
- Debenture
- Margin
- Net worth

and scores more.

An Example of One of My "Systems"

To get a glimpse of one of my stock-picking systems, let's look at a typical list of 50 blue-chip stocks, as of year-end 1987. This list appears frequently in *Barron's.*

The first step is to calculate the average yield of these 50 stocks on that date. It was 3.73 percent. The second step was to segregate the stocks that had a yield no lower than 3.73 percent. As you can imagine, there were quite a few—21 in fact.

The next step was to average the number of institutional owners. They ranged from a high of 1750 (for IBM) to a low of 80 (for GATX). Those that had the fewest institutional owners (such as mutual funds, banks, and pension plans) were put into one group. Here they are and how they performed in the following 12 months (from year-end 1987 to year-end 1988):

AlliedSignal	+ 15.94%
American Brands	+ 57.83
Boeing	+ 63.85
Citicorp	+ 38.93
CSX	+ 9.01
Detroit Edison	+ 29.91
GATX	+ 46.75
Norfolk-Southern	+ 19.52
Southern California Edison	+ 6.15
United Technologies	+ 21.40
Weyerhaeuser	− 2.74
Wisconsin Energy	+ 20.00
Average performance	+ 27.14%

Now, let's look at the stocks preferred by institutions (also taken from the same list of 50 stocks). This is how they performed in the one-year period ending December 31, 1988:

AT&T	+ 6.48%
Amoco	+ 8.70
BellSouth	+ 9.62
Du Pont	+ 1.00
General Motors	+ 36.05
IBM	+ 5.52
Mobil	+ 16.29
Pfizer	+ 24.40
Schlumberger	+ 13.48
Average performance	+ 13.50%

This method of picking stocks, as you can see, is extremely simple. Yet it seems to work most of the time. To be sure, no method works all the time. That's why it is necessary to validate a method before presenting it to my readers. I keep prior issues of the *Stock Guide* and *Value Line* so that I can verify an idea before I start to use it.

This is but one method presented in this book of building a portfolio. In Chapter 5 I present additional systems that you may find illuminating. I have given a summary of five tests that show how an investor could have designed a portfolio using just two financial factors. In five verification or back tests, these portfolios outpaced the Dow Jones Industrial Average four times. This is no mean feat as any veteran investor will tell you. If you can outperform the Dow Jones Industrial Average—and do it on a consistent basis— you can pat yourself on the back. Very few individual investors— and only a handful of professionals, for that matter—have been able to do it.

But, getting back to the table, in the one instance in which this stock selection method failed to do better than this popular index, the results were extremely close. If we take the five tests and average them, the results are quite impressive. The portfolios created by my systematic stock picking method advanced 16.57 percent in the indicated one- and two-year periods. By contrast, the Dow Jones Industrial Average climbed only 11.51 percent. As you can appreciate, that's a considerable edge in favor of the "Slatter System" for building a portfolio.

Years	Slatter System (%)	Dow Jones Industrial Average (%)
1985–1987	+ 32.51	+ 22.82
1988–1989	+ 29.88	+ 30.49
1991–1992	+ 13.83	+ 7.49
1972–1973	− 9.27	− 13.06
1992–June 1993	+ 16.39	+ 9.80
Averages	+ 16.57	+ 11.51

If you are not convinced that this method is your cup of tea, you might like to examine another technique for constructing a portfolio. The table below illustrates further back-checking of my method against the Dow Jones Industrial Average.

Years	Slatter System (%)	Dow Jones Industrial Average (%)
1975–1976	+ 32.27	+ 22.67
1976–1977	− 6.85	− 12.87
1986–1987	+ 10.80	+ 5.88
1991–1992	+ 11.92	+ 7.49
1992–August 27, 1993	+ 26.92	+ 13.58
Averages of five periods	+ 15.01	+ 7.35

Throughout the book, I will present tables showing how a particular method of investing has worked in prior years. A skeptic might infer that I have selected years in which the system was successful, while omitting years in which it failed.

Admittedly, no system works to perfection all the time. In my illustrations, however, I have tried to select years that will give you the flavor of the system. It goes without saying that I would not include the system if it did not have a good record, but to include an exhaustive table for each year would turn this book into a research paper rather than a readable book.

How to Build or Restructure Your Portfolio

This book also presents several chapters on portfolio restructuring. To explain this concept, I dramatize a number of situations, showing exactly how I have helped individual investors make the changes necessary to turn their portfolio into a diversified list of stocks that will outperform the market in most years. Each of these chapters takes a hypothetical investor, such as a widow or a middle-aged couple, and dramatizes how I would help them restructure their portfolio or show them a method of stock selection.

Case Histories to Guide and Entertain You

None of these case histories, incidentally, involves an actual person or any of my clients. Rather, they are imaginary persons with imaginary names. For instance, I do not know a man named Bryce Glabrous

Wicker, the farmer from upstate New York whom I describe in Chapter 12. The entire story is fictional and is used to demonstrate a method of building a stock portfolio. Nor do I know a detective named Succo D. Pomodoro—he prefers to be called Dan—who appears in Chapter 9. He is a figment of my imagination. On the other hand, the method of stock selection discussed in this chapter is one that you might find valuable.

Exit fees are poison to investors. The minute you buy a fund with a 5% deferred sales charge, for example, you are 5% poorer. Either you pay this fee now to escape, or you will have to stay long enough for the fund operator to gouge the same sum out of your portfolio through annual 12b-1 charges.

Moral: Stick with fund sponsors that have a long history of keeping their expense ratios below average. Among the no-load fund families that consistently charge 1% or less per year in expenses are Vanguard, USAA, Twentieth Century, Federated, and Nicholas.

SOURCE: Jason Zweig in *Forbes*, June 21, 1993.

Summary

If you are looking for a book that explains the world of common stocks, you will find *Straight Talk about Stock Investing* extremely helpful, regardless of whether you are a novice or an experienced investor. What's more, this book will convince you that the road to financial security and wealth can be achieved by investing in common stocks. It will show you how to diversify, how to avoid the pitfalls, why you should not be trapped into thinking mutual funds are the best investment, and how to select stocks that will enable you to do better than the general market.

You will also learn that very few investors can gain financial security and wealth—including the so-called professionals, such as banks, insurance companies, pension plans, mutual funds, and stock brokers. On the other hand, it is likely that many individual investors do even worse than the professionals.

In short, *Straight Talk about Stock Investing* will help keep you from making some of the same blunders that less enlightened investors are making.

If All Else Fails...

One final note. If you want further clarification on anything that appears in this book, again, feel free to call me at (216) 781-5600 (my office). Or, you may write to me at Hickory Investment Advisors, 1801 East 12th Street, Suite 210, Cleveland, Ohio 44114.

Annual Reports

The Public Register's Annual Report Service offers current financial information on over 2000 publicly held companies. To receive free annual reports, dial 1-800-426-6825. Information requested will be processed within 24 hours and sent by overnight courier to you at no charge. Or, you can fax your request directly to the Bay Tact Corporation, fax number: (203) 974-2229.

1
Setting Goals

Unless you have an exceptionally high income or have inherited great wealth, you will be faced with the onerous task of planning your financial future. The big problem: there is rarely enough money to do all the things you want to do. If you are a well-educated, ambitious, and serious person, you have any number of things to spend your current income on:

- Food, shelter, and clothing
- Insurance
- Car repairs and gasoline
- Lunches
- Dining out
- Newspapers and magazines
- Entertainment
- Gifts and donations
- Domestic help
- Club and association dues
- Savings for college
- Money for medical emergencies (because health coverage never pays it all)
- Money for the unexpected (such as a new roof, new appliances, money to support your aging parents—and there are plenty more)

- Vacations
- Cash to tide you over when you are looking for a new job

Don't Shortchange Your Retirement Plans

Admittedly, I left out a few things. But it all adds up to one conclusion: saving money for retirement is not easy—with planning or without. Even if you are fortunate enough to make a substantial income, let's say $200,000 a year, you can still end up shortchanging your retirement plans. The reason? If you make big bucks, you tend to spend big bucks.

I'm not a psychologist, so I cannot explain why people spend more than they make. Could it be vanity or pride? If you make a huge income, you aren't going to be satisfied with the same house that someone making $50,000 would buy. Your peers are spending $500,000 or $1 million for houses—which means you feel foolish if you don't.

The same holds true for the vacation spots or foreign travel you select. Or the clothes you buy.

Will You Be Forced to Retire?

I won't belabor the point, which is simply this: eventually you will grow old and want to slow down or retire. In some companies, you will be forced to retire at age 65. That's assuming you don't get the ax at age 53.

And, of course, there is always the threat of disability. To be sure, it doesn't hit a large percentage of people, but if it does, the impact on your finances can be devastating. Some people buy insurance for such contingencies. Self-employed individuals are particularly vulnerable.

The important first step in setting goals is to start setting aside a fixed percentage of your income for such future goals as education and retirement. Of the two, I think that education is the most daunting. When my son attended Dartmouth College, the annual tuition was $3000. When I attended Colgate University, it was $400. Obviously, the current costs are many times these amounts. And they will escalate even further as the years go by. If you plan to pay for this, you had better be aware that the task will be Herculean.

If you have already passed this stage in your life, then you are facing the equally significant problems of having enough money to maintain some semblance of your preretirement standard of living.

Some Flaws in Your Thinking

Of course, you may be convinced that there is no problem because your company has a good retirement program, and the federal government will assist by doling out your Social Security.

There could be some flaws in your thinking, however. For one thing, not every company will honor its commitments. Increasingly, companies are dropping their retirement plans. They are also canceling their pledges to pay for the health care of their retired employees. My wife, a nurse, worked for a large Cleveland hospital that took this route to save money.

What it all adds up to is this: there are a lot of "bad guys in black hats" out there who don't give a hoot what happens to you. Therefore, it is up to you to make plans that do not depend on the company or the government.

Social Security—Can You Count on It?

Even the government cannot be trusted. The latest tax law took another swipe at Social Security by making higher-income folks pay an increasing amount of income tax on payments received. As the federal deficit gets further out of whack, who knows what will happen to Medicare or Social Security?

Admittedly, this is scary talk. But is it really unrealistic?

If you have read this far, you might be feeling a little shell-shocked. I hope so, because my objective has been to convince you that you can't continue to buy $1200 suits, $40,000 cars, and million-dollar homes. You are not that rich. And if you are, you probably don't have to read *Straight Talk about Stock Investing*.

Living in a $300,000 Shanty

The first step in setting goals is to decide *now* that you are going to save and invest some money for the future. If it means whittling down your standard of living a half notch, so be it. Of course, your friends, neighbors, and business associates will be shocked when they find out that your finances are so shaky that you are now forced to wear shoddy $500 suits, drive a $20,000 car, and live in a shanty worth only $300,000.

On the other hand, they probably won't notice because they have problems of their own. And even if they do notice, it won't necessarily ruin your life. True, they may feel somewhat superior to you, but that is good. If they felt *inferior* to you, they would be envious. They might even loath you. All things considered, it is better for your friends, neighbors, and business associates to feel superior to you because you can't afford $1200 suits, $40,000 cars, and million-dollar domiciles.

Dividend Checks Rarely Get Smaller

Then again, you can feel superior to them because you are saving your money and buying stocks on a systematic basis. When you own over 40 stocks—as I do—you feel rather good about yourself. If Social Security doesn't work out at least you have companies all over the world sending you quarterly dividend checks. Best of all, these dividend checks rarely get smaller. They just keep growing, growing, and growing. Which is more than you can say for bonds, CDs, annuities, or most any other asset.

It's clear that your first step is to do something about your financial situation. It doesn't matter whether you're making $40,000 a year, $80,000 a year, or $120,000 a year. It's not the amount you bring home that matters—it's how you handle it.

Admittedly, it will be tough, though not impossible, to send your offspring to college and save for retirement on $40,000 a year. Perhaps part of your planning, then, is to do something about your income. It could entail getting more education, working harder, or becoming more serious about your career. Because this book is not geared to helping you manage your career, I won't dwell on this very long. Instead, I will assume that your income is large enough for you to save for retirement by making some changes in what you spend.

The Years Are Rolling By—Are You Ready for Retirement?

Once you get to the age of 50, retirement looms ever more imminent. Given a normal retirement at age 65, you have 15 years to get things rolling. If your kids are through college and your mortgage is out of the way, you should be able to set aside some meaningful amounts. At a very minimum, you should be able to save 15 to 25 percent of your after-tax income. Let's say you are making $75,000 a year, after taxes. If you save 20 percent, that's $15,000 a year. At age 65, assuming it grows at 10 percent a year, you will end up with $476,593.

To be sure, that doesn't sound like a big fortune. However, let's say you put the same money in the bank at 3 percent. This annual deposit of $15,000 will build up to only $278,986 by age 65. Neither of these calculations has taken into consideration inflation, taxes, or commissions. Obviously, none of the latter are your friends in your quest to amass a fortune.

Because I have no knowledge of your salary, your age, or your ability to save, I cannot give you very exact advice on how to proceed.

Did You Pick Some Wealthy Parents?

My main objective is to convince you that you *do something about the problem.* It may not be enough, but it will be better than simply drifting along waiting for someone to die and leave you a ready-made portfolio. On the other hand, that could happen. Some of my friends and neighbors are doing quite well precisely because they were lucky enough to pick wealthy parents, aunts, uncles, or whatever. I was not. Every cent I have was amassed by savings made by my wife and me. Despite this handicap, we are not worried about retirement. That's because these benevolent companies are going to send me fat checks for the rest of my life. A partial list includes: General Electric, Peoples Energy, Detroit Edison, British Telecomm, Elf Aquitaine, Amoco, Royal Dutch Petroleum, Eli Lilly, Sara Lee, Banc One, Cedar Fair, American Water Works, Hanson, PLC, Indiana Energy, Houghton-Mifflin, United Technologies, ConAgra, and others.

You will notice some unfamiliar names. Most of them are foreign. The reason I own foreign stocks is simple: it means less risk to my portfolio. Each of those foreign markets is influenced by factors that are peculiar to that country, its economy, its politics, and its way of life. No two markets act the same. In addition, most of those markets have stocks that are cheaper than those available in the United States. They have lower P/E ratios and higher yields.

But this is getting a little far afield. The point to be made is this: I have not inherited any money. I have never made a huge annual income. On the other hand, I enjoy a good standard of living, have an excellent home, and more suits of clothes than I will ever need. In other words, I did not buy stocks at the expense of my standard of living.

But I did buy stocks. And I will continue to buy stocks until I run out of money. If I can do it, I see no reason why you can't do it as well.

If you have never bought stocks, you may get a sinking feeling in your stomach every time someone tells you to start buying stocks. You may be fearful that you will pick the wrong one, and it will drop out of sight. After all, you could have been unlucky enough to buy IBM at $100 a share. As this is written, it is $45. If IBM isn't safe, why should any sane person want to buy stocks?

Just to make you feel a little better, I am one of the people who bought IBM at $100 a share. But I didn't sink my life's savings into it. Most of the rest of my stocks have done far better. To be sure, my Eli Lilly has been rather mistreating me of late. Even so, I have owned it long enough to be well ahead of the game. As you can see, even a so-called expert like John Slatter takes his lumps once in a while.

If you are fiddling around and not willing to take the plunge, I can understand your fears. Stocks go up and down—that's what they have been doing for decades. And they are not about to stop just because you have decided to become an investor.

Stocks Have Been Kind to Investors

As I point out in later chapters, stocks have been kind to investors in the past. Far kinder than the alternatives.

In other chapters, you will learn ideas that will guide you in making stock selections. But even if you ignore all of this advice, you can make money in the stock market simply by buying *something*. Let's say, for instance, that you decide to buy two stocks every year. If you are now 50 years old, you will own 30 stocks by the time you retire. Let's further assume that you know nothing about stocks and don't intend to learn. You simply buy the 30 stocks in the Dow Jones Industrial Average, painstakingly, alphabetically. I don't necessarily recommend this idea, but I am sure it would work reasonably well if you stuck with it until you owned all 30.

Let's further assume that you started such a program five years ago. Thus, you now own 10 stocks. Suppose you invested $2000 in each of these stocks and you did it on December 31st of each year. In other words, you bought two stocks each time, beginning at year-end 1988. Table 1-1 shows what your portfolio would look like.

My strategy was to buy about $2000 of each stock, rounded to the nearest share. The total amount invested after five years came to $20,073.63. Table 1-2 shows the values at the end of June 1993.

One of the biggest fears about investing is the thought that you may be plunging into the market at exactly the wrong time. It seems that this fear exists even when stocks are at their nadir. Back in late 1974, for instance, after the market had lost about 40 percent of its value, many analysts were not convinced that it was a good time to buy. The fear existed that stocks were still vulnerable. In retrospect, we now know that this low point presented investors with one of the greatest opportunities of all time. But it wasn't apparent to those who lived

Table 1-1

Stocks purchased, two a year, beginning at year-end 1988, using the 30 stocks in the Dow Jones Industrial Average. Stocks chosen alphabetically.

	Date purchased	Price of stock ($)	Value of purchase ($)
AlliedSignal	12-31-88	32.50	2,015.00
ALCOA	12-31-88	56.00	2,016.00
American Express	12-31-89	34.88	1,987.88
AT&T	12-31-89	45.50	2,002.00
Bethlehem Steel	12-31-90	14.75	2,006.00
Boeing	12-31-90	45.38	1,996.50
Caterpillar	12-31-91	43.88	2,018.25
Chevron	12-31-91	69.00	2,001.00
Coca-Cola	12-31-92	41.88	2,010.00
Disney, Walt	12-31-92	43.00	2,021.00
Total invested			20,073.63

through it. Similarly, today seems like a high point, with only limited upside potential. Time will tell whether this is the case.

If you are just about to begin an investment program, it is probable that you are a timid soul, fearful that your life's savings will be swallowed up in a cataclysmic abyss.

I am not able to offer you any advice, since my 30-odd years on the investment scene have not given me the power to view the future. The only advice I can offer is this: if you have money to invest, you should invest it. In the long run, you will fare better than the milquetoasts who buy CDs and other bland fixed-income instruments.

To demonstrate how this could have worked out in the recent past, I went back to year-end 1986—just 10 months prior to the infamous Crash of 1987. Suppose you had $45,000 to invest and wondered whether it was a safe time to put your money to work. For some answers, refer to Table 1-3. It is assumed that you invested $3000 in each of 15 stocks. For simplicity, I used the first 15 that were in the Dow Jones index at that time.

This performance was not particularly impressive because the market, as represented by the Dow Jones Industrial Average, actually did considerably better. During the 1986–1993 period, the index climbed from 1895.95 to 3516.08, a gain of 85.45 percent.

Table 1-2

Value of 10 stocks on June 30, 1993.

	Price of stock ($)	Value of purchase ($)
AlliedSignal	66.75	4,138.50
ALCOA	70.00	2,520.00
American Express	32.25	1,838.25
AT&T	63.00	2,772.00
Bethlehem Steel	18.75	2,550.00
Boeing	37.00	1,628.00
Caterpillar	74.88	3,444.25
Chevron	87.75	2,544.75
Coca-Cola	43.00	2,064.00
Disney, Walt	40.75	1,915.25
Total value		25,415.00

NOTE: Money deposited in bank at 3 percent yields $21,236.

The Importance of Selectivity

On the other hand, the purchase of these 15 stocks demonstrates that you have nothing to fear from the market itself. To be sure, it has its share of rallies and sinking spells, but the performance of its individual components has a greater bearing on how well you will fare. Some stocks more than doubled during this period; others actually lost ground. This is good evidence that *selectivity* is more important than market forecasting. For its part, forecasting is a no-win game. No so-called expert—at least not to my knowledge—has a consistent record of forecasting the course of stock prices.

If you are curious about what the annual percentage gain was in this $7\frac{1}{2}$-year period, it was 7.34 percent. This alone would have been better than most fixed-income instruments such as CDs. But if you add in the dividends, the gain would have been much more impressive. Because doing this would entail countless calculations, I have not made this determination. Suffice it to say, the results would have been impressive because even the beginning yield was 3.75 percent. Although not all of these stocks have increased their dividends in the period, most have. The total picture of these 15 stocks is shown in Table 1-4.

Table 1-3

Stocks from the Dow Jones Industrial Average, as of December 31, 1986. Stocks selected alphabetically.

	Stock price change 12-31-86 to 6-30-93 (%)
AlliedSignal	+ 66.36
ALCOA	+ 106.54
American Can (now Primerica)	− 6.17
American Express	+ 13.91
AT&T	+ 152.00
Bethlehem Steel	+ 200.00
Chevron	+ 93.39
Du Pont	+ 68.30
Eastman Kodak	+ 9.29
Exxon	+ 88.59
General Electric	+ 122.67
General Motors	+ 34.85
Goodyear Tire	+ 102.99
Inco	+ 91.49
IBM	− 59.06
Average price change of 15 stocks	+ 72.34

But enough about setting your goals. The message should be clear. If you have not already done so, it is high time that you began buying common stocks to ensure a secure and comfortable retirement. If you live to be 90, you will be glad you heeded this advice.

Before investing, create an emergency reserve of up to three months' living expenses, says Harold Evensky, an investment adviser in Coral Gables, Florida. Keep it in liquid form—money-market funds or, for slightly higher yields, short-term bond funds.

SOURCE: Carole Gould in "Successful Investing," *The New York Times*, August 8, 1993.

Table 1-4

Number of shares, current value, and annual dividends of the 15 stocks selected as of year-end 1986.

Shares owned, 6-30-93	Current dividend ($)	Current value ($)	Annual dividend ($)
75 AlliedSignal	1.16	5,006	87.00
89 ALCOA	1.60	6,230	142.40
53 Primerica	0.64	2,789	33.92
106 American Express	1.00	3,419	106.00
120 AT&T	1.32	7,560	158.40
480 Bethlehem Steel	None	9,000	None
66 Chevron	3.50	5,792	231.00
108 Du Pont	1.76	5,090	190.08
66 Eastman Kodak	2.00	3,300	132.00
86 Exxon	2.88	5,687	247.68
70 General Electric	2.52	6,703	176.40
91 General Motors	0.80	4,040	72.80
144 Goodyear Tire	0.60	6,120	86.40
255 Inco	0.40	5,738	102.00
25 IBM	2.16	1,234	54.00
Totals		77,718	1,820.08

Saving naturally and necessarily comes before investing because we can only invest what we have previously saved. Buying straw hats in the fall or Christmas cards in January and saving through the many other daily forms of conscientious underspending can make a splendid difference over the years—particularly when matched with a sensible long-term approach to investing.

SOURCE: Charles D. Ellis in *Investment Policy, How to Win the Loser's Game,* Second Edition, 1993, Business One Irwin.

Write out your long-term goals and your long-term plans—and stay with them. As every great coach advises his or her athletes: "Plan your play—and play your plan!"

If your long-term investment policy is not working out in the short run (e.g., stocks dropped sharply in price), your first assumption should be that you will "double up"—because you *know* you took considerable time and care in making your original policy decision.

SOURCE: Charles D. Ellis in *Investment Policy, How to Win the Loser's Game*, Second Edition, 1993, Business One Irwin.

2
Where to Find Information

Unless you are going to do exactly what your broker tells you to do, it's necessary to do some reading. Brokerage houses generally provide reports on the stocks they like. Many novice investors fail to read this material because it is often written for the more sophisticated institutional investor.

These reports tend to assume that you are already familiar with the company. As a consequence, they may not explain the nature of their business, their products, or their services. Usually, these write-ups concentrate on recent developments, which can be meaningless if you are not familiar with what has gone on in the past. If you are an uninformed investor, this may leave you in the dark and confused as to how to proceed.

At the other extreme are so-called basic reports, which are exhaustive and filled with tables, graphs, and arcane language. I have come across treatises that were 50 to 100 pages long. It is unlikely that you will ever see one, however, because they are reserved for portfolio managers at institutions.

Written by analysts with in-depth knowledge, some of these analyses are real masterpieces, which is a pity because no one ever reads them except the author's boss. On the other hand, these gems are so impressive that no one would dare throw them away. It would be like pitching the Holy Bible in the trash bin.

In most instances, these erudite creations are carefully filed away for future reference. Then, if the portfolio manager's boss asks him why he bought XYZ company—which turned out to be an unmitigated dud—he quickly goes to the file and whips out the 89-page report to cast the blame where it belongs: on the heinous cad who conned him into this monumental blunder.

What about Brokers?

One thing I would like to make clear: very few brokers are vultures, although they seem to have this reputation. At least many brokers tell me this. Since I was a broker myself for several years, I rather doubt that the average investor views his or her own broker in this light.

In any event, there are capable brokers, and there are those that should be banned from the business. I suspect that this applies as well to doctors, storekeepers, engineers, politicians, secretaries, haberdashers, men of the cloth, teachers, plumbers, accountants, baby sitters, and street cleaners.

Your job is to find one who has a good reputation and who is interested in *your* welfare. I have been dealing with brokers for 32 years and have the highest regard for many of them. The ones who helped me edit this book, for instance, all fall in that category.

Above all, you want a broker who likes stocks and is not peddling "packaged products." The minute your broker begins to promote new issues, secondary offerings, convertibles, preferred stock, options—or anything else that is not a pure-and-simple common stock—make a hasty retreat. One more caution: when your broker tells you there is "no commission," scream for the cops. The price of the product being foisted on you will drop by 10 percent a few days after the stock has been sold to the public. No matter what the broker tells you, there is, indeed, a commission—and a big one.

What Lies Ahead?

But, getting back to where to look for information. This chapter will show you where to find important sources of information: the *Standard & Poor's Stock Guide* and "tear sheets" and *Value Line Survey*. I will also explain what to look for in the financial pages of *The Wall Street Journal* and *Barron's*.

In case you are curious about what I read, here is a complete list of the publications I subscribe to or have access to at my office:

The Wall Street Journal

The Financial Analysts Journal

The New York Times (particularly the Sunday business section)

Barron's

Financial World

Fortune

AAII Journal

The Economist

U.S. News and World Report

Newsweek

Time

The Cleveland Plain Dealer

Business Week

Forbes

In addition to these publications—most of which are readily available to investors—I also scan or read all reports issued by a host of Wall Street firms, including:

Merrill Lynch*

Cowen*

PaineWebber

Legg Mason

Josephthal Lyon & Ross

Morgan Stanley*

Smith Barney Shearson

*my favorites

Admittedly, to read all of these publications would make a normal person go blind. It would also imply that my ability to read fast is highly developed. Since I am not blind and do not know how to speed-read, you can conclude that I don't read this material cover to cover.

Instead, like most people I pick and choose. For instance, I read every word written about the Cleveland Indians, since I am a lifelong baseball freak. Except for articles on tennis (I have a wicked serve) and football, I skip everything in the sports section on golf, basketball, hockey, and soccer.

The same thing applies to the magazines I subscribe to. If an article strikes a responsive chord, I may read it to the bitter end. If not, I may not get beyond the headline.

Of all the material that crosses my desk, the following are the items that I deem most valuable. First and foremost is *The Wall Street Journal*. I am such a nut on this periodical that I even seek it out when I am on vacation. On a recent trip to London, for instance, I first read the London *Times* (now available for 30 pence), noting with particular disgust that they devoted very little space to baseball. (It was during the playoffs, and the only mention was a short paragraph each day, saying who had won the game. On Sunday, the coverage was slightly better. Even so, you could tell the reporter usually covered cricket, not baseball.)

Surprisingly, *The Times* does not ignore American stocks. Every day they list nearly 400 stocks, giving the latest price and the price the prior day. Fortunately, *The Wall Street Journal* did not abandon me. For 1 pound (about $1.50), you can buy a copy of *The Wall Street Journal Europe*. It gives all stock prices for the stocks listed on the New York, American, and OTC (over-the-counter) issues. Although not as complete as the U.S. edition, the European version is reasonably good. In any event, I devoured each issue as I sped in a British train to such cities as Oxford, Cambridge, York, and Portsmouth. While other people looked at scenery, I checked to see how rich I was becoming. At that particular time, my stocks were leaping merrily upward. If we were bounding about London itself on the Underground, I had my *Wall Street Journal Europe* clutched close to my vest while my wife kept track of when it was time to disembark and go look at a cathedral, dine at a pub, buy a mug at Harrods, look at books in Dillon's, or visit the British Museum.

The Magic of *The Wall Street Journal*

But getting back to the domestic version of *The Wall Street Journal*. To my way of thinking, it stands head and shoulders above everything else. The *Journal* is authoritative, well written, and interesting. It not only covers financial subjects but has a variety of articles on economics, politics, books, movies, sports, and almost any other subject you can think of. Even if I didn't own a single stock, I would not want to miss *The Wall Street Journal*.

The first thing I read is the front page of the first section (there are three). There are two columns on the left side, one on investments and one on general news. Each brief, one-paragraph article touches on an important development, with a page number if the topic is treated in full elsewhere.

After reading these two columns, I glance at the two stories on either side of the front page. They are in-depth articles on topics that are usually of importance to readers interested in a particular company, industry, or political or economic subject.

In addition, the front page also contains a column near the right side that varies from one day to the next. One day a week, for instance, this column deals with taxes. Another day it deals with labor news. If you read nothing else, the front page is worth the price of the paper.

After a brief reading of this page, I quickly flip to the third section, which deals more specifically with stocks and contains the price changes of every stock you ever heard of—plus many you have never heard of. This is the section that consumes most of my reading time. I first want to check the "New Highs" and "New Lows." Maddeningly, the *Journal* often tries to hide this column—it is rarely in the same place two days running. But, rest assured, it is in there somewhere.

Keep a Good Supply of Felt-Tip Pens Handy

Once I find it, I get out my green felt-tip pen and check off every stock I have an interest in that has hit a new high. These are the stocks that I own personally or that we have in our clients' portfolios. A new high takes place when a stock reaches its highest level in the past 52 weeks. In the old days, the new highs were based on the highest price in the calendar year. The new method makes more sense. I also look at the new low list and cringe if I see one of my stocks there. Fortunately, I don't do much cringing.

I am not sure how important these two lists are because I have never seen a study of what happens to stocks that appear there. I suspect, however, that you should not run out to sell one of your stocks when it hits the new high list. The chances are that it will pop up there again and again before it finishes its ascent.

A good friend of mine—Dick Niemiec, a broker of great sophistication and ironclad integrity with Kemper Securities in Wooster, Ohio—thinks that the best place to find bargains is the new low list. Since Dick has picked a lot of winners, he may be on to something. If you have lots of time, you might find it interesting to find out which of us is right.

Just for the fun of it, I made a ministudy of this concept, that is, however, far from definitive. Even so, you might like to examine my handiwork.

New Highs and New Lows

Out of the 2600-odd stocks listed on the New York Stock Exchange, only a handful will appear on this list on any given day. A typical number might be 50 or 100. The list of new lows is, of course, an embarrassment.

I have often wondered if it would make sense to invest in the stocks on the new high list. You have often heard the axiom, "buy low and sell high." How could you logically think it astute to buy a stock that was selling at its highest price in the past 12 months? I decided to check on this idea.

To do so, I grabbed an old issue of *Barron's* because we don't save *Wall Street Journal*s for more than a few weeks. The one I pulled out was dated November 23, 1992, or nearly a year earlier. I selected the first 15 stocks that seemed somewhat familiar. In other words, I ignored those that were obscure.

Table 2-1 shows the 15 selected, along with the price on the prior Friday, November 20, 1992. I then checked the price in the current *Wall Street Journal* of August 25, 1993. During that period of time, these stocks performed quite well, advancing an average of 20.14 percent.

Table 2-1

Stocks reaching new highs on November 20, 1992, and how they performed from that date until August 24, 1993.

	Price 11-20-92 ($)	Price 8-24-93 ($)	Stock price change (%)
AT&T	47.62	58.38	+ 22.57
Baldor Electric	21.33	22.62	+ 6.05
Bank of New York	49.25	54.25	+ 10.15
Beckman Instruments	23.75	22.25	− 6.32
Berkshire Hathaway	10,075.00	17,100.00	+ 69.73
Blockbuster	17.50	26.88	+ 53.57
Capital Holding	33.00	41.38	+ 25.38
Carlisle	23.00	31.62	+ 37.50
Cedar Fair	27.75	29.62	+ 6.76
Central Hudson G&E	30.88	35.00	+ 13.36
Century Telephone	26.67	29.38	+ 10.16
Chrysler	29.00	42.25	+ 45.69
Church & Dwight	35.75	23.88	− 33.22
Citizens Utility A	29.38	33.12	+ 12.77
Comsat	24.12	30.88	+ 27.98
Average performance of 15 stocks			+ 20.14

During the same period, the Dow Jones Industrial Average also advanced but not as much, only 12.75 percent.

You may think that the price of Berkshire Hathaway is a misprint. It is not. This is Warren Buffett's company. It demonstrates rather dramatically that avoiding high-priced stocks can be a mistake.

Trying to Stop a Freight Train

So much for the stocks on the new high list. They seem to do quite well, which says something for momentum. It may be analogous to trying to stop a freight train.

You may be curious as to what happened to the stocks on the new low list (see Table 2-2). After all, these stocks hit the list because investors were fed up with them. They had reverse "momentum."

Table 2-2
Stocks reaching new lows on November 20, 1992, and how they performed from that date until August 24, 1993.

	Price 11-20-92 ($)	Price 8-24-93 ($)	Stock price change (%)
Alcatel	23.25	24.88	+ 6.99
Boeing	34.25	39.12	+ 14.23
Borden Inc.	26.50	16.12	− 39.15
Boston Celtics	16.75	19.12	+ 14.18
British Steel	7.50	17.00	+ 126.67
Broken Hill	30.00	42.00	+ 40.00
Canadian Pacific	10.88	15.75	+ 44.83
Digital Equipment	32.38	40.00	+ 23.55
EG&G	18.38	20.12	+ 9.52
Elf Aquitaine	30.00	37.00	+ 23.33
Homestake Mining	10.62	19.88	+ 87.06
Humana	19.38	34.50*	+ 78.06
IBM	62.25	43.88	− 29.52
Interstate Power	28.75	29.50	+ 2.61
Lands End	24.88	32.00	+ 28.64
Average performance of 15 stocks			+ 28.73

*Including value of spin-off.

NOTE: During this period, the Dow Jones Industrial Average climbed from 3227.36 to 3638.96, a gain of 12.75 percent.

As it turned out, these stocks did even better. How can one explain this? Perhaps the selling had been overdone and now they were "value stocks."

One illustration, to be sure, does not prove very much. I continued my ministudy by looking at another group of stocks, in this instance those in the Dow Jones Industrial Average or those in the *Barron's* 50 (see Table 2-3).

Although the list is small, it shows that stocks hitting new highs don't necessarily keep climbing. In the next test, I picked stocks that

Table 2-3

Stocks reaching new highs on November 20, 1992, and how they performed from that date until August 24, 1993. All selected from Dow Jones 30 or *Barron's* 50.

	Price 11-20-92 ($)	Price 8-24-93 ($)	Stock price change (%)
AT&T	47.62	60.38	+ 26.77
Donnelley, R.R.	31.38	30.38	− 3.19
Procter & Gamble	54.25	48.62	− 10.37
Union Pacific	58.00	66.50	+ 14.66
Weyerhaeuser	37.62	41.12	+ 9.30
Wrigley	37.75	40.00	+ 5.96
Average performance of six stocks			+ 7.19

Table 2-4

Stocks reaching new lows on November 20, 1992, and how they performed from that date until August 24, 1993. All selected from Dow Jones 30 or *Barron's* 50.

	Price 11-20-92 ($)	Price 8-24-93 ($)	Stock price change (%)
Boeing	34.25	39.25	+ 14.60
IBM	62.25	44.00	− 29.32
United Technologies	42.50	58.12	+ 36.76
Westinghouse Electric	9.75	15.88	+ 62.82
Average performance of four stocks			+ 21.22
Dow Jones Industrial Average	3227.36	3652.09	+ 13.16
Action of all 10 stocks*			+ 12.78

*These are the 10 stocks listed in Tables 2-3 and 2-4.

had hit the new low list and were also from one of the lists mentioned above. See Table 2-4.

Shifting gears, I decided to test the concept by using a different beginning date: February 19, 1993. See Tables 2-5 and 2-6.

As you can see, neither list provided many candidates for great profits. So far, we haven't proved much. Let's try still another beginning date: April 30, 1993. See Tables 2-7 and 2-8.

Although this look at new highs and new lows is not exactly scientific, it may convince you that there is no magic involved in either list. Some stocks continue to surge ahead from the new high list, and some stocks from the new low list change directions and bounce back.

Some Other Features to Look at in *The Wall Street Journal*

After looking at the new high list, I check the list of most active stocks. Active stocks are those that are heavily traded because of some dramatic and unexpected development, such as a comment made by a corporate executive or a report being circulated by a brokerage firm. These stocks often react to news by going up or down a point or two. Big moves of this magnitude might shake you up a bit, but I am not convinced you should either buy or sell after these price changes take place. A week from now, everyone will have forgotten the incident and will be latching on to something else. Meanwhile, the stock that was battered a week ago will start to creep back up. And the stock that bounded ahead will begin to sag back. What it amounts to is this:

Table 2-5

Stocks reaching new highs on February 19, 1993, and how they performed from that date until August 24, 1993. All selected from Dow Jones 30 or *Barron's* 50.

	Price 2-19-93 ($)	Price 8-24-93 ($)	Stock price change (%)
Amoco	55.75	57.62	+ 3.36
Chevron	77.75	91.88	+ 18.17
SCEcorp	23.81	24.62	+ 3.41
Sears, Roebuck	54.00	68.27*	+ 26.43
Vulcan Materials	54.62	45.88	− 16.02
Average performance of five stocks			+ 7.07

*Includes spin-off shares.

Table 2-6

Stocks reaching new lows on February 19, 1993, and how they performed from that date until August 24, 1993. All selected from Dow Jones 30 or *Barron's* 50.

	Price 2-19-93 ($)	Price 8-24-93 ($)	Stock price change (%)
American Brands	34.50	32.62	− 5.43
Baxter International	28.00	26.38	− 5.89
Merck	36.88	31.75	− 13.90
Pfizer	54.50	62.00	+ 13.76
Philip Morris	68.00	48.88	− 28.13
Average performance of five stocks			− 7.90
Dow Jones Industrial Average	3322.18	3652.09	+ 9.93
Action of all 10 stocks			− 0.42

Table 2-7

Stocks reaching new highs on April 30, 1993, and how they performed from that date until August 24, 1993. All selected from Dow Jones 30 or *Barron's* 50.

	Price 4-30-93 ($)	Price 8-24-93 ($)	Stock price change (%)
Caterpillar Tractor	69.25	82.50	+ 19.13
Chevron	86.12	91.88	+ 6.68
Mobil	70.88	77.88	+ 9.88
Timken	31.25	33.50	+ 7.20
Average performance of four stocks			+ 10.72

Don't start taking sleeping pills every time one of your stocks gets whacked. And don't think you are about to become a millionaire because one of your stocks shot up three points yesterday.

In most instances, if you don't do anything, you'll end up rich. Constantly making changes in your portfolio is not the way to amass a fortune. Every time you switch, you enrich two people: the IRS and your broker.

Table 2-8

Stocks reaching new lows on April 30, 1993, and how they performed from that date until August 24, 1993. All selected from Dow Jones 30 or *Barron's* 50.

	Price 4-30-93 ($)	Price 8-24-93 ($)	Stock price change (%)
Donnelley, R.R.	27.25	30.38	+ 11.47
Philip Morris	47.00	48.88	+ 3.99
Average performance of two stocks			+ 7.73
Dow Jones Industrial Average	3427.55	3652.09	+ 6.55
Action of all six stocks			+ 9.73

After I have examined the most active stocks, I then proceed to look at all the stocks that I have an interest in. For some strange reason, this is exciting. When I look at the Big Board issues listed under A, I know there are three stocks that I want to check: Alcatel, American Water Works, and Amoco. Then, I look at the Bs to see how these stocks are doing: Banc One, Banco Bilbao, Banco Santander, BellSouth, Bristol-Myers Squibb, British Gas, and British Telecommunications. Similarly, I proceed through the alphabet until I have finished those listed on the Big Board. I never look at the Os, since I don't own any, and none of them are among those we use in our clients' portfolios. I skip the American Stock Exchange; there aren't any that I have an interest in. Next, I look at the Nasdaq issues—stocks traded over the counter— where I look at Ericsson Telecomm, J.B. Hunt, Kimball, and Reuters.

What to Look at When You Go Through the Stock Listings

When you check your stocks, there are a few items that you should understand. The first two figures refer to the high and low price over the past 52 weeks. After the name of the stock (which, incidentally, is abbreviated, which means you have to be able to figure out what the full name is), you will find the ticker symbol. If you have an interest in a stock, it's a good idea to memorize the symbol. It will impress your broker and will enable you to obtain information on her branch office quote machine. Ticker symbols are not hard to remember because they are usually derived from the name. For instance, Bristol-Myers is BMY. Similarly, Ford Motor is F. General Motors is GM. Houghton

Mifflin is HTN. Eli Lilly is LLY. Merck is MRK. Southern Indiana Gas & Electric is SIG. NICOR is GAS. National Fuel Gas is NFG. And so on. Most brokers know hundreds of symbols, but they may not know yours. Be ready to give her the symbol if you ask her to check it out. She will think you are more than just another country bumpkin.

Next comes the annual dividend. In some instances, this will be omitted, particularly if the stock has been recently split. I've never understood why this is so, but it is a bit maddening. (As you may have observed, I am easily irritated.)

The dividend is followed by the yield (the dividend divided by the price) and then the P/E ratio (the price divided by the latest 12-month's earnings per share).

The volume of trading is the next entry and is the number of round lots traded that day. A round lot is 100 shares. Investors often call me and ask what is happening to their stock because the volume is much higher than usual. This is often a difficult question to answer, although it is sometimes mentioned in *The Wall Street Journal*. Otherwise, it often remains a mystery—and probably not very important. Which all boils down to the fact that I am not impressed by volume. It does not figure in my stock picking strategies.

Next comes the high and low for the day and the closing price. If the stock has hit a new high, you will see an up arrow to left of the entry. If it hit a new low, there will be a down arrow. If the stock has been split recently, you will see an *s* to the left of the entry.

There is no end to the information in this section of *The Wall Street Journal*. For instance, you will see data on interest rates. Investors like falling interest rates and get panicky when interest rates start to climb. Market experts try to forecast interest rates but most have an erratic record. You might as well predict which dog will win at the track.

Here are some interest rate definitions that might come in handy:

Prime Rate. The rate posted by large banks as a base rate for loans to consumers and smaller businesses.

Discount Rate. The interest rate charged by Federal Reserve banks on loans to depository institutions.

Federal Funds. The rate for overnight loans among financial institutions.

Incidentally, if you want to get a better understanding of *The Wall Street Journal*, you can read a book on this very subject. It's called *The Dow Jones–Irwin Guide to Using The Wall Street Journal*, Second Edition, by Michael B. Lehmann. With that tidbit of cogent advice, I think I will leave well enough alone and go on to another topic.

Forbes Magazine

This is another one of my favorites. It is published twice a month. I particularly enjoy reading the columns in the back of the magazine. My favorites are David Dreman, Kenneth L. Fisher, and Mark Hulbert. Once I finish reading the wisdom of these pundits, I push my way toward the front. Invariably, I come across well-written pieces on companies or concepts of interest. Outside of *The Wall Street Journal, Forbes* is a "must" for me.

Close to *Forbes* is *Barron's*, which is owned by Dow Jones & Company, who also publish *The Wall Street Journal.* I enjoy *Barron's.* It is entirely different from any other Wall Street periodicals and contains a tremendous amount of statistical information.

Among the articles is often an interview with a prominent analyst or portfolio manager. Twice a year, the editors line up a panel of experts and quiz them on their views of the economy, the market, and individual securities. I have no idea how accurate the forecasts of these gurus are, but their comments make stimulating reading.

Finally, I don't want to forget the *AAII Journal,* a monthly publication of the American Association of Individual Investors. It is completely different from any other investment periodical. For one thing, there is no advertising, which means you can hold it up to read even if you don't have enough muscles to do push-ups.

The *Journal* is also unique in that it does not make specific recommendations. Rather, it is devoted to ideas and concepts. In other words, it helps you become a better and more sophisticated investor.

I like the *AAII Journal* so much that I am a lifetime subscriber. A few years ago, when they were just getting started, they made an offer that has never been repeated—at least to my knowledge. I plunked down a couple hundred dollars for my lifetime subscription; now I don't have to worry about becoming too poor to keep renewing my subscription.

They Could Cancel Your Subscription, George

At the bottom of my list of magazine subscriptions is the *Financial Analysts Journal,* published every two months. It is written largely by college professors and people with high IQs—and a vast knowledge of complex mathematical equations—who are trying to impress mere mortals with their erudition. Somehow I suspect that it is an excellent publication for those who are extremely erudite and sophisticated.

I have yet to meet anyone who could understand what these people are talking about. And this includes George Morris, CFA, one of my close buddies, a broker in Cleveland with Kemper Securities. George, I might add, is a veteran analyst who gave it all up to become a broker. He is a crafty tennis player and a man whose Wall Street wisdom knows no bounds. Despite all this, George Morris claims he throws his copy of the *Financial Analysts Journal* out without even looking at the titles of the articles. How crass! I hope the *Journal* cancels his subscription. It would be a lesson to him for his uncouth, high-handed arrogance.

In case I haven't made my point, the *Financial Analysts Journal* is a little bit above my feeble mind's ability to fathom. If someone could find out what these writers are trying to say, the *Journal* might be a great publication.

Beyond these helpful magazines are three services that you should be familiar with. All are readily available in most brokerage offices and public libraries. If you are a substantial investor, you might consider buying your own *Value Line Survey* or *Standard & Poor's Stock Guide.*

The *Standard & Poor's Stock Guide*

Of all the tools I use, the *S&P Stock Guide* is the most useful. Conceivably, you could pick stocks without resorting to *The Wall Street Journal, Barron's,* brokerage house reports, or advice from your cleaning lady. Nearly everything you need to build a portfolio is right here in this handy guide, which is issued monthly by one of the largest purveyors of investment information in the country.

To be sure, you will probably want to investigate further before you make up your mind whether or not to buy or sell a stock. But, the *Stock Guide* is your first stop. You can tell almost at a glance whether you want to go further. But more about that later.

The *Stock Guide* is readily available in nearly all brokerage offices and libraries. It is issued once a month and costs about $100 a year. Or, if you are a good customer, your broker may give you one. If not, you can call 1-800-221-5277. Or, you may write to Standard & Poor's at 25 Broadway, New York, N.Y. 10004. McGraw-Hill also reprints the *Stock Guide*'s valuable year-end issue and makes it available through bookstores around the country. Look for *Standard & Poor's Stock and Bond Guide.* (As the title indicates they package both the *Stock Guide* and the *Bond Guide* in one book.)

The reason I like the *Stock Guide* is because it provides the essence of what I want to know about a company before I investigate in further detail.

In brief, here is what you can find in the *Stock Guide:*

- The earnings per share (EPS) in each of the past four years. These numbers are found on the right-hand page and are listed under the heading *Earnings $ Per Shr.*

- The EPS in the most recent 12 months is given in the same section at the far right, under the heading *Last 12 Mos.*

- Quite often, there is an estimate of the EPS for the current year. Look just to the left of the latest 12-month's EPS.

- The indicated dividend. This tells you what the company is likely to pay in the year ahead. To arrive at this figure, S&P normally multiplies the quarterly dividend by four. The indicated dividend is also found on the right-hand page, under *Dividends.* Look at the right-hand column under Dividends and you will see the heading *Ind. Rate.*

The *Stock Guide* also contains abbreviated information on mutual funds. The most valuable information is the record of the fund during the past five years. For instance, if you look at the September 1993 issue of the *Stock Guide*, it will tell you that the Investment Company of America turned $10,000 into $21,433 (including reinvested dividends and capital gains), assuming you invested your $10,000 on December 31, 1987. If you believe that past records have a predictive value (I'm not sure they do), you can look at other funds in this section and make appropriate comparisons.

My only regret about this part of the *Stock Guide* is this: they don't include enough names. However, since there are now about 5000 different funds, this shortcoming is understandable.

Value Line Survey

If *Value Line* ever goes belly-up, I would be first among the mourners. No other service provides the wealth of information found in *Value Line.* If you are a subscriber, you receive three things each week:

- A new index
- A specific stock recommendation
- A booklet containing vital information on well over 100 stocks, broken down by industry.

The third item is the key to *Value Line.* Each week, *Value Line* reviews the prospects for six or seven industries. Over the course of 13 weeks, about 1700 stocks are reviewed. At the beginning of each industry section is a one-page discussion of the developments that are occurring in that industry. Next are one-page reports on each company. About one-half of the page is devoted to a statistical history of the company over the past 15 years. Thus, at a glance, you can see how the company has done in terms of earnings per share, dividends per share, cash flow, and so forth. *Value Line* also provides estimates of what it thinks will transpire in the balance of the current year as well as the following year. As noted earlier, I am not impressed with estimates by analysts.

Balance sheet numbers are also provided but not for the entire 15 years. They normally cover the preceding 10 years, which is certainly sufficient.

The beauty of *Value Line* is that all the companies in each industry are grouped together. Thus, if you are intent on buying shares in an oil company, for instance, you can easily compare one against another. This is not true of Standard & Poor's tear sheets or *Moody's Handbook of Common Stocks*. In those services, stocks are listed alphabetically.

A great deal of vital information is provided by *Value Line*, including what insiders are doing with their shares. It tells you how many insiders (such as corporate officers and board members) are buying and selling. Although I always look at this activity, I am not sure it is helpful. For one thing, these transactions occurred several weeks before. For another, I have read studies of insiders' buying and selling and did not find their actions particularly predictive.

For those who need guidance in making up their minds, *Value Line* has an opinion on nearly every stock. The top 100 stocks are graded a *1*. The bottom 100 are graded *5*. A score of *3* falls in the middle. According to *Value Line*, their number 1s do much better than 2s, 2s do better than 3s, and so on. For my part, I pay very little attention to these scores, preferring to make up my own mind.

The Standard & Poor's Tear Sheets

One of the major statistical services is Standard & Poor's. They provide "tear sheets" on thousands of stocks. You can find them in most brokerage offices and libraries. It is doubtful, however, that you would want to sign up for this service yourself. A collection of tear sheets covering the companies in S&P's two major stock indices is available in the bookstores. Look for *Standard & Poor's 500 Guide* and *Standard & Poor's MidCap 400 Guide*.

The advantage of the tear sheets is that they cover more stocks than *Value Line*. Each sheet is devoted to one company. Unlike *Value Line*, the tear sheet does not offer specific advice. However, it gives you a good deal of information concerning the company's business and recent developments. Tables are provided with a history of dividends, earnings, and balance sheet data. Although I like *Value Line* better, the tear sheets are better as far as background is concerned. They also give you the name of the investor contact. Don't feel shy about calling this person if you have any questions. For best results, tell the person that you own 4000 shares and are considering adding to your holdings. Above all, don't let on that you are a novice with only $1500 to invest.

The best time to call the investor contact is at 1 p.m. Whether she eats early or late, she is certain to be at lunch at 1 p.m. The secretary will ask you the purpose of your call. Tell her that you are a major stockholder seeking clarification on some crucial points. Leave your name and phone number. This way, you save the price of the call.

Once the contact returns your call, be prepared with a list of sophisticated questions. I realize that you may not be financially sophisticated, but you must at least pretend to be. The best way to accomplish this is by having the *Value Line* sheet in front of you. But don't let on that you do. Instead, say this, "I have been reading an analysis of your company, and it is not clear exactly what is meant by some of these comments. Would you be willing to help me?"

"Yes, of course."

"For instance, this report says that results this year might benefit from the completion of the Lebanon-to-Leidy project. I wonder if you might elaborate on that."

"Elaborate" is the key word here. Every question you ask must be open-ended. Never ask a question that can be answered with a simple yes or no. You want detailed information. Once you ask the question, sit back and listen. Never interrupt until the line falls silent. When the investor contact finally runs out of steam, have your next question ready.

Next, say this: "If you were to select three or four reasons why your stock is attractive at this time, what would they be?"

Then, at the very end, say this: "I don't like to be negative, but I am sure your company has a few problems. What problems do most analysts stress?"

If you use your imagination, you can really milk one of these interviews. But, for heaven's sake, don't do it if you are paying for the call.

3

Why Common Stocks Are Your Best Investment

A friend of mine—I'll call him Hans Aschenbecher—sells used cars. You might wonder why I choose to call him Hans Aschenbecher when his real name is Barry Yagour. Simple: to protect his privacy.

By Hans's own admission, used car salesmen are not at the top of the social or economic scale. Still, this particular used car salesman is extremely talented.

Hans has been selling Buicks for 22 years. Nearly every year, he is singled out for some sort of sales honor. One reason he does well is that he knows what he is talking about, and he doesn't try to sell you a car that is not going to make you happy. If you have any complaints, he is quick to rectify them. As a result, his customers return time and time again to do business with him.

Not a bad way to carve out a career.

The other day, I stopped at Hans's used car lot at Friedman Buick to discuss the purchase of another Park Avenue. Knowing that he is making good money and is now in his mid-40s, I asked him if he had started to purchase stocks.

"The only stock I have ever owned is Centerior Energy," he told me. "But I sold it for a small profit and no longer own any stocks."

What You Don't Understand, You Avoid

Perhaps Hans is typical of people in general. Here is an intelligent and successful person with an excellent income who does not own common stocks. I can only assume that somewhere along the way, he became convinced that common stocks are too risky.

The ordinary individual cannot afford to buy major corporations for his personal portfolio, but he does have the opportunity to buy shares in such corporations through the stock market. What the investor sacrifices in his lack of control in management decisions, he benefits from gaining liquidity. If the investment goes sour, he has an instant market for selling his shares. The businessman, by contrast, is stuck with a poor investment which can take months or longer to unload. This wonderful aspect of liquidity is the investor's advantage over the businessman.

SOURCE: Lawrence M. Stein, *Value Investing*, John Wiley & Sons, 1988.

If Hans were 27 years old and just getting started, I could understand that he was not ready to initiate an investment program. But how can a person in middle age neglect to do something about retirement?

Is it fear of loss that prevents people from venturing into the world of common stocks? It may well be. It could also be that the whole idea of common stocks is too complicated for anyone to understand.

Admittedly, Your Career Comes First

After all, earning a living requires steadfast attention to your own career. It may mean taking courses in the evening. It may mean reading trade journals. It may mean extensive travel and working late at the office. Or all of the above.

If so, perhaps most people don't want to spend the time to read books on common stocks plus *The Wall Street Journal, Forbes, Barron's, Business Week,* and annual reports.

In short, what you don't understand you don't get involved with. To draw an analogy, I don't profess to know much about plumbing, car repairs, or shoe repair. Nor am I motivated to read about these things in order to handle these chores myself. It may be that noninvestors feel the same way about stocks.

Although I can understand the reluctance to delve into this complex sphere, I am hoping that you, dear reader, are cut from different cloth.

> Cash gives you absolutely no inflation protection; bonds give you very little. The risk in cash and bonds is greater than usual—and the risk in stocks is not.
>
> SOURCE: John Templeton in *The Wall Street Journal,* July 23, 1993, from *Heard on the Street,* by Suzanne McGee.

"There Is Nothing to Fear But Fear Itself"

To be sure, the stock market may seem intimidating, but it doesn't have to be. For my part, computers used to be intimidating, but along came Mary Clink, one of my associates, and soon I was reveling in word processing and spreadsheets. It took some effort, and it took a lot of crises, nail biting, frustration, and fuming, but now I wonder how I ever existed before my transformation to the modern world. Thank you, Mary Clink.

Let's hope I can convince you that "there is nothing to fear but fear itself" when it comes to common stocks.

Perhaps I was fortunate in my selection of parents. My father was an inveterate and enthusiastic investor. Long before I had any money to invest—and long before I became a stock broker—I was reading *Barron's* and *The Financial Analysts Journal* as well as such books as *The Intelligent Investor* by Benjamin Graham.

Why Not Blame the Media?

So far, I have not given you any reason to banish your fear of stocks. Perhaps we can put the blame on journalists. Typically, the only time you read about stocks is when they are crashing. Similarly, you don't hear much about stocks that are doubling or tripling—only when they are about to declare Chapter 11 or when the CEO has been fired because he has bungled his job. That usually means the price of the stock has plummeted.

There is no question that stock prices decline every now and then, and there is no doubt that some stocks collapse and cut their dividends. Even electric utilities and banks fall in price and slash their dividends. If these "safe" stocks are risky, why should anyone venture into this maelstrom?

The Alternatives Are Lackluster—Or Worse

One reason is that the alternatives are not very attractive. Money-market funds and bank accounts don't keep up with inflation. Bonds may be a bit better, but they don't increase their payout. If you buy a 20-year bond, the interest paid to you never changes. Meanwhile, the cost of living keeps climbing.

This leaves common stocks and real estate. I can remember vividly that noninvestors often told me they were not interested in the stock market because they preferred to invest in real estate. I wonder how many of them feel the same way today?

Perhaps one reason some people fear the stock market is because they dipped their toe in and came away with a bad blister.

Not infrequently, the uninformed investors take their first plunge into stocks at exactly the wrong time. Here again, I might blame the newspapers because soaring stock prices can prompt them to print articles that might entice people to invest. Usually, these stories appear when stocks are temporarily too high. Those who buy at this time see their holdings sink in value. As a consequence, they vow never to get involved again.

Even Experts Suffer Losses

For my own part, I have been investing for three decades, which means that I have witnessed a host of bear and bull markets. I have seen my own stocks climb and retreat. Admittedly, I have suffered some losses along the way. On the other hand, I would be hard put to compile a list of my losses.

Still, there have been some. Most recently, I bought some Ericsson Telecomm, a Swedish company that makes telephone equipment. I paid $35 a share in March 1991. Not long after, the stock skidded below $20. But I hung on, and it came back and recently got as high as $50, at which time I sold, only to see it shoot up to $60 before falling back to $42, where it is at this writing.

My Experience with the
Drug Stocks

Eli Lilly is another stock that has been a concern—at least in the last year or so. I bought Lilly in July 1980 for $51.25. Since then, the stock has been split two-for-one twice, which means the adjusted cost price is $12.813. To be sure, Lilly is a long way from its high of $90.38 (it is currently about $60).

It is well known, of course, that nearly all drug stocks have tumbled because of the furor over a change in the health care system. But despite all these gyrations, the fact is that my Lilly stock has been a great investment, rising from about $13 to $60 (not to mention the tons of dividends I have received over the years).

No Contest

Consider an investor who put $10,000 in the market (as measured by the S&P 500) in 1946 and another investor who put down ten times as much, $100,000, in long-term government bonds. Forty-three years later, after inflation and taxes, the stock investment would be worth more than $63,000, the bond position just under $25,000.

Was it any different for tax-free accounts? Not much. Ten thousand dollars placed in stocks in 1946 would have become $158,076 in 1988 after adjusting for inflation ($1,049,210 in 1988 dollars). By comparison, $10,000 put into long-term governments at the same time would have shrunk to $8,350 after inflation.

SOURCE: David Dreman's "The Contrarian" column in *Forbes*, May 15, 1989.

Two Bad Years with
Houghton Mifflin

Still another stock that might be considered a problem is the book publisher Houghton Mifflin, which I bought in 1979 for $31.25. In the interim, this stock has also split two-for-one on two separate occasions, which means my adjusted cost was $7.813.

So, why am I complaining? At the beginning of 1989, the stock reached a high of about $50. For the next two years, it declined steadily until it bottomed out at just under $20. Since then, it has rebounded smartly and is now about $47. In summary, my shares have climbed from just under $8 to about $47. Maybe I should quit complaining.

I began by telling you about my stock market losses. As you can see, none of them were exactly devastating.

It would not be difficult to regale you with a series of big winners, but I will refrain. Perhaps the point to be made is this: stocks fluctuate, and you can get a bit exasperated at times, but in the long run, you will make a ton of money.

The Purpose of This Chapter

Of course, you may be thinking that I am an expert on the stock market and therefore *should* be able to pick winners without much effort. Meanwhile, you, an amateur, might not fare as well. The purpose of this book, however, is to show you a number of methods for picking stocks that will outperform the market. But the purpose of this chapter is to convince you that stocks are your best investment and that you should try to convince yourself that the long-term trend of stocks is up and that dividends will also climb over the years. At least, that is what has happened in the past.

You'll Be Amazed by What Lies Ahead

You are now ready to learn more about how to build a successful portfolio of stocks that will make you wealthy.

Later on in the book, moreover, you will learn about several tested techniques for picking stocks that outperform the market.

Mark that word carefully: *outperform.*

Beating the Market Is Tough—Even for Professionals

Books written by college professors, incidentally, deny that investors as a group can consistently do better than the market averages, such as the Dow Jones Industrial Average or the Standard & Poor's 500. Included in such academic work is the contention that even the professionals, such as mutual funds, pension plans, and bank trust departments *cannot* do any better than the general market. In fact, two-thirds of these full-time professionals actually do *worse* than the market.

Even though outperforming the market is difficult, my methods of stock selection are far superior to anything you have ever seen before.

Table 3-1

	Stocks selected by my super system (%)	Group average (%)
	− 6.45	− 13.4
	+ 92.65	+ 68.60
	+ 229.40	+ 113.00
	+ 71.82	+ 36.60
	+ 46.00	+ 62.30*
	+ 206.90	+ 50.60
	+ 97.25	+ 56.50
	+ 36.10	+ 22.58
	+ 5.47	+ 4.17
	+ 32.68	+ 16.97
Averages of these 10 stocks:	+ 81.18	+ 41.79
Average of all 30 stocks:	+ 75.20	+ 40.21

*Test in which the group outperformed the Super System.

What's more, they are not complicated and do not require forecasting the future.

One method is particularly intriguing. It is described in great detail in Chapter 17, a point in the book when you are ready for it. Needless to say, it has produced astounding results in the past. In Chapter 17 are also a number of impartial tests. All told, the system has been tested 30 times, in various periods, from 1974 to the present.

Overall the results have shown that you can outperform the market by—brace yourself—87 percent. In only three tests out of 30 did this system fail to do as well as the general market.

To give you an idea of what to èxpect, Table 3-1 shows 10 tests made at random. The performance of the selected stocks is compared with the group that they were a part of.

I hope you will continue reading until you, too, are convinced that you *can* pick stocks with equal success.

4
The Glossary

You may think it odd that I am placing the glossary near the beginning of this book rather than at the end. The reason is this: I am assuming that many readers are new to the world of common stocks and thus do not understand all of the terms and themes that I will be discussing.

This glossary is not merely a dry list of definitions. In many instances, these definitions give strong hints of my thinking and philosophy. I urge you to take the time to read this section before proceeding—unless, of course, you are a grizzled veteran of the investment scene.

If you are looking for a better—or at least more complete—glossary, there are two books that you might want to look at: *Wall Street Words: Basics and Beyond* by Richard Maturi (Probus Publishing Co., 1991) and *The Wall Street Dictionary* (5000 entries) by R.J. Shook and Robert L. Shook (New York Institute of Finance, 1990).

account executive: A salesperson who deals with the clients of a brokerage house. Other terms are sometimes used such as customer's man (now obsolete), broker, investment consultant, or sales executive.

American depositary receipts (ADRs): A representation of the shares of a foreign company. They may be traded on an exchange or over the counter. ADRs facilitate the trading of foreign stocks because they make it unnecessary to open an account with a brokerage house abroad.

American Stock Exchange: Sometimes referred to as The Curb, which is descriptive of its earlier days when stocks were traded outside rather than on the floor of a building. The American Stock Exchange is the nation's second-largest exchange but is much smaller than the New York Stock Exchange. Stocks listed there are often foreign stocks and energy stocks.

analyst: A person trained to analyze securities who may work for a brokerage house, a bank, an insurance company, a mutual fund, or any other enterprise involved in the investment business. Analysts are often called securities analysts. Most analysts have college degrees that reflect training in accounting, statistics, corporate finance, and portfolio management. Typical degrees are MBA and CFA. Analysts have limited direct contact with the investing public. However, their reports are available describing developments in stocks and industries. Most analysts specialize in one or two industries.

annual reports: Publications issued by all companies whose shares are traded in the open market. They are usually available two or three months after the end of the fiscal year. Annual reports are a good source on the products and services of the company. They are rarely objective, however, and can lead you astray as to the merits of the company because they lack the analysis that can be provided by a securities analyst.

appreciation: An increase in price. You might say that a stock "appreciated" 45 percent in 1993.

asset: The opposite of a liability. Assets represent the investments of the company. Typical assets are plants, real estate, furniture, and equipment. An intangible asset would be an asset such as a copyright, a patent, or a trade name.

asset allocation: The manner in which investors divide up their holdings. The most common segments are stocks, bonds, and money-market funds but others include real estate or convertible bonds. Proper asset allocation can make a big difference in the performance of one's holdings. In the long run, the best performance occurs in a portfolio with a high concentration of common stocks.

balance sheet: A formal accounting statement, showing the breakdown of assets, liabilities, and net worth of a corporation. In effect, it is a snapshot of how a company looked on a specific day, such as year-end or at the end of a quarter. The term "balance" refers to the balance sheet equation, Assets = Liabilities + Net Worth. The balance sheet, however, does not give you any information on how much profit the company made during the period. That is dealt with in the income statement.

balanced mutual fund: A fund that is invested in common stocks, bonds, and money-market funds. A typical breakdown might be 50 percent in stocks, 40 percent in bonds, and 10 percent in money-market funds.

basis point: An interest rate term. A point is 1 percent. A basis point is 1 percent of a percentage point. If, for instance, interest rates declined from 6.15 percent to 6.05 percent you would say that interest rates declined by 10 basis points.

bear market: The opposite of a bull market; refers to a market that is declining. In 1973 and 1974, we experienced an extreme bear market in which stocks declined more than 40 percent. A "bear" is an investor who expects stocks to decline.

belly-up: A slang term referring to a company that is bankrupt. You are advised to avoid companies that are poised to go "belly-up."

Big Board: A slang term referring to the New York Stock Exchange. Most companies that you are familiar with—about 2600 in all—are listed on the Big Board.

blue chip: A large, well-established company usually well known by most investors. It might be assumed that blue chips are safe, but this is sometimes incorrect. Blue chips such as IBM, Westinghouse, American Express, and Philip Morris have experienced sinking spells in recent years. In poker, the blue chips are worth more than white or red chips.

bond: A debt instrument, generally issued to raise money for expansion or perhaps to pay for an acquisition. Bonds are usually issued in denominations of $1000 but are quoted in the press as if they were in hundreds For instance, a bond selling for $98 is actually worth $980. Unlike stocks, bonds have a maturity date, such as 10, 15, or 30 years. At maturity, the company or government body is expected to redeem the bond at its face value— which is the same price it was issued at, usually $1000. During the period it is in the hands of investors, a bond pays semiannual interest. This interest never changes unless the company is prepared to declare bankruptcy.

bond ratings: Provided by such organizations as Moody's, Standard & Poor's, Duff & Phelps, or Fitch. Each has its own method of assessing the financial strength of the issuer, which could be a corporation or a government body such as a state or city. A strong bond would be rated AAA or AA. The lowest rating that would be deemed "investment grade" is BBB or its equivalent.

book value: The net asset value of a corporation after deducting liabilities from assets. If assets are less than liabilities, a company could have a negative book value. Book value is often expressed as book value per share. This is calculated by dividing the outstanding common shares into the book value. If, for instance, the book value is $100 million and there are 10 million shares outstanding, the book value per share would be $10. Some investors like to examine the relationship of the price of the stock to the book value per share. It is often two or three to one. When a stock sells below book value per share, value investors might be attracted to the stock.

bull market: A market that is rising. It is the opposite of a bear market. A bull is an investor who expects stocks to rise and is optimistic about the outlook for stocks.

buy and hold: A strategy involving buying a stock and holding it, regardless of future developments. A buy-and-hold strategy often works better than a trading strategy, since it minimizes taxes and commissions. Time and patience are two of the most important ingredients of a successful investment.

call price: The price that the issuer (the company or a government body) can call in (refund) its bonds. It is often a few points above par (the issue price), such as $106. If a bond is issued when interest rates are high, the company wants the right to call the bond and redeem it so that it can sell new bonds at a lower rate of interest. In 1993, a large number of companies took advantage of low interest rates to refinance their debt. In some instances, investors are protected against this because the bond may have a guarantee that it cannot be called for a specified period of time after issue, such as 5 or 10 years. U.S. government bonds are usually not callable.

capital gain: The profit on a stock or bond that is selling at a higher price than when it was purchased. Investors are often reluctant to sell a stock that has a large capital gain because of the income tax consequences. After taxes are paid, there is less to invest in a different security. Unless you are quite sure that you can find a stock that is much better than the one already owned, it may not be wise to sell. On the other hand, if the stock is clearly overvalued or becomes too large a percentage of the portfolio, selling makes sense because a decline in price would result in a loss—and the loss could even exceed the capital gains tax.

capital-intensive: Might be contrasted with labor-intensive. A good example of a firm in a capital-intensive industry is an electric utility because it costs a great deal of capital to build a new generating plant. By contrast, an example of a firm in a labor-intensive industry would be an advertising agency. The amount of capital needed to run an agency is small, but the number of people is great.

capitalization: The way the capital structure of a corporation is organized, and capital is derived from two sources, equity capital from the sale of bonds or from bank debt. These are the source of long-term capital. Short-term and intermediate are also useful sources, but they are not of interest to the individual investor. The balance sheet is made up of three items: assets (on the left side of the balance sheet) and debt and net worth (on the right side). These two sides are always in balance because, by definition, net worth is the difference between assets and debt.

cash flow: By one definition, cash flow is earnings, plus noncash items such as depreciation and amortization. Some analysts like to calculate the relationship of the price of the stock to cash flow per share. A relationship in excess of 10 to 1 might be a red flag denoting the stock is too expensive.

certificate of deposit (CD): A very conservative financial instrument often issued by a bank. The investor is guaranteed a certain rate of interest as long as the CD is held to maturity, which could be for one year, two years and sometimes up to five years but rarely for as long as a bond. In years past, these CDs were popular with extremely conservative individuals, particularly those who would be reluctant to buy a common stock.

chartered financial analyst (CFA): A degree earned by securities analysts after a period of intensive study. It might be compared to an MBA. The big difference is that the CFA is earned by way of self-study rather than enrolling in a university. Three all-day examinations are given to CFA candidates. They must be taken at least one year apart.

chief executive officer (CEO): The highest-ranking corporate officer. A CEO could be chairman of the board or president. In some instances, the chairman of the board is not the CEO.

chief financial officer (CFO): The highest-ranking financial officer; may also be the treasurer.

chief operating officer (COO): Usually the second-ranking corporate executive. The COO may be the president but would be subordinate to the CEO.

churning: A pejorative term denoting excessive portfolio turnover, often caused by an aggressive stockbroker who is trying to generate commissions. Churning may lead to a depletion of the value of a portfolio if carried too far. The firm's compliance department (a regulatory department) tries to minimize churning and would be expected to discipline anyone guilty of this unethical activity.

clean balance sheet: A balance sheet essentially free of debt. The opposite would be a leveraged balance sheet.

closed-end investment company: Similar to the so-called mutual fund. Both investment companies are engaged in the management of financial assets, such as stocks and bonds. A closed-end fund has one difference: it does not issue new shares nor does it redeem shares when investors elect to liquidate their holdings. Once a closed-end fund gets under way, it is then traded like a stock on an exchange or over the counter. Thus, it can neither grow nor shrink from new infusions of cash or sales by unhappy shareholders. In one sense, it is advantageous. Regardless of how many shareholders liquidate their holdings, it does not alter the size of the closed-end fund. In other words, it is not forced to liquidate its own holdings in order to satisfy shareholders. By contrast, an open-end mutual fund could get into serious trouble if too many shareholders demand to have their shares liquidated, especially in a declining market.

common stock: Represents ownership. All corporations have common stock. Owners of common stock are owners of the corporation. In actual practice, they cannot exercise this right because there are usually thousands of owners. The board of directors is the true source of power. To be sure, in isolated instances, incensed shareholders can combine their strength and demand to be heard.

common stock fund: An investment company that invests in common stock rather than bonds or other fixed-income securities.

compound annual growth rate: A calculation that assumes that growth is compounded not linear. Although the calculation of compound growth can be done manually, it is much easier to use a financial calculator. If a company earned $2.34 per share in 1982 and earned $5.89 per share in 1991, the earnings-per-share compound annual growth rate would be 9.67 percent. This is entirely different from calculating the average annual growth rate, which would be 7.33 percent.

convertible debenture: A form of bond that will be converted into common stock at the option of the bondholder or on a specified date. Corporations issue convertibles in order to raise money less expensively. If straight (nonconvertible) bonds are yielding 8 percent, for instance, a company might issue a convertible bond for less, let's say 6 percent. Of course, eventually the bond will be converted into stock and will dilute earnings, but that could be several years in the future. By that time, the bond money would have been invested profitably and would mitigate the dilution.

coupon: A bond term. Unlike stocks, bonds are often not registered directly with the company. Ownership is determined by the person who has possession. In order to receive the semiannual interest, this person has to clip the coupon, take it to a bank or broker, and get the cash. It is important to note that new bond issues do not have coupons attached because they are registered in the name of the holder.

coverage ratio: The ability of a company to pay its bond interest. It is calculated on a pretax basis because bond interest is a tax-deductible expense. In order to determine how strong the company is, you divide the annual interest cost into pretax earnings. For a public utility, a coverage of three times would be average. A coverage of only two times would be a sign of weakness. For a nonutility, a coverage of at least six times would be considered reasonable. Strong companies might have a coverage of 30 times.

cumulative preferred stock: The guarantee that a company makes to its preferred shareholders. Because owners of preferred stock are conservative investors, they are assured that if the dividend is not paid, it will be paid at some time in the future—unless the company files for bankruptcy. In the interim, the company is restricted from paying dividends on its common stock. However, it might well pay interest to its bondholders.

current assets: Assets that will be converted into cash within one year. Cash itself is a current asset, as are most receivables and inventories.

current liabilities: Liabilities that must be paid within one year, such as rent, insurance policy premiums, and other short-term obligations.

current ratio: The ratio of current assets to current liabilities. A ratio of two-to-one is considered satisfactory. This does not mean that a higher ratio is necessarily better. A ratio of five-to-one, for instance, might indicate the company is too cautious and has idle cash not being utilized effectively.

debenture: A bond that is not tied to actual property. Instead, its safety is based on the full faith and credit of the company.

debt-to-equity ratio: A measure of a company's financial strength. Although it is not necessary for a company to be debt-free, too much debt can be onerous and a sign that the company may be in trouble. A debt-to-equity ratio of one-to-four would be fine, but a one-to-one ratio would be indicative of excessive leverage. One notable exception: public utilities can tolerate a higher debt-to-equity ratio than most industrials.

deficit: Another word for red ink. When a company loses money, it has suffered a deficit.

depreciation: An accounting term having to do with the proper allocation of a capital asset over its expected life. Let's say a company purchases a machine for $100,000. Since this machine may last 10 years, it would not be deemed an expense in the year of purchase. If "straight-line" depreciation is used, the income statement would be charged with an expense of $10,000 in each of the next 10 years. In other words, the machine would be depreciating during that period. Many companies prefer accelerated depreciation, which means charging more than $10,000 a year initially, gradually reducing the amount charged in later years. Most companies use accelerated depreciation because it reduces taxes in the early years.

dilution: Can occur when a company makes an acquisition—using common stock—and pays more for the company than the new company can contribute to profits in the first year or two. The acquiring company justifies dilution by telling shareholders that future growth will justify this action.

diversification: Spreading the risk inherent in owning common stock. If an investor invests everything in one stock, the risk is high. By owning 15 or 20 different stocks (preferably in diverse sectors of the economy), the investor achieves diversification.

dividend payout ratio: A relationship between the earnings per share and the dividends per share. If the company earns $4 and pays out $2, the payout ratio is 50 percent, a rather typical ratio. A growing company might pay no dividend or only a small percentage. A more mature company might pay out $3. In the short run, some shareholders might like a high payout ratio. In the long run, such a policy could be self-defeating because it deprives the company of funds for expansion and acquisitions.

dividend reinvestment plan: A method of acquiring more shares by reinvesting dividends. Normally, there is only a modest fee for this service or no fee at all. Quite often, it is also possible to send in additional money for the purchase of more shares. Some investors enjoy this privilege because they avoid having to pay a brokerage commission. Unfortunately, there are some shortcomings to this idea. When the shares are sold, the cost basis (which is needed to calculate your tax) of every purchase—and every dividend—has to be determined. If proper records have not been kept, the chore can be onerous. There is also the delay factor. A payment sent in today to buy more shares may be invested a week or a month later when the price has changed substantially.

dividend yield: Calculated by dividing the price of the stock into the annual dividend. As an example, if the dividend is $2 and the stock price is $50, the dividend yield is 4 percent.

dividends: Paid to shareholders by corporations when they make a profit. The amount they pay is never guaranteed. The board of directors can raise or lower the dividend at its own discretion. If the corporation is successful, dividends will follow and may be raised periodically.

dollar cost averaging: A method of investing that allows the investor to add to holdings on a regular basis, for example, $100 a month, $500 a quarter, and so on. If the investor keeps up the plan for a long period, let's say 10 years, results can be good. It is assumed that stock is purchased at various prices, sometimes low, sometimes high. Nearly all mutual funds permit this type of investing, as do many corporations. Although dollar cost averaging sounds intriguing, it has some drawbacks. For instance, it does not work as well as lump-sum investing when the price of the stock is lower at the beginning of the period than it is at the end. Another flaw is that it assumes an investor would always be able to continue the set amount of investing. It might be impossible during periods of, for instance, unemployment, high expenses, or emergencies. Still another flaw is its assumption that an investor would want to maintain the same regular investing ($100 a month, for instance) for 10, 15, or 20 years. It ignores the probability that the person will be earning more money as his or her career progresses.

Dow Jones Averages: Stock market indices well known to most investors. The one most often quoted is the Industrial Average, which consists of 30 large companies, such as General Motors, Bethlehem Steel, Woolworth, Merck, Philip Morris, IBM, and ALCOA. The Dow Jones Averages are published every weekday in *The Wall Street Journal*, most daily newspapers, and in *Barron's* every Monday. The Dow Jones Industrial Average is a good gauge of how stocks are performing and is often used as a benchmark. If your stocks do better than the Dow 30, you can congratulate yourself. Some investors are also interested in the other two averages that make up the 65-stock index. One is the Transportation Average, made up of 20 stocks, such as Union Pacific, Delta Air Lines, Federal Express, and Carolina Freight. The other 15 stocks are public utilities, including Detroit Edison, Consolidated Natural Gas, and Peoples Energy. Taken together, these 65 stocks give you a good idea how stocks in general are performing.

earnings: The same as profits. If a company's expenses are less than its revenues (or sales), the company makes a profit. This is usually expressed as earnings per share. Stocks are very sensitive to earnings. Stocks often fall when "the Street" perceives that earnings will be disappointing, even when they will be up. If they do not match analysts' expectations, the stock usually falls.

Exchange Rate Mechanism (ERM): Most currencies in the European Community are part of the Exchange Rate Mechanism, an agreement to keep each country's money within a fixed range of values against the others.

federal funds rate: The interest rate charged by one Federal Reserve branch when it loans money overnight to another Federal Reserve branch.

fixed-income securities: These securities come in many forms. Basically, they are bonds or short-term instruments, such as notes or CDs. Fixed-income securities pay a fixed rate of interest, which does not normally fluctuate.

front-end load mutual funds: Mutual funds that have a commission, such as 4 percent. This is in contrast to no-load mutual funds or rear-load funds. Front-end load funds are generally distributed by brokerage houses. Although no-load funds have records that are similar to load funds, it should not be assumed that it is always wise to ignore load funds. Some, such as the Templeton and American Funds groups, are well managed and well worth considering.

fundamental analysis: The analysis of stocks with emphasis on company, industry, and economic factors and may include the strength of the balance sheet, the caliber of the company's management, its products and services, its share of the market, or its marketing arm and research capability. It is the opposite of technical analysis, which looks at stock prices and trading volume factors.

greenmail: A term that applies to the financial payment made to a predatory investor in a hostile takeover attempt. When greenmail is paid, the takeover attempt is thwarted—but at a price.

hemline theory: A method of forecasting the stock market based on whether women's hemlines are rising or falling. According to the theory, hemlines and stock prices rise and fall in tandem.

income statement: An accounting statement that shows how a company has been doing, listing its revenues and expenses in the previous quarter or year. These numbers are generally compared to the same period a year earlier to see whether the company is doing well or poorly.

index fund: A mutual fund that has no active management. Instead, the fund simply buys all of the stocks in an index such as the S&P 500. Index funds are geared to track the market. They will rarely do better or worse than the index. Surprisingly, index funds tend to outperform the average mutual fund. One reason is low expenses because they don't have to pay the salaries of analysts and portfolio managers.

indicated yield: The dividend yield that is expected based on the current quarterly dividend. If the company was paying 90 cents a share and has just raised its payout to $1 per quarter, you would assume that the total annual dividend will be $4. If the stock is selling for $100, the indicated dividend yield would be 4 percent.

insider buying and selling: The action insiders (mostly company officials) are taking concerning their own stock. Whenever a high official or board member (or some other major shareholder) buys or sells stock in the company, this transaction must be reported to the government and made public. Some investors follow these transactions, figuring it would make sense to buy when management is buying and to sell when management is selling. Studies on this topic are not very conclusive, however. One reason is the time period that elapses after the transaction is made public. Insiders are sometimes quite tardy about reporting their transactions. By the time you learn about it, the price of the stock may be quite different.

investment advisor: A firm that manages the portfolios of investors. There is usually a minimum portfolio size, such as $300,000 or perhaps several million dollars. Most investment advisors are registered with the Securities and Exchange Commission (SEC). Investors sometimes shun investment advisors because they are wary of paying the annual fee (typically 1 percent). Yet, they don't seem to be aware that bank trust departments and mutual funds have similar fees. For their part, brokers charge commissions that may be equally as high. In short, all investing involves fees of one sort or another.

junk bonds: Low-quality bonds that have a high yield. The risk is greater because some of them are destined to default. It is probably best not to get involved unless you are prepared to suffer an occasional loss of principal.

leverage: Among its several meanings, the one most often heard refers to the amount of debt on the balance sheet. If a company has a high percentage of debt in its capital structure, it is said to be highly leveraged. Capital can be acquired by a corporation by selling either debt or equity instruments. In this way, capital can be acquired at a low fixed rate and, as earnings increase, funds available for dividends are leveraged up.

limit orders: Given to brokers to protect you against a sharp change in the price of the stock after you have instructed your broker to buy or sell a particular stock. You might tell the broker to buy 200 shares but only if it can be accomplished at $42 a share or less. Most investors prefer market orders because they are executed at the current price.

limited partnerships: These are investment partnerships that invest in oil and gas ventures, real estate, cable TV, movie production companies, or even airplane leases. The idea is to earn income from the rent, leases, or business cash flow, then get capital gains when the business or property is sold at some future date.

liquidity: Another term that has more than one meaning. If you have all of your wealth tied up in real estate—which can take months to sell— you are not very liquid. By contrast, if you are invested in cash, stocks, and bonds, you are very liquid because these assets can be converted to cash within a few days.

margin: Can mean the percentage of income that is revenues or sales. It might also refer to the percentage of an investment one must put up when buying stock "on margin" by borrowing part of the purchase price from a broker. Most conservative investors avoid buying stocks on margin. To be sure, they multiply their profits if the stock advances, but they also multiply their losses if the stock plummets.

market letters: Published by self-proclaimed stock market experts who profess to know a lot about a subject or have a particular system they believe works in beating the market. There are hundreds of stock market letters being sold for $25 a year to as high as $500—and a few are even higher than that. Studies indicate that these letters fall short of guiding you on the road to riches. Read Mark Hulbert's column "Wall Street Irregular" in *Forbes* to gain a good understanding of this topic. Beware of stock market letter advertising claims. The SEC has not been very successful in preventing some market letter writers from fraudulent claims. If the record of a market letter sounds too good to be true, you can be sure something is amiss. As a group, market letter advice does less well than the Dow Jones Industrial Average or the S&P 500.

market timing: This concept sounds like a good idea because it implies you can sell stocks at the top and get back in when they hit bottom. The flaw is that you have to be right twice. If you are lucky enough to sell at the top, there is no assurance you will be fortunate enough to recognize the bottom. If you fail and merely leave your proceeds in a money-market fund, stocks may take off and leave you at the starting post.

money-market funds: Highly liquid mutual funds providing interest to short-term, idle funds; they are invested in short-term financial instruments. For the most part, there is little risk.

moving average: A term used by technical analysts—those who rely on charts and graphs in making their investment decisions. One such average is a 200-day moving average. Each point on the moving average represents the average price of the stock for the past 200 days. If you believe in this strategy, it would be wise to stay out of the stock when the stock is selling below its moving average. While the concept is quite popular, there is not much evidence that it will enable you to time your buy-and-sell decisions. This is particularly true when you factor in taxes and commissions.

municipal bond: Refers to a bond issued by a government or government agency other than the federal government. It could be a city, county, state, or toll road, for example. Investors are attracted because interest payments are free of federal income tax. They may also be free of state or local taxation if the bond is issued by that particular state or local government. On the other hand, if an Ohio resident buys a Michigan municipal bond, it would be subject to taxation in Ohio. For further information on municipal bonds, you might like to read *The Municipal Bond Market* by Wilson White (The Financial Press, 1985) or *The Municipal Bond Handbook* by Sylvan G. Feldstein, Frank J. Fabozzi, and Irving M. Pollack (Dow Jones-Irwin, 1983).

mutual fund: An investment company that pools the resources of hundreds or thousands of investors. Such funds are often worth several hundred million dollars and are invested in a variety of investment vehicles, such as stocks, bonds, and money-market funds. The advantages of mutual funds are professional management and diversification. The disadvantages are the cost of management and the built-in tax liabilities. Two excellent books on mutual funds are *Straight Talk about Mutual Funds* by Dian Vujovich (McGraw-Hill, 1992) and *Bogle on Mutual Funds* by John C. Bogle (Richard D. Irwin, Inc., 1994)

net worth: Calculated by deducting debt from assets. If debt exceeds assets, the company has a negative net worth.

New York Stock Exchange: Located in New York City and is the site of trading of the shares of about 2600 corporations. Most smaller companies are traded on the American Stock Exchange or over the counter. There are also a number of small, regional exchanges.

no-load mutual fund: One in which the sales charge is not deducted from the dollars initially invested and is sold by the fund itself rather than by a broker. There are, however, no-load funds sold by brokers, but they generally have trailer fees that are paid to the broker, which means they are not precisely no-load funds.

odd lot: Less than 100 shares of stock. A round lot is 100 shares. In years past, investors were less reluctant to buy an odd lot than they are today. Small investors tend to prefer mutual funds today. The cost of buying an odd lot can be high if the brokerage house has a minimum commission charge, such as $50.

options: Agreements allowing an investor to buy or sell shares of stock within a certain period for a specified price. "Puts" are options to sell, and "calls" are options to buy.

over the counter (OTC): Refers to stocks that are not listed on an exchange. Rather, the shares are bought and sold by dealers, normally brokerage houses. These brokerage houses actually buy and sell for their own account the stocks that they make a market in. They make a profit because of the spread between the bid and asked price. This spread is normally much higher on an inactive stock. An active stock may have a bid of $25 and an asked price of $25.25. An inactive stock may have a one- or two-point (dollar) spread. Some investors are reluctant to buy a stock that is not listed on a major stock exchange. This fear of over-the-counter stocks is not justified. Some fine companies are quite happy to stay OTC, including Ericsson, J.B. Hunt, Roadway, Intel, Kimball, and Reuters Holdings.

payout ratio: A company's dividend and earnings per share. If the dividend is $1 and the earnings per share is $3, the payout ratio would be 33.3 percent. In this example, if the dividend is $2, the payout ratio would be 66.7 percent. A low payout ratio is often indicative of a company that is plowing back its profits into new products, research, acquisitions, or expansion, which would enhance its growth and prove to be a good investment.

penny stock: Low-priced stocks that are extremely speculative. There may be no earnings and a shaky financial structure. Boiler-room (illegal sales operations) operators often call unsophisticated investors and pitch them on the merits of buying these low-priced stocks. Don't be gulled into falling for their most convincing palaver. Your own broker—a person of integrity, such as Steve Lazarides in Canton, Ohio, a Merrill Lynch account executive I know and trust—is the one to do business with.

point: The same as $1. If a stock declines two points, it has fallen in price by $2.

poison pill: A strategy written into a company's articles of incorporation and used by the company's management to discourage a hostile takeover. Shareholders don't benefit from poison pills because they miss out on a takeover at a price that is usually well above the current market. Management, on the other hand, tries to fend off a takeover because the new owners might dispense with their services.

portfolio manager: A person who manages a portfolio of stocks, such as a mutual fund or the portfolio of a major investor. Portfolio managers may be employed by investment advisors, banks, insurance companies, or pension funds among others.

preferred stock: Stocks that are not issued by all corporations. Common stocks are. Preferred stocks are more like bonds than they are like common stock. They differ from bonds in that they don't have a maturity date. Most preferred stocks have a fixed dividend that does not change. Management does not have to pay the dividend if profits do not warrant it. Preferred stocks are among the world's *worst* investments and should be avoided by individual investors. On the other hand, they have more appeal to corporate investors who derive a tax break on the dividends.

price/earnings (P/E) ratio: Calculated by dividing the price of the stock by the earnings per share. If the stock sells for $30 and the company is earning $1.50 per share, the price/earnings ratio would be 20. Investors sometimes call it the P/E ratio or the price/earnings multiple. The P/E may also be calculated by using the projected earnings rather than the most recent 12-month's figure. I do not subscribe to the use of future earnings because I have no faith whatsoever in estimated earnings.

price range: May refer to the high and low price of the stock within a certain period of time, such as the past 52 weeks. Some investors try to buy stocks that are selling well below the 52-week high. There is no assurance, however, that such a strategy will prove profitable.

prime rate: The interest rate charged by banks to customers with good credit ratings. It is important because it may influence other interest rates, such as those charged for mortgages or car payments.

prospectus: A required document drawn up to comply with the SEC's requirements governing when a new issue is to be sold to the public. Unless you understand legal jargon, you will find these weighty documents difficult to read and interpret. In any event, it is best to avoid investing in an issue that requires a prospectus. Buying stocks already trading on an exchange or over the counter is a much better way to invest your money.

public utilities: Normally regulated by state governments and occasionally by the federal government. This is because they often have a monopoly to sell their product or service in a prescribed geographic area. Because they have very little direct competition, it is necessary to regulate the price they charge as well as other actions they take. The four main public utilities are electric, natural gas, telephone, and water. For more information on this group of stocks, I recommend *Plugging into Utilities* by Donald L. Cassidy (Probus Publishing Company, 1993).

random walk theory: An idea dreamed up by college professors. It is their contention that stock prices cannot be accurately forecast; that is, share prices are reached in a random fashion. No matter how hard you try, you will not be able to outperform the general market—so the theory goes. Although this has been true of mutual funds and most other institutional investors, it does not follow that it is impossible to be a successful investor.

rate base: A public utility's major assets, such as electric generating plants. The state commission uses this rate base to help determine whether it will grant a rate increase to the utility.

round lot: One hundred shares of stock, as opposed to an odd lot, which is less than 100 shares.

short selling: The sale of borrowed stock (from a broker) by an investor who hopes to make a profit by buying an equal number of shares later at a lower price to replace the borrowed stock. The experts liken this to casino gambling and crap shoots. "I've never sold a stock short in my life," says Peter Lynch, former manager of Fidelity's successful Magellan Fund. He says it makes more sense spending time figuring out what stocks to buy.

standard deviation: A statistical term used throughout this book to help you determine what is good and what is bad or what is low and what is high. What it amounts to is this: the standard deviation measures the dispersion in a distribution of data. It is difficult to calculate unless you have a good calculator. If you wanted to determine if a stock had too high a P/E ratio, you might compare its P/E ratio with 30 or 40 other stocks selected at random. In a normal curve, about 16 percent will be in the high area—which means they are more than one standard deviation above the mean (a fancy term for the average).

stock dividend: Not a cash dividend. Some companies will declare a 2 percent stock dividend when they would prefer not to pay out any more cash. If you start out with 100 shares, you will now have 102 shares. You might think you are richer, but this would be an illusion. Since every other shareholder also has 2 percent more shares, you have gained nothing.

stock splits: These occur when the price of a stock gets too high to be attractive to investors. A stock selling for $80, for instance, might be split four-for-one. Thus, an investor who owned 100 shares would now own 400 shares. But the value of these shares would remain the same.

subsidiary: Part of a company, for example, one engaged in a different business. Many companies diversify by buying companies that make a product different from their main line of business. Such a business would be called a subsidiary.

symbol: An abbreviation for the company name used to differentiate a company from all others. The full term is the *stock ticker symbol*. If you are in a broker's branch office, you will need to know the symbols of any stocks you want to check on the quote machine in the lobby. Every broker has access to a quote machine. They often know the symbols of hundreds of stocks.

take-or-pay contract: One that obligates the buyer of a product to take delivery of a certain volume of goods or services. If the company does not take the required amount, it must be paid for nonetheless. A good example is the take-or-pay contracts negotiated by natural gas distributors. When there is a shortage of gas, the price is high. Contracts negotiated at these high prices have to be honored later when spot prices are much lower. Contracts such as these caused the bankruptcy of Columbia Gas.

tax-loss carry forwards: These enable a company to pay lower taxes because it can use losses of prior years to offset profits being generated currently or in future periods.

technical analysis: Different from fundamental analysis. A technical analyst may not care what a company's business is or what its prospects or earnings are. Such an analyst reaches a decision to buy or sell by using charts and graphs as well as other numbers that would be foreign to a fundamental analyst.

variable annuity: An annuity sold by an insurance company. It is less conservative than a fixed annuity because it lacks the usual guarantees. This is because it uses mutual funds that invest in stocks and bonds as its primary investment vehicles.

white knight: A slang term referring to a company that could rescue another company from a hostile takeover. Recently, IPALCO Enterprises, an electric utility based in Indianapolis, tried to make a hostile takeover of PSI Resources, another electric utility situated nearby. Since PSI did not want to be taken over by IPALCO, it made a concerted effort to support another takeover offer by Cincinnati Gas & Electric, the "white knight."

wire house: A large brokerage house with branches in many cities and states. Merrill Lynch, PaineWebber, and Dean Witter are wire houses. By contrast, McDonald & Company, for example, would not be a wire house because its scope is more regional.

working capital: The excess of current assets over current liabilities. If these two numbers are equal, or if current liabilities exceed current assets, a company has no working capital and cannot pay its bills out of current funds.

yield to maturity: A bond term. If a bond has a 6 percent coupon, it will have a different yield to maturity if the price of the bond is other than $100. Let's say the price is $90. The bond will gradually rise in price as the maturity date approaches. This capital appreciation has to be taken into account when you calculate yield to maturity. Bond experts have tables that help provide the answer. Or a computer may be used.

zero coupon bond: A bond that pays no current interest. Rather, it is purchased at a large discount to the maturity (face) value. Such bonds are preferred by investors who have no need for current income. The federal government taxes this profit each year even though the investor is not receiving any cash. The best way to avoid this tax is to put zero coupon bonds in an IRA or some other qualified retirement plan. You might also buy a municipal (tax-free) zero coupon bond.

5

Diversification and Asset Allocation

Most investors are well aware that common stocks involve risk because they fluctuate almost every day, sometimes a point or more. A point, of course, is one dollar. It's rather like poker, where colored chips represent real money. You flinch less when you lose a few chips.

Even blue chips fluctuate. One day recently, one of the bluest of blue chips, Minnesota Mining and Manufacturing (3M), dropped 10 points. More often, however, the changes are less than a point. But, over a period of weeks, these small moves can translate into a substantial change in price.

This volatility is what drives skittish people up the wall with fear. They can see their life's earnings going down the drain. In bad years, losses can amount to 10, 20, and even 30 percent.

Some Strict Rules to Follow

In order to reduce this risk, diversification is absolutely necessary. A well-diversified portfolio should contain at least 15 names. In a small portfolio, moreover, no two stocks should be from the same industry—and not more than 10 percent should be invested in any industry.

Unfortunately, very few investors follow this advice. They tend to concentrate on utilities, banks, and oil stocks. Even worse, they sometimes have nearly all their assets in *one* stock—generally a local stock because a member of the family has close ties to the company or spent many years working there.

Such disregard for diversification can be fatal if someone pulls the rug out from under that stock. This has happened to such stocks as U.S. Surgical, Avon, Westinghouse Electric, Philip Morris, American Brands, Merck, Syntex, American Home Products, IBM, General Motors, and hundreds of others. Diversification is the first rule of investing. It cannot be overemphasized.

Asset Allocation

Closely allied is asset allocation. Common stocks are one group of investments, but there are others such as bonds, preferred stocks, and money-market funds. What is the best mix of assets? In the pages that follow, I will discuss this aspect of investing in considerable detail.

If you have never owned a common stock and are now contemplating your first purchase, how is it possible to achieve diversification? The obvious answer is to buy a mutual fund. Most funds own scores of different stocks in many different industries. There are, to be sure, specialized mutual funds that do not offer much in the way of diversification because they confine their investing to a narrow sector of the economy such as health care, automotive, utilities, or oil. You would have to invest in several of these funds to achieve diversification.

Because you are reading a book on common stocks, I will assume you don't have a strong interest in mutual funds. If you would like more information on this method of investing, you may find it useful to read my discussion on this subject in the Introduction. But don't read it if you are looking for a favorable treatise on mutual funds. Although I am not exactly rabid on the subject, I make it crystal clear that I much prefer individual common stocks.

A Tough Ailment to Cure

As a professional money manager, I see the folly of poor diversification. It is by far the toughest problem to cure, once it has gone too far. It's like trying to quit smoking or give up cocaine. In the early stages, it is easy to treat but not after it has become an ingrained habit.

Here's what I am talking about. Let's say you live in Cincinnati, the headquarters of one of America's premier corporations, Procter & Gamble. It is not difficult to find a worker in one of their plants who owns one stock worth $300,000. No amount of cajoling will convince that person that Procter & Gamble stock might decline some day.

In one sense, the problem has already progressed too far. Because the stock was purchased over a long period of time, there is a huge capital gain to deal with whenever the shares are sold. Thus, $300,000, after taxes are paid, is no longer $300,000. It might be only $250,000 or $225,000.

Even a hardened advocate of diversification finds it difficult to solve the problem at this late date. If, for instance, you split up the $225,000 into 20 different stocks, there is no assurance these 20 stocks will perform well enough to make up for the $75,000 paid to the IRS.

The best way to solve the problem is not to get trapped into it in the first place. Whenever you buy a stock, make sure you don't buy more of what you already have. If you already have a utility, don't rush out to buy another one—at least not until you have purchased at least 10 stocks in other industries.

Are You Fixated on Public Utilities?

Even this advice can lead you astray. Let's say, for instance, that you already own SCEcorp, a major electric utility serving Southern California. You are aware that you should not buy another electric utility so you buy Washington Gas Light, which distributes natural gas. Then you buy BellSouth, a telephone company, followed by American Water Works.

In one sense, these four stocks are in different industries. Even so, they are all public utilities. To be sure, they provide you with a measure of diversification but not enough. It would be better to buy a bank stock, an oil stock, a drug stock, and a railroad. These are distinctly different industries. More than that, they are in different "sectors."

It is important to understand this. Although there are 70 or 80 industries, there are only 12 sectors. Each sector is comprised of several industries. This can be tricky because you might think you are diversifying when you buy Merck (pharmaceuticals), Coca-Cola (beverages), Gillette (cosmetics and toiletries), Dun & Bradstreet (publishing), Walgreen (drug stores), and Melville (shoes).

Industries and Sectors Are Not the Same

Admittedly, these stocks are in different industries, but they are all in the same sector: *consumer growth*. Although these might seem like great companies in great industries, it was a poor place to be during 1993. If you were highly concentrated in this sector in 1993, your performance was below average. Unfortunately, these particular industries have a great deal of intuitive appeal, and conservative investors found out the hard way that they were not nearly as safe as they had imagined them to be.

Still another sector that seems safe and sane is *consumer staples.* It contains such stocks as Unilever, N.V., a Dutch company that competes against Procter & Gamble. Neither one has set the world on fire lately. Here is a sample of lackluster stocks in this sector that were major disappointments in 1993: Kellogg, H.J. Heinz, American Brands, Philip Morris, and Borden. They all seem like sensible and prudent investments. Unfortunately, they haven't been.

That Warm and Cozy Feeling

By contrast, you probably ignored a sector called *credit cyclicals.* It contains such names as Armstrong World, Snap-On Tools, H.F. Ahmanson, and Fleetwood. Some rather hefty gains have been recorded by this group. The chances are that these stocks don't ring a bell. In other words, they are not household names that give you that warm and cozy feeling. Thus, like most investors, you ignore them.

I learned early in my adult life that successful people often do the things that failures are unwilling to do. When I originally heard this admonition, I was a salesman. Good salesmen do the things that will make them successful, such as calling on lots of prospects—most of whom will give them the cold shoulder. Poor salesmen, by contrast, can't stomach this constant rejection.

The same thesis holds true in investing. If you always buy stocks that are "comfortable," you won't make much money.

A few examples of "comfortable" stocks that bit the dust are IBM, Borden, Avon Products, Long Island Lighting, Commonwealth Edison, Eli Lilly, ConAgra, Baxter International, Philip Morris, American Brands, and Anheuser Busch, to name a few of the obvious ones.

This brings us back to sectors. As noted earlier, there are 12 of them. A well-diversified portfolio should be in all 12 sectors but not necessarily with the same percentage. If you had equal amounts invested in each sector, you would have 8.33 percent in each one. I see no reason to believe that this is necessary—or even desirable. A good rule of thumb is to invest at least 4 percent in each sector but no more than 12 percent. Even 12 percent is too much if it happens to be concentrated in the sectors that are suffering from a sinking spell.

There is one problem with the sector idea: it is not always convenient to get a list to go by. We use one provided by Merrill Lynch, which I assume is available to anyone who deals with that firm. Since you may prefer to do business elsewhere, let me discuss each of these sectors and give you some representative names.

Credit cyclicals is a sector already mentioned and one that you may want to ignore. I sometimes feel the same way, but I force myself to use the stocks in the portfolios that we manage. This paid off handsomely in 1993. If you are building a portfolio, you might want to look at the three stocks in Table 5-1.

Consumer growth is a huge sector, with all the stocks you would love to own. This sector is broken down into a host of industries, such as broadcasting, drugs, hospital supplies, entertainment, publishing, cosmetics, soft drinks, and restaurants. You won't have much trouble finding something to make you feel warm and cozy here. But don't make the mistake of loading up on these favorites. Three stocks that appeal to me at the moment are shown in Table 5-2.

Consumer cyclicals is a group that tends to be more affected by what happens in the economy, such as autos, footwear, retail, advertising,

Table 5-1

Stock	Symbol	S&P rating	P/E ratio	Institutional owners	Dividend yield (%)	Price 8-31-93 ($)
Snap-On Tools	SNA	B+	25.95	233	2.6	42
Fleetwood Enterprises	FLE	B+	18.15	222	2.2	22½
Skyline Corp.	SKY	B+	18.75	134	2.8	17¼

Table 5-2

Stock	Symbol	S&P rating	P/E ratio	Institutional owners	Dividend yield (%)	Price 8-31-93 ($)
Dun & Bradstreet	DNB	A+	19.49	698	3.9	62⅜
Bristol-Myers Squibb	BMY	A+	12.81	1147	5.1	56⅛
Reuters	RTRSY	NR	26.57	286	1.6	69⅝

NR = no rating

and textiles. It is not a good sector when stocks are at their apex. On the other hand, it is where the action is when there are indications that the economy is coming back to life. Table 5-3 shows three such stocks that I find attractive.

Conglomerates are companies that have a stake in several different industries. Table 5-4 shows three that appeal to me.

Financials includes mostly banks, savings and loans, and insurance companies. Table 5-5 shows three that might do well in the year ahead.

Transportation, as you might suspect, consists largely of railroads, airlines, and trucking firms. Table 5-6 shows three that seem attractive.

Utilities is made up of four sectors: electric, natural gas, telephone, and water. Table 5-7 shows three to consider.

Basic industries is made up of stocks that are geared to serving other industries rather than the consumer. This includes chemicals, papers, metals, and steel. Table 5-8 shows three that should work out.

Capital goods companies are those that make machinery that is sold to other companies, which they will use in producing their products. Table 5-9 shows three that appeal to me at the moment.

Table 5-3

Stock	Symbol	S&P rating	P/E ratio	Institutional owners	Dividend yield (%)	Price 8-31-93 ($)
Genuine Parts	GPC	A+	18.63	406	2.8	37¼
Interpublic	IPG	A+	18.71	305	1.7	29¾
Kmart	KM	A−	12.99	714	4.2	23

Table 5-4

Stock	Symbol	S&P rating	P/E ratio	Institutional owners	Dividend yield (%)	Price 8-31-93 ($)
Alcatel	ALA	NR	13.40	75	1.4	26⅛
Hanson, PLC	HAN	NR	13.96	362	5.1	19⅛
Textron	TXT	A	14.54	373	2.2	57⅛

Table 5-5

Stock	Symbol	S&P rating	P/E ratio	Institutional owners	Dividend yield (%)	Price 8-31-93 ($)
Jefferson-Pilot	JP	A−	13.56	281	2.8	55⅞
Lincoln National	LNC	B+	11.63	347	3.3	46⅝
National City Corp.	NCC	A−	11.61	325	4.1	26⅛

Table 5-6

Stock	Symbol	S&P rating	P/E ratio	Institutional owners	Dividend yield (%)	Price 8-31-93 ($)
Conrail	CRR	B−	15.36	427	2.4	53¾
J.B. Hunt	JBHT	B+	23.08	83	0.8	24
Roadway Services	ROAD	A−	17.87	237	2.4	59½

Capital goods–technology combines the characteristics of the previous group but includes more sophisticated technology. Table 5-10 presents three of these for you to look at.

Consumer staples sounds like a conservative group because it consists of items that are essential, such as food. In the past year or two, however, these stocks have been big losers. Perhaps it's about time they came back to life. Three that I have been recommending lately are shown in Table 5-11.

Energy consists of oil and related stocks. Most investors like this group, probably because dividend yields are sometimes above average. You might find the stocks in Table 5-12 of interest.

If you have considerable resources, let's say at least $100,000, you might like to use all 36 of these stocks. It is difficult to imagine that you would regret this decision. Because this portfolio was originated about a year prior to the publication of this book, about a year will have elapsed before you set your eyes on it. Just for the fun of it, you might check *The Wall Street Journal* to see how my portfolio has fared. When you do, make sure you adjust for any stock splits that occurred between August 31, 1993, and the date you make your calculations.

Table 5-7

Stock	Symbol	S&P rating	P/E ratio	Institutional owners	Dividend yield (%)	Price 8-31-93 ($)
British Gas	BRG	NR	20.87	69	4.8	49⅞
IPALCO	IPL	B+	15.30	176	5.3	38¼
KU Energy	KU	A	15.72	131	5.0	31¾

Table 5-8

Stock	Symbol	S&P rating	P/E ratio	Institutional owners	Dividend yield (%)	Price 8-31-93 ($)
Great Lakes Chemical	GLK	A−	19.13	500	0.5	68½
Kimberly-Clark	KMB	A+	23.33	597	3.5	49
Lubrizol	LZ	B+	23.42	325	2.4	35⅛

Table 5-9

Stock	Symbol	S&P rating	P/E ratio	Institutional owners	Dividend yield (%)	Price 8-31-93 ($)
Dover	DOV	A−	21.36	324	1.8	52¾
Emerson Electric	EMR	A+	19.76	740	2.4	61¼
Hubbell A	HUB.A	A+	16.82	312	3.2	50⅝

Table 5-10

Stock	Symbol	S&P rating	P/E ratio	Institutional owners	Dividend yield (%)	Price 8-31-93 ($)
EG&G	EGG	A	12.50	236	2.7	19½
Intel	INTC	B	15.75	1030	0.3	64¼
United Technologies	UTX	B	NM	502	3.2	56⅞

NM = not meaningful

Table 5-11

Stock	Symbol	S&P rating	P/E ratio	Institutional owners	Dividend yield (%)	Price 8-31-93 ($)
American Brands	AMB	A	7.96	546	6.0	32⅝
Grand Metropolitan	GRM	NR	17.93	87	3.0	27¼
Unilever, N. V.	UN	A−	13.58	368	2.6	108

Table 5-12

Stock	Symbol	S&P rating	P/E ratio	Institutional owners	Dividend yield (%)	Price 8-31-93 ($)
Elf Aquitaine	ELF	NR	17.08	89	2.3	37¾
Royal Dutch Petroleum	RD	A	16.38	838	4.2	100¾
Texaco	TX	B−	15.05	898	4.9	64⅞

The Ultimate Portfolio

I realize that you may not be rich enough to buy all 36 stocks. Assuming you have enough cash on hand to buy 12 of these stocks, which ones should you buy? That would depend on what type of investor you are. Obviously, if income is your sole consideration, you would pick the stock with the highest yield from each sector, so I won't bother to make up a portfolio for you. If, however, you are like many investors, you would feel most comfortable with a portfolio that offered some income as well as reasonable growth. Table 5-13 shows my selections.

If you are a more aggressive investor and are looking primarily for growth and don't care much about income, Table 5-14 presents yet another portfolio.

Falling in Love with Local Stocks

From what I have been able to observe over the years, investors like two types of stocks: those they are familiar with and those that are

Table 5-13

Stock	Symbol	S&P rating	P/E ratio	Institutional owners	Dividend yield (%)	Price 8-31-93 ($)
Genuine Parts	GPC	A+	18.63	406	2.8	37¼
Snap-On Tools	SNA	B+	25.95	233	2.6	42
Dun & Bradstreet	DNB	A+	19.49	698	3.9	62⅜
Hanson, PLC	HAN	NR	13.96	362	5.1	19⅛
Lincoln National	LNC	B+	11.63	347	3.3	46⅝
Roadway Services	ROAD	A−	17.87	237	2.4	59½
KU Energy	KU	A	15.72	131	5.0	31¾
Kimberly-Clark	KMB	A+	23.33	597	3.5	49
Emerson Electric	EMR	A+	19.76	740	2.4	61¼
United Technologies	UTX	B	NM	502	3.2	56⅞
Unilever, N.V.	UN	A−	13.58	368	2.6	108
Texaco	TX	B−	15.05	898	4.9	64⅞

Table 5-14

Stock	Symbol	S&P rating	P/E ratio	Institutional owners	Dividend yield (%)	Price 8-31-93 ($)
Fleetwood Enterprises	FLE	B+	18.15	222	2.2	22½
Reuters	RTRSY	NR	26.57	286	1.6	69⅝
Interpublic	IPG	A+	18.71	305	1.7	29¾
Textron	TXT	A	14.54	373	2.2	57⅛
Lincoln National	LNC	B+	11.63	347	3.3	46⅝
J.B. Hunt	JBHT	B+	23.08	83	0.8	24
KU Energy	KU	A	15.72	131	5.0	31¾
Great Lakes Chemical	GLK	A−	19.13	500	0.5	68½
Dover	DOV	A−	21.36	324	1.8	52¾
Intel	INTC	B	15.75	1030	0.3	64¼
Unilever, N.V.	UN	A−	13.58	368	2.6	108
Elf Aquitaine	ELF	NR	17.08	89	2.3	37¾

local. A good many of the stocks I have mentioned do not fall into either category. For that reason, I am providing you with a thumbnail sketch of each stock.

Alcatel Alsthom (*AKA—New York Stock Exchange [NYSE]*) is the second-largest French company. Alcatel has a major stake in three businesses—telecommunications equipment, power company generators, and high-speed train manufacture. With sales of about $31 billion, Alcatel ranks in the top 40 companies in the world.

American Brands (*AMB—NYSE*) is primarily a tobacco company, although it has a number of nontobacco businesses, including distilled spirits, life insurance, hardware, and office products. American Tobacco Co. manufactures cigarettes in the United States. Brand names include Lucky Strike, Pall Mall, Tareyton, Carleton, Malibu, Montclair, and Misty. Gallagher Limited makes cigarettes outside the United States, primarily in the United Kingdom.

Bristol-Myers Squibb (*BMY—NYSE*) is a major health care company, with strong participation in a number of sectors of the industry, including pharmaceuticals, over-the-counter drugs, nutritional products, surgical instruments, medical devices, toiletries, and skincare products. The company's product line is vast, including such well-known brands as Ban, Bufferin, Excedrin, Mum, Miss Clairol, Nuprin, Enfamil, Theragram, and Loving Care. In pharmaceuticals, its largest product is Capoten, a drug to control hypertension (high blood pressure).

British Gas (*BRG—NYSE*) provides about 90 percent of the natural gas used in Britain and is the largest supplier of gas in the world.

Consolidated Rail Corporation (*CRR—NYSE*) operates the largest freight railroad system in 14 northeastern and midwestern states as well as the District of Columbia and the Canadian province of Quebec. Conrail is one of the largest rail transporters of auto parts and finished vehicles. What distinguishes Conrail from the other rails is its aggressive growth plan, its track record, and its ability and desire to buy in its own shares.

Dover Corporation (*DOV—NYSE*) is comprised of nearly 70 diverse companies that manufacture a variety of specialized industrial products marketed nationally to such industries as building, petroleum, electronics, and aerospace. Products include elevators, petroleum production equipment, surface mount electronic assembly products, automotive lifts, kettlers, steamers, and food service equipment.

Dun & Bradstreet (*DNB—NYSE*) is the world's leading marketer of information, software, and services for business decision making. Its operations include Nielsen Media Research, D & B Business Credit Services, and Donnelley Directory publishing.

EG&G (EGG—NYSE) is a Fortune 200 company, with annual sales in excess of $2.7 billion. It designs and manufactures laboratory and field test instruments and electronic and mechanical components for commercial customers. EG&G provides engineering, precision component manufacturing, and test site operating and management services to many government agencies and laboratories.

Elf Aquitaine (ELF—NYSE) is the largest corporation in France and the sixth-largest integrated oil and gas company in the world. The company is an integrated producer, refiner, and marketer; it is self-sufficient in crude oil. Elf conducts a specialty chemical business, primarily in North America. It has withstood the economic decline well.

Emerson Electric (EMR—NYSE) is a diversified manufacturing company, with an emphasis on electrical equipment. Commercial and industrial products include process control instrumentation and systems, integral horsepower motors, industrial machinery, and equipment and components as well as computer support products. Earnings have increased for 34 consecutive years. Management is a stickler for tight cost controls and has implemented a strategy of seeking growth in niche markets and timely acquisitions.

Fleetwood Enterprises (FLE—NYSE) is the largest domestic manufacturer of recreational vehicles and manufactured housing. Fleetwood's motor homes, travel trailers, and folding trailers are used for leisure time activities, including vacations, sightseeing, and fishing trips.

Genuine Parts (GPC—NYSE) distributes automotive replacement parts throughout the nation. This is accomplished through 6100 independent outlets and 475 company-owned jobbers. The company also operates in Canada. Auto replacement parts tend to be far more stable than original equipment. The company also sells industrial replacement parts and distributes information processing supplies, furniture, and machines.

Grand Metropolitan PLC (GRM—NYSE), headquartered in London, England, specializes in branded consumer businesses, primarily food, drinks, and retailing. Its businesses include Pillsbury, Green Giant, Häagen-Dazs, Burger King, and J&B Scotch whisky.

Great Lakes Chemical (GLK—NYSE) is the world's leading producer of bromine, brominated specialty chemicals, and furfural derivatives. Bromine specialties include fire control chemicals (flame retardants used in plastic resins for electronic devices, construction, textiles, and appliances). The company has been notably successful in a succession of antidilutive acquisitions.

Hanson, PLC (HAN—NYSE), headquartered in London, England, operates over 150 businesses—cranes, golf clubs, kitchenware, light fixtures, leisure products, and tobacco. It participates in extractive industries through the production of bricks, cement, aggregates, and coal.

Hubbell Inc. (HUB.A—NYSE) produces a wide variety of electrical products, including fixtures and devices for hazardous locations. Hubbell avoids commodity-type products, preferring to benefit from the wider margins on its line of specialties. The company does not make products for the consumer but prefers to concentrate on the industrial sector, which is less vulnerable to foreign competition.

J.B. Hunt (JBHT—Over-the-Counter [OTC]) is one of the largest domestic irregular route, truckload carriers. The company has been increasing its intermodal business by replacing trailers with containers and chassis. Equipment utilization should improve as Hunt learns how to operate its growing intermodal network.

Intel (INTC—OTC) was founded in 1968. The company's first products were semiconductor memory chips. In 1971, Intel introduced the world's first microprocessor. Intel sells its microprocessor components, modules, and systems directly to companies that incorporate them into their products, such as computer systems manufacturers, makers of automobiles, and a wide variety of industrial and telecommunications equipment.

The Interpublic Group of Companies, Inc. (IPG—NYSE) is one of the largest organizations of advertising agencies in the world. The firm's largest clients are General Motors; Unilever, N.V.; and Coca-Cola. The principal functions of the company's advertising agencies are to plan and create advertising programs for clients and to place the advertising in various media, such as radio, television, magazines, and newspapers.

IPALCO Enterprises (IPL—NYSE), based in Indiana (an excellent state for regulation), is a medium-sized electric utility serving the capital of the state, Indianapolis, a city that is both diversified and strong economically. IPALCO has extremely low rates, making its territory attractive to industry.

Jefferson-Pilot (JP—NYSE) is a holding company whose subsidiaries provide a variety of insurance, financial, and communications products and services. The company's largest subsidiary, Jefferson-Pilot Life Insurance Co., traces its history back to 1903.

Kimberly-Clark (KMB—NYSE) is principally engaged in the manufacturing of a wide range of products for personal, business, and industrial uses. The company's products are sold under a variety of well-known names, including Kleenex, Huggies, Pull-Ups, New Freedom, Kotex, Spenco, Lightdays, Depend, Hi-Dri, Kimguard, Kimwipes, and Classic.

Kmart Corporation (KM—NYSE) is the world's second-largest retailer. There are 2383 general merchandise and 2022 specialty retail outlets in the United States. Specialty retail operations include the nation's largest book chain, Walden Book Co., with 1275 stores. Kmart also operates Builders Square, Pay Less Drug Stores, PACE Membership Warehouse Clubs, Office Max, and Sports Authority stores.

KU Energy Corporation (KU—NYSE) is a holding company whose main subsidiary is Kentucky Utilities. The company is one of the nation's lowest-cost power companies. Its low rates help attract industry to the territory. KU is strong financially, with an excellent balance sheet and utility bonds that are rated AA.

Lubrizol Corporation (LZ—NYSE) is a specialty chemical company and leading producer of additives for engine oils, automatic transmission fluids, gear oil, machine oils, metalworking fluids, and fuels. Lubrizol serves the transportation, industrial, and agricultural markets. Lubrizol is the acknowledged market leader in lubricant additive technology. Lubrizol will benefit from the impact of the technological push on product requirements because manufacturing equipment technology requires more sophisticated lubrication.

National City Corporation (NCC—NYSE) is a major bank holding company based in Cleveland, Ohio. National City is the second-largest bank holding company in Ohio and about the 25th-largest in the United States. The company owns 16 commercial banks with almost 500 offices in Ohio, Kentucky, and Indiana. Fee income, which represents 37 percent of total income, includes trust fees, credit card fees, processing fees, and mortgage banking fees.

Reuters (RTRSY—OTC) is the world's foremost electronic publisher. The company provides business news, market prices, and historical data on currencies, securities, and futures through a global communication network.

Roadway Services (ROAD—OTC) is a holding company engaged in trucking and related operations. Roadway Express, Inc., the company's largest operating company, is a long-haul, unionized motor carrier. It primarily hauls long-haul, less-than-truckload general freight, serving all 50 states, Puerto Rico, Guam, Canada, Mexico, Europe, and the Pacific Rim through 611 terminals.

Royal Dutch Petroleum (RD—NYSE), based in the Netherlands, is the world's largest international oil company with revenues in excess of $100 billion. In the United States, the company's service stations operate under the Shell banner. Royal Dutch has a stake in such businesses as oil production, marketing and refining, natural gas, chemicals, coal, and metals.

The Sherwin-Williams Company (SHW—NYSE) is a 125-year-old worldwide manufacturer and distributor of paint, varnishes, coatings, home decor products and industrial finishes as well as related products and tools. The company operates a chain of some 2000 paint and wallpaper stores in 48 states, in addition to 154 auto coatings outlets. Besides its Sherwin-Williams trade name (sold only in company outlets), the company sells paint under such labels as Dutch Boy, Krylon, Duplicator, Martin-Senour, and KemTone.

Snap-On Tools (SNA—NYSE) is a leading manufacturer and distributor of high-quality hand tools and equipment, primarily for use by professional mechanics and technicians. In recent years, it has expanded its product lines and its targeted markets to include automotive shop equipment, aerospace, electronic equipment service, and medical applications.

Texaco Inc (TX—NYSE) is primarily engaged in the worldwide exploration for and production, transportation, refining, and marketing of crude oil, natural gas, and petroleum products. It recently sold its petrochemicals business. Margin improvement is noteworthy in Latin America and the Far East. While downstream results in Europe will probably continue to reflect the recession there, that shortfall is being more than offset by gains where economies are more robust.

Unilever, N.V. (UN—NYSE) is one of the world's largest producers and marketers of branded and packaged consumer goods. The company operates in 90 countries through 500 operating companies. Its principal products are margarine, edible fats and oils, salad dressings, dairy products, frozen foods, ice cream, instant soups, and detergents.

United Technologies Corporation (UTX—NYSE) produces high-technology products and support services to the aerospace, building, and automotive industries. Worldwide Power produces Pratt & Whitney commercial and military aircraft engines and parts. Flight Systems includes Sikorsky military and commercial helicopters and

Hamilton Standard controls. Building Systems consists of Carrier air conditioning and Otis elevators.

The Essence of Asset Allocation

While most investors at least understand what diversification is all about—even though they flagrantly ignore its application in their own portfolio—they are less able to come to grips with asset allocation.

Instead, they concentrate their efforts on picking stocks and other assets that they hope will give them income, safety, and growth. They incessantly fret about what the market is about to do, and they try to pick stocks that will outperform the market. In both instances, they will probably fail to do the right thing.

The truth of the matter is this (at least according to some people who seem to have good credentials): you can't predict what the market will do; you can't build a portfolio that will outperform the market—at least not on a consistent basis.

I certainly agree that you can't predict the market. But I am not convinced that the market will do better than I will. These experts maintain that the really important decision revolves around asset allocation. This is tantamount to saying you should shift your assets around so that you will be in cash before every crash and in stocks just before the beginning of every bull market. This doesn't exactly ring true because these same people claim you can't predict the market. If that is the case, how will you be able to change your asset allocation?

If you are like most investors, you are constantly fretting that a ghastly bear market is lurking around every corner. During my several decades in the investment business, I have listened to countless investors tell me that they didn't want to deal with me because "I don't like the looks of the market."

At no time have I ever heard someone say, "come on over—the market is ready to take off for the stratosphere. I want to buy a bucket full of common stocks."

If you are a worrier, you are not alone.

Since this book is primarily about common stocks, you can assume that I am a devout believer in this form of investing. In my own portfolio, to be sure, I have a few bonds and a few thousand dollars tied up in money-market funds. But the bulk of my emphasis is on common stocks. Over the years, common stocks tend to go up. Perhaps more important, common stock companies keep paying dividends, and they raise them periodically, sometimes once a year. When you retire, you won't have to worry about inflation. For one thing, your Social Security is geared to track the rising cost of living. What it amounts to is this: if your income from Social Security and stock dividends is high enough the day you retire, it will see you through to the bitter end.

Avoiding the Fixed-Income Trap

By contrast, if all your holdings are in bonds, you are in deep trouble. Bonds do not raise their payments. True, they don't fluctuate as much as stocks, but that's not nearly as important as the income they provide.

It is precisely for this reason that I think it is imperative that the bulk of your assets be in stocks—not bonds or money-market funds. In fact, if you never owned any fixed-income instruments, you would be far better off.

I realize, of course, that most people are not ready to accept this advice. They can't get over their fear of a crash that will wipe them out. Admittedly, stocks will fluctuate, and perhaps a bear market is just around the corner. But, does that mean it is the end of the world? Hardly. Most companies continue to pay their dividends regardless of what the price of their shares do. If you are getting $30,000 a year from your stocks, for instance, you will still be getting $30,000 even if the value of your holdings drops down by 30 percent. In any event, bear markets always end, usually in less than two years.

A Formula for All Seasons

If all this sounds like crazy palaver, let me give you a few hints on how to deal with the ups and downs of the stock market. A good friend of mine has solved the problem by dividing his assets into three equal parts: one-third in stocks, one-third in bonds, and one-third in money-market funds. He readjusts the percentages once a year. Thus, if stocks have done well and are now 40 percent, while bonds are 30 percent and money-market holdings are 30 percent, he switches things around to get back to the original configuration.

If you are a gold-plated worrier, you should use this approach. No matter what happens, at least one-third of your holdings will have done well.

If you are a little less of a worrier, here is another way to handle your portfolio. If you are 60 years old, you should have 70 percent of your holdings in common stocks. The rest can be in a combination of bonds and money-market funds, perhaps fifty-fifty.

As you grow older, you increase the percentage in the fixed-income sector but reduce the common stock part by 1 percent each year. Thus, when you are 70, you will have 60 percent in common stocks and 40 percent in fixed income. When you are 80, you will have 50 percent in each sector.

Suppose you are younger than 60. In that case, you increase the percentage in common stocks by 1 percent each year. For example, a person who is 50 will have 80 percent in stocks and only 20 percent in bonds and money-market funds.

Finally, if you are not a nervous Nellie, you should have 90 percent in stocks and 10 percent in fixed income from now until the day you die. Your children will end up rich. And so will you.

6
A Simple Way to Play the Stock Market

As you continue to read this book, you will realize that it is different from most others because it contains a host of stock selection strategies. Most of them are simple to use and do not require any extensive reading or research. All that is required is a pen and paper, a calculator, and a *Stock Guide*.

One of the most intriguing ideas I ever created will take less than 30 minutes to implement. You simply check the current yield on each of the 30 stocks that make up the Dow Jones Industrial Average. Five days a week, these 30 stocks (along with 20 transportation issues and 15 utilities) are listed on page 3 of the third section of *The Wall Street Journal*. No calculations are needed because the yield is given in the stock tables.

This extensively tested system involves investing equal sums of money in the 10 stocks from the Dow with the highest yield. Once a year, the stocks are rebalanced. Normally, this entails selling three or four stocks and replacing them with a similar number with higher yields. It's as simple as that.

This method of investing has been well documented historically. In fact, at least three writers have used my idea as the basis for a full book. My favorite is *The Dividend Investor* (Probus Publishing, 1992) by Harvey C. Knowles III, a Merrill Lynch broker in Cincinnati. The coauthor is Damon H. Petty, a financial consultant with a major brokerage house in San Diego. See also Chapter 18 in my book *Safe Investing* (Simon & Schuster, 1991).

Still Trying to Develop
Better Methods

To be sure, the method does not work every year, but the long-term results (it has been back-checked, or verified, to 1957) are generally about 40 percent better than the market. No mutual fund or bank trust department (at least to my knowledge) can come close to this. Even though this is a sound method, I have not been content. It didn't work in 1992 because IBM and Westinghouse pulled it down. As a consequence, I am constantly trying to develop even better methods.

One of the most interesting involves picking the 15 or 16 highest-yielding stocks from the Dow and then eliminating the two or three that have the most institutional owners. This may seem strange, but it turns out that institutional owners are not always "good judges of good horseflesh." What it amounts to is this: if a stock becomes too popular, it is best to avoid it. Had you followed this advice in 1992, you would *not* have owned IBM, Merck, or Philip Morris. All were losers.

To make this idea crystal clear, let's look at some concrete examples. For instance, suppose we go back to year-end 1985, when the Dow Jones Industrial Average was 1546.67. Next, let's focus on the 16 Dow stocks with the highest yield at that particular time. The number of stocks used depends on which ones have above-average yields. It's generally about 15 but can vary slightly, depending on when you make your calculations. In order to determine what the average is, simply add up all the yields and then divide by 30.

The following comments refer to Table 6-1. If you examine the current list of 30 Dow stocks, you may notice that it does not contain USX although this stock was part of the average at the end of 1985. From time to time, *The Wall Street Journal* adds or subtracts stocks. About two years ago, for example, it added J.P. Morgan, Walt Disney, and Caterpillar Tractor. To do this, the *Journal* had to delete three stocks (Navistar, USX, and Primerica) so the total would remain at 30. In all of my illustrations, I will use the stocks that were in the Dow at that particular time rather than those that are now in the Average.

Avoiding Stock Market Favorites

The important thing is to eliminate any stocks that are extreme favorites of institutions, such as mutual funds, pension plans, and banks. My thesis is that these stocks will not perform as well as others because nearly everyone already owns them. Thus, they are potential sellers rather than buyers.

Table 6-1

Sixteen stocks with the highest yield from the Dow 30, as of year-end 1985. Stocks with too many institutional owners excluded.

Stock	Institutional owners	Dividend yield 12-31-85 (%)	Stock price percentage change 12-31-85 to 12-31-87 (%)
AlliedSignal	481	3.9	− 39.57
American Can	209	4.8	− 19.58
AT&T	760	4.8	+ 8.00
Chevron	662	6.3	+ 3.93
Du Pont	618	4.4	+ 28.73
Eastman Kodak	804	4.8	+ 93.58
Exxon	906*	6.5	+ 27.56*
General Motors	947*	7.1	− 12.79*
Goodyear Tire	414	5.1	+ 92.00
International Paper	366	4.7	+ 66.50
Minnesota Mining & Manufacturing	710	3.9	+ 43.45
Philip Morris	801	4.5	+ 93.20
Sears, Roebuck	616	4.5	− 14.10
Texaco	571	10.0	+ 24.17
Union Carbide	355	4.8	− 7.94
USX	274	4.5	+ 11.74
Average performance of 14 stocks			+ 27.44
Average beginning yield			5.07
Total return			32.51
Dow Jones Industrial Average in same period			+ 18.89
Average beginning yield of 30 stocks			3.93
Total Return of Dow Jones Industrial Average			+ 22.82

*Stocks excluded because of high institutional ownership.

The Magic of the Standard Deviation

The next step may slow you down a little if you have never studied statistics. For whatever reason, I missed out on statistics during my college days. I have been trying to catch up ever since and have pur-

chased a dozen books—each supposedly easier to fathom than the last. One of the few things I came away with was something called "the standard deviation."

It is an intriguing concept because it enables you to break down a group of numbers into four distinct groups:

- Those that are much better than average (there are 16 percent in this group).

- Those that are better than average but are not good enough for the first group (34 percent normally fall here).

- Those that are below average but not horrible (another 34 percent fall in this category).

- Those that are truly horrible (the bottom 16 percent).

Suppose, for instance, that you were from outer space and someone said you should speak to the tall man with red hair. He would ask what a tall man was. To determine this, you gather together a group of men, let's say 50 or 75, and measure each man's height. You will find that a certain number are "more than one standard deviation from the mean." This is your 16 percent who are tall. The next 34 percent are above average and so on.

The above paragraph, however, does not explain how you arrive at the "standard deviation number." Although you could figure it out by some painstaking arithmetic, it is not necessary if you have a fancy calculator such as the Hewlett-Packard 12C.

If all this talk of standard deviation is baffling to you, you could probably survive by simply taking 16 percent of the number you are trying to select or eliminate. In the first illustration (Table 6-1), you would eliminate three stocks, which would be OK, except that one of them (Eastman Kodak) was a big winner. Using the calculator, you would have retained this stock but would have eliminated two potential losers, IBM and General Motors. In this particular illustration, IBM was a modest winner, but GM did poorly. The rest of the stocks would have been purchased, giving you above-average performance. In the year that followed, the stocks held did very well, climbing 27.44 percent. If you add in the average beginning dividend, your total return was a very respectable 32.51 percent.

In order to determine if this is good or bad, you should determine how the Dow Jones Industrial Average performed in the same period. As it happened, the Dow was 1546.67 at the end of 1985. It closed two years later at 1838.83, for a gain of 18.89 percent. Add in the average yield of the 30 stocks in the Dow, and your total return was 22.82 percent. This is a far cry from the performance of the 14 stocks my system recommended. (I realize, of course, that my "total return" figure is somewhat suspect because the period used is two years rather than one. Thus, it might have made more sense to double the beginning yield before adding it to the price appreciation. On the other hand, I have treated both groups the same way). You can give me a C– for questionable use of statistics!

Follow These Steps

Before we go on to another example (Table 6-2), let's review what we have done here. Here are the steps:

- Start with the 30 stocks that make up the Dow Jones Industrial Average. As noted above, they are listed in *The Wall Street Journal* on page 3 of the third section.

- Check the stock tables in the *Journal* to find out the dividend yield on each stock. No calculations are needed. The yield is given to the right of the name of each stock.

- Pick approximately 15 stocks with the highest yield.

- Using the standard deviation, eliminate the two or three stocks with the most institutional owners.

What to Do If You Are Still Baffled.   If all this is still Greek to you, feel free to call me at (216) 781-5600. As long as you're paying for the call, I will try to bail you out of your misery. Make sure you have your Hewlett-Packard 12C handy, along with some numbers you want to work with. Under no circumstances should you try to frustrate me by using some other brand of calculator. My knowledge does not extend beyond the H-P 12C.

Assuming you haven't yet decided to burn this book, let's proceed to look at some more examples of this method of stock selection.

In this illustration, I have used a one-year holding period, rather than two—for no particularly good reason except to demonstrate that the holding period is not that important.

By referring to a year-end 1988 *Stock Guide* (like a pack rat, I have shelves piled high with them), we have 16 stocks with yields varying between 6 and 3.6 percent. Among this group, the one with fewest institutional owners was AlliedSignal with 484. At the high end of the spectrum were General Electric (1349) and IBM (1758). Incidentally, IBM, despite its grave difficulties in the past couple of years, still has well over 1000 institutional owners. You might infer from this that institutional managers are not exactly clairvoyant.

Table 6-2

Sixteen stocks with the highest yield from the Dow 30, as of year-end 1988. Action of stocks that were not institutional favorites.

Stock	Institutional owners	Dividend yield 12-31-88 (%)	Stock price change 12-31-88 to 12-31-89 (%)
AlliedSignal	484	5.5	+ 7.31
AT&T	842	4.2	+ 58.26
Chevron	811	5.7	+ 48.09
Du Pont	792	4.3	+ 39.38
Eastman Kodak	955	4.4	− 8.86
Exxon	1072	5.0	+ 13.64
General Motors	920	6.0	+ 1.20
General Electric	1349*	3.7	+ 44.13*
IBM	1758*	3.6	− 22.77*
Minnesota Mining & Manufacturing	710	3.9	+ 43.45
Philip Morris	1154	4.4	+ 63.44
Sears, Roebuck	762	4.9	− 6.73
Texaco	599	5.9	+ 15.16
United Technologies	625	3.9	+ 31.91
Westinghouse	678	3.8	+ 40.62
USX	600	4.8	+ 22.22
Average performance of remaining 14 stocks			+ 26.36
Average beginning yield			4.76
Total return			+ 31.12
Dow Jones Industrial Average in same period			+ 26.96
Average beginning yield of 30 stocks			3.53
Total return of Dow Jones Industrial Average			+ 30.49

*Stock excluded because too many institutional owners.

Assuming we continue to use the standard deviation concept, two stocks would be eliminated: General Electric and IBM. If you did not have a calculator, you could take 16 percent of 15, and your answer would be 2.4. In other words, you would still be eliminating two stocks.

The Hewlett-Packard 12C

If you can beg, borrow, or steal one of these calculators, the process of determining the standard deviation is easy. Here are the steps:

- Turn on the calculator by pressing the *ON* button in the extreme lower left-hand corner.

- Clear out the "garbage" by pressing the yellow button with an *f* on it. Then press the button labeled *CLX,* which is just to the left of the *Enter* button. Every time you do a standard deviation study, you must clean out the "garbage."

- Now you are ready to enter your numbers. Let's refer back to Table 6-1. The first stock is AlliedSignal, which has 481 institutional owners. Punch out this number and then press *Enter.* Next, press the button directly to the left of the + button, down in the right-hand corner. Its called the *sigma+.*

- From this point on, do not press the *Enter* button again. Instead, enter the number of institutional owners for the rest of the list—making sure you press the *sigma +* button after each entry. Incidentally, if you make a mistake, you have to start over (although I understand there is a way to save yourself but I have forgotten how to do it). So be careful. Every time you make an entry, it is recorded in the window. By the time you have entered your 16 numbers, a "16" will flash on the screen before you press the *sigma+.* If the number is not 16, you have made a mistake. Back to square one, as they say.

- Now that you have entered all 15 or 16 numbers, you're almost done. Press the blue button (it has a *G* on it). Next press the zero. This gives you the "mean," which is the fancy name for the average. In this illustration, the mean is 593.38. In other words, in this group of 30 stocks, the average institutional ownership is 593.38.

- Next you are going to discover the standard deviation by pressing the blue button again, immediately followed by pressing the period directly to the right of the zero. As it turns out, the standard deviation is 225.25.

- The final step is to add the mean to the standard deviation, which means adding 593.38 to 225.24, giving you a total of 818.62.

- You have now determined that any stock with 818 institutional owners is too popular and should not be purchased.

No System Is Infallible

In this test, the 15 stocks selected had an average gain during 1989 of 25.05 percent. If we add back the average beginning yield of 4.83 percent, the total return would have been 29.88 percent. This may appear to be an excellent return, but you still have to compare it with the Dow itself, which advanced from 2168.57 to 2753.20, a gain of 26.96 percent. Add in the beginning yield of 3.53 percent and your total return would have been 30.49 percent, which is modestly better than that turned in by the 13 stocks.

This proves that nothing works every time.

Now, let's look at Table 6-3, which goes back to year-end 1972. No, that's not a typo. The reason I use 1972 is because that was a poor time to set up a portfolio. The market sagged badly in 1973 and 1974. It was a bear market to remember. (Let's hope history doesn't repeat itself.)

Nothing Is As Constant As Change

You may recall that at the beginning of this chapter I told you that the stocks in the Dow change from time to time. This is clearly evident in this list in that several of these stocks have been taken out such as American Brands, General Foods (part of Philip Morris), Johns-Manville (now known as Manville), U.S. Steel (now two companies), and International Harvester (now called Navistar). As someone once said, nothing is as constant as change. It's certainly true of the stock market. When I came into the business in 1961, for instance, the average daily trading volume was three million shares—a far cry from today, when some days 300 million shares change hands.

But, getting back to my system of picking stocks. In this instance, no system would have protected you from losses. On the other hand, those losses were quite a bit less than you might have experienced had you owned all 30 stocks in the Dow Jones Industrial Average. During 1973, the Dow fell from 1020.02 to 850.86, a loss of 16.58 percent. If you add in the average beginning dividend, the loss amounted to 13.06 percent. The damage, incidentally, was even worse the following year.

That Devastating Bear Market

By using our Hewlett-Packard 12C, we would have eliminated four stocks. The mean was 273. Add this to the standard deviation of 250 and you get a total of 523. Among those that remained a few actually went up during that devastating bear market of 1973. Notably, for instance, Allied Chemical (now AlliedSignal) shot up 68.97 percent. Even so, there were some big losers. However, the average loss, at 10.63 percent, was quite a bit less than the Dow's loss of 16.58 percent. After adding in the beginning yield of 4.42 percent, your net loss was only 6.21 percent. The system wins again!

Table 6-3

Seventeen stocks with the highest yield from the Dow 30, as of year-end 1972. Action of stocks that were not institutional favorites.

Stock	Institutional owners	Dividend yield 12-31-72 (%)	Stock price change 12-31-72 to 12-31-73 (%)
AlliedSignal	106	4.1	+ 68.97
American Brands	82	5.4	− 23.44
American Can	78	7.0	− 17.00
AT&T	677*	5.3	− 4.98*
Bethlehem Steel	122	4.1	+ 12.34
Exxon	733*	4.3	+ 7.57*
General Foods	202	4.9	− 16.67
General Motors	760*	5.5	− 43.14*
International Harvester	125	3.9	− 32.90
International Paper	218	3.6	+ 26.51
Johns-Manville	93	3.8	− 47.20
Standard Oil CA	276	3.6	− 12.64
Texaco	596*	4.4	− 21.67*
Union Carbide	293	4.0	− 31.75
US Steel	63	5.2	+ 23.36
Woolworth	121	3.8	− 41.20
United Technologies	625	3.9	+ 31.91
Average performance of remaining 13 stocks			− 10.63
Average beginning yield			4.42
Total return			− 6.21
Dow Jones Industrial Average in same period			− 16.58
Average beginning yield of 30 stocks			3.52
Total return of Dow Jones Industrial Average			− 13.06

*Stock excluded because of high institutional ownership.

Now, let's jump ahead to modern times, year-end 1991. After you had reduced your list to the 15 stocks with the highest yield, you were able to eliminate Exxon and IBM because they were too popular with institutions. You may recall that owning IBM in 1992 was not a happy experience. See Table 6-4.

The 13 remaining stocks did well, with an average appreciation of 9.2 percent. Because the beginning yield was 4.63 percent, the total

Table 6-4

Fifteen stocks with the highest yield from the Dow 30, as of year-end 1991. Action of stocks that were not institutional favorites.

Stock	Institutional owners	Dividend yield 12-31-91 (%)	Stock price change 12-31-91 to 12-31-92 (%)
American Express	732	4.9	+ 21.34
AT&T	891	3.4	+ 30.35
Chevron	793	4.8	+ 0.72
Du Pont	808	3.6	+ 1.07
Eastman Kodak	760	4.1	− 16.06
Exxon	1003*	4.4	+ 0.41*
General Motors	782	5.5	+ 11.69
IBM	1254*	5.4	− 43.40*
Minnesota Mining & Manufacturing	860	3.3	+ 5.64
Sears, Roebuck	561	5.3	+ 20.13
Texaco	907	5.2	− 2.45
Union Carbide	285	4.9	+ 64.81
Westinghouse Electric	568	7.8	− 25.69
Woolworth	419	4.1	+ 19.34
United Technologies	527	3.3	− 11.29
Average performance of remaining 13 stocks			+ 9.20
Average beginning yield			4.63
Total return			+ 13.83
Dow Jones Industrial Average in same period			+ 4.17
Average beginning yield of 30 stocks			3.32
Total return of Dow Jones Industrial Average			+ 7.49

*Stock excluded because of excessively high institutional ownership.

return was 13.83 percent. During that particular year, the Dow Jones Industrial Average advanced very modestly, from 3168.83 to 3301.11, a net gain of 4.17 percent. If we tack on the 3.32 percent yield, we get a total return of 7.49 percent. Once again, my system succeeded in helping you outperform the overall market.

Table 6-5

Fifteen stocks with the highest yield from the Dow 30, as of year-end 1992. Action of stocks that were not institutional favorites.

Stock	Institutional owners	Dividend yield 12-31-92 (%)	Stock price change 12-31-92 to 6-30-93 (%)
American Express	694	4.0	+ 29.65
Chevron	796	4.7	+ 26.26
Du Pont	836	3.7	Nil
Eastman Kodak	777	4.9	+ 23.46
Exxon	1077	4.7	+ 8.18
IBM	1189*	9.6	− 1.99*
J.P. Morgan	747	3.7	+ 3.23
Minnesota Mining & Manufacturing	897	3.2	+ 7.33
Philip Morris	1445*	3.4	− 37.12*
Sears, Roebuck	605	4.4	+ 20.88
Texaco	911	5.4	+ 5.86
Union Carbide	315	4.5	+ 15.79
United Technologies	557	3.7	+ 12.21
Westinghouse Electric	426	5.4	+ 18.69
Woolworth	422	3.5	− 14.23
Average performance of remaining 13 stocks			+ 12.10
Average beginning yield			4.29
Total return			+ 16.39
Dow Jones Industrial Average in same period			+ 6.51
Average beginning yield of 30 stocks			3.29
Total return of Dow Jones Industrial Average			+ 9.80

*Stock excluded because of high institutional ownership.

And don't forget that you were spared the agony of owning Exxon (up only 0.41 percent, and IBM, down a sickening 43.4 percent).

Our final illustration (Table 6-5) advances forward to year-end 1992. Our cutoff date is June 30, 1993.

Once again, the yield/institutional-owners idea has triumphed over the Dow Jones Industrial Average. Next, let's go back a few years and see how my system fared in 1988 and 1989. In this illustration, I have assumed that you bought your qualifying stocks at the end of 1987 and held them for two full years. See Table 6-6 for the details.

Table 6-6

Fourteen stocks with the highest yield from the Dow 30, as of year-end 1991. Action of stocks that were not institutional favorites.

Stock	Institutional owners	Dividend yield 12-31-87 (%)	Stock price change 12-31-87 to 12-31-89 (%)
AlliedSignal	537	6.4	+ 23.45
AT&T	882	4.4	+ 68.52
Boeing	584	3.8	+ 140.71
Chevron	793	6.1	+ 70.98
Du Pont	801	3.9	+ 40.77
Exxon	1045	5.2	+ 31.15
General Motors	933	8.1	+ 37.68
Philip Morris	1037	4.2	+ 95.02
Primerica	295	6.6	+ 18.13
Sears, Roebuck	779	6.0	+ 13.81
USX	575	4.0	+ 20.17
Union Carbide	359	6.9	+ 6.90
United Technologies	637	4.1	+ 60.15
Woolworth	350	3.8	+ 85.14
Average performance of 14 stocks			+ 50.90
Average beginning yield			5.25
Total return			+ 56.15
Dow Jones Industrial Average in same period			+ 42.00
Average beginning yield of 30 stocks			3.71
Total return of Dow Jones Industrial Average			+ 45.71

What about Ancient History?

Now, let's look at some more ancient history. In this test, I have gone back nearly 20 years, to year-end 1975. If the stocks were chosen at that point and held one year, here is how your portfolio performed (see Table 6-7). You will probably notice that there are some strange names here because the makeup of the 30-stock average has changed considerably during this stretch.

Although the results shown in Table 6-7 are indeed impressive, we must face the unpleasant fact that nothing works every time. For

Table 6-7

Thirteen stocks with the highest yield from the Dow 30, as of year-end 1975. Action of stocks that were not institutional favorites.

Stock	Institutional owners	Dividend yield 12-31-75 (%)	Stock price change 12-31-75 to 12-31-76 (%)
AlliedSignal	121	5.4	+ 22.30
American Brands	89	6.9	+ 18.45
American Can	65	7.0	+ 24.30
Bethlehem Steel	137	6.1	+ 22.81
Esmark	48	4.8	+ 13.94
General Foods	174	5.1	+ 9.50
Goodyear	270	5.1	+ 9.20
Inco	234	6.3	+ 29.21
International Harvester	77	7.6	+ 47.49
Johns-Manville	83	5.2	+ 44.09
Standard Oil California	292	6.8	+ 39.57
Westinghouse	211	7.3	+ 31.78
Woolworth	77	5.5	+ 17.05
Average performance of 13 stocks			+ 25.14
Average beginning yield			6.08
Total return			+ 31.22
Dow Jones Industrial Average in same period			+ 17.86
Average beginning yield of 30 stocks			4.78
Total return of Dow Jones Industrial Average			+ 22.64

instance, 1990 was a rough year for my system. It was also a rough year for the market because a good many stocks tumbled. Table 6-8 shows how the high-yield/institutional-ownership system fared. Be prepared to grit your teeth.

As you can see, Goodyear was the bad buy in this test. The following year, however, it atoned for all of its evil doings in 1990, bounding up a lusty 183.44 percent. Here is how the list as a whole performed (Table 6-9).

In Table 6-10 is my final test. It assumes that you were investing at the end of 1991 and held your stocks until the end of 1992. Two stocks would have been eliminated because they had too many institutional

Table 6-8

Twelve stocks with the highest yield from the Dow 30, as of year-end 1989. Action of stocks that were not institutional favorites.

Stock	Institutional owners	Dividend yield 12-31-89 (%)	Stock price change 12-31-89 to 12-31-90 (%)
AlliedSignal	481	5.2	− 22.58
ALCOA	573	3.6	− 23.17
Chevron	854	4.1	+ 7.20
Du Pont	845	3.9	− 10.37
Eastman Kodak	940	4.9	+ 1.22
Exxon	1048	4.8	+ 3.50
General Motors	950	7.1	− 18.64
Goodyear	401	4.1	− 56.61
Sears, Roebuck	745	5.2	− 33.44
Texaco	758	5.1	+ 2.76
USX	609	3.9	− 14.69
Union Carbide	389	4.3	− 29.57
Average performance of 12 stocks			− 16.20
Average beginning yield			4.68
Total return			− 11.52
Dow Jones Industrial Average in same period			− 4.34
Average beginning yield of 30 stocks			3.96
Total return of Dow Jones Industrial Average			− 0.98

Table 6-9

Fifteen stocks with the highest yield from the Dow 30, as of year-end 1991. Action of stocks that were not institutional favorites.

Stock	Institutional owners	Dividend yield 12-31-90 (%)	Stock price change 12-31-90 to 12-31-91 (%)
AlliedSignal	426	6.7	+ 62.50
ALCOA	551	5.2	+ 11.71
American Express	783	4.5	− .61
AT&T	837	4.4	+ 29.88
Chevron	795	4.3	− 4.99
Du Pont	756	4.6	+ 26.87
Eastman Kodak	790	4.8	+ 15.92
Exxon	956	5.2	+ 17.63
General Motors	875	8.7	− 16.00
Goodyear	301	9.5	+ 183.44
Sears, Roebuck	573	7.9	+ 49.26
Texaco	854	5.3	+ 1.24
USX	538	4.6	− 1.70
Union Carbide	321	6.1	+ 23.66
Westinghouse	686	4.9	− 36.84
Average performance of 15 stocks			+ 24.13
Average beginning yield			5.78
Total return			+ 29.91
Dow Jones Industrial Average in same period			+ 20.32
Average beginning yield of 30 stocks			4.20
Total return of Dow Jones Industrial Average			+ 24.52

Table 6-10

Fifteen stocks with the highest yield from the Dow 30, as of year-end 1991. Action of stocks that were not institutional favorites.

Stock	Institutional owners	Dividend yield 12-31-91 (%)	Stock price change 12-31-91 to 12-31-92 (%)
American Express	732	4.9	+ 21.34
AT&T	891	3.4	+ 30.35
Chevron	793	4.8	+ 0.72
Du Pont	808	3.6	+ 1.07
Eastman Kodak	760	4.1	− 16.06
Exxon	1003*	4.4	+ 0.41*
General Motors	782	5.5	+ 11.69
IBM	1254*	5.4	− 43.40*
Minnesota Mining & Manufacturing	860	3.3	+ 5.64
Sears, Roebuck	561	5.3	+ 20.13
Texaco	907	5.2	− 2.45
Union Carbide	285	4.9	+ 64.81
Westinghouse Electric	568	7.8	− 25.69
Woolworth	419	4.1	+ 19.34
United Technologies	527	3.3	− 11.29
Average performance of remaining 13 stocks			+ 9.20
Average beginning yield			4.63
Total return			+ 13.83
Dow Jones Industrial Average in same period			+ 4.17
Average beginning yield of 30 stocks			3.32
Total return of Dow Jones Industrial Average			+ 7.49

*Stock excluded because of excessively high institutional ownership.

Table 6-11

Summary of all five tests.

Period	Institutional-yield system (%)	Dow Jones Industrial Average (%)
1985–1987	+ 32.51	+ 22.82
1988–1989	+ 29.88	+ 30.49
1972–1973	− 6.21	− 13.06
1991–1992	+ 13.83	+ 7.49
1992–June 1993	+ 16.39	+ 9.80
Averages	+ 17.28	+ 11.51

owners: Exxon (which didn't move much) and IBM (which plunged 43.4 percent). Once again, this illustration demonstrates that the high-yield idea works best when you avoid stocks that are too popular with institutions.

Now that we have examined several examples of this method of stock selection, it is appropriate to add up the results for all five periods (Table 6-11). In each instance, I have used the total returns. What it amounts to is this: if you had used the system in these particular years, your average total return was +16.57 percent. By contrast, the Dow Jones Industrial Average gained 11.51 percent. If we divide 16.57 by 11.51, it would appear that this system beat the market by 44 percent.

7

Some Thoughts on Analyzing Stocks

Ideally, a stock you plan to purchase should have all of the following characteristics:

- A rising trend of earnings, dividends, and book value per share.
- A balance sheet with less debt than other companies in its particular industry.
- An S&P rating of A− or better.
- A P/E ratio no higher than average.
- A yield that suits your particular needs.
- A stock that insiders are not selling in significant quantities.
- Below-average payout ratios.
- Low popularity with institutions.
- A history of earnings and dividends that are not pockmarked by erratic ups and downs.
- Companies whose return on equity is often 15 percent or better.
- A ratio of price to cash flow that is not too high when compared to other stocks in its industry.

Obviously, it is just about impossible to find a stock that fits this pattern. You might compare it to picking a baseball player. Ideally, you would like him to be a flawless fielder who never makes errors, hits 45 home runs a year, has a batting average of .326, steals 40 bases, and knocks in 110 runs. Outside of Barry Bonds, there aren't many who fit this description.

It's the same way with stocks. You have to pick the ones that come closest to your dream stock.

The best way to do this is with the aid of *Value Line Survey,* which as I've said is available in many brokerage house branch offices and public libraries. Although it costs a few hundred dollars per year, it might be a good investment if you have a substantial portfolio and want to refer to *Value Line* frequently.

In order to get you started, I will refer to issue 6, dated July 23, 1993. Initially, I will confine my analysis to stocks rated A, A+, or A++. This refers to *Value Line*'s financial strength designation. A B++ grade might be considered average.

Although you can certainly make money by buying lower-quality stocks, you are increasing your risk. Being of a cowardly persuasion, I normally like to stick with above-average quality. To be sure, I miss out on some big winners, but I also avoid some big losers.

Consolidated Papers

In order to introduce you to the world of fundamental analysis, I opened up my copy of *Value Line* and leafed my way to the first one with an A financial strength rating. It happened to be Consolidated Papers, which is not a company I know much about. As a consequence, I should be able to analyze it objectively.

Timeliness

Starting in the upper left-hand corner, I notice that *Value Line* gives this stock a rating of 3 for timeliness. Its best ratings are 1 and 2. Its worst ratings are 4 and 5. Thus, a 3 is neutral and indicates that *Value Line* thinks the stock will rise or fall at about the same pace as the market. Frankly, I do not worry too much about their timeliness ratings. I prefer to make up my own mind in this regard.

Safety

Next, I looked at safety. *Value Line* gives Consolidated a score of 1, its best rating. Safety is another way of saying the stock is not too volatile. This is borne out by the beta coefficient, which is 0.95. A beta of more than one would indicate greater volatility. Volatility can help you in a rising market and hurt you when stocks are falling. If you are a conservative investor, you would prefer a beta of less than one.

Insider Purchases and Sales

Just below the beta is a box with insider transactions. An insider, as you might suspect, is someone closely connected with the company, such as an officer or board member or someone with a very large holding. It is assumed that such persons would know more about the company than an outsider.

If such people are buying or selling, it might be an indication that you should do the same. However, this may not necessarily be the case. By the time this action is made public, several weeks have elapsed, and the stock may have already reacted. In this instance, two insiders sold the stock in March. Because this issue is dated July 23, you can see that their action was taken quite a few weeks before. During that time, the stock spurted upward. It would seem that the insider who sold did not do the right thing.

(On this score, it might seem that insider selling is a red flag. On the other hand, the reason for selling might be easily explained and does not always denote an aversion to the stock. Whole books, incidentally, have been written on this topic—and I still don't know if insider buying and selling should concern an investor.)

How to Determine Value

No matter how good a stock may seem, you should be reluctant to buy it unless there is some indication of good value. There are essentially five ways to get a feel for value:

- The dividend yield
- The price/earnings (P/E) ratio
- The price-to-revenues ratio
- The price-to-book-value ratio
- The price-to-cash-flow ratio

Dividend Yield

Let's start with dividend yield. On this particular date, Consolidated Papers had a yield of 2.5 percent. Although you would not reject a stock with a low yield, at least you can say that this stock is not attractive for anyone looking for income.

Price/Earnings Ratio

The price/earnings ratio, as given by *Value Line*, is 25.5. *Value Line* calculates the P/E using the earnings per share for the prior six months, combined with its estimate for the next six months. In any event, a P/E of 25.5 is an indication that this is not a cheap stock. A good way to look at the P/E is to compare it with the general market. If stocks in general are selling at 18 times earnings (as they are now), it would make sense to invest in stocks with multiples below this level. Another approach is to compare the P/E with other stocks in the same industry.

Why Low-P/E Investing Works

Low-P/E investing works because growth-stock investors are not as good at forecasting the future as they think they are. Investors are betting that they can find companies that will achieve superior growth over an extended period of time. As a result, they bid up the prices of stocks with good future growth prospects ("growth" companies) and force down the prices of stocks with poor future growth prospects ("value" companies). The superior growth prospects of the growth companies are reflected in their high P/Es, and the poor growth prospects of the value companies are reflected in their low P/Es.

When expectations meet reality, investors discover that the growth companies, on average, grow slightly faster than the average companies, but not as fast as required to justify their lofty prices. Hence, investors are disappointed, and these stocks underperform. Although value companies grow slightly slower than the average company, their earnings growth is better than expected. Hence, investors are positively surprised, and these stocks outperform.

SOURCE: William E. Jacques, CFA, Partner, Executive Vice President and Chief Investment Officer, Martingale Asset Management.

Price-to-Revenues Ratio

The price-to-revenues ratio is calculated by dividing the price of the stock ($51) by the revenues per share ($20.63). A stock selling for more than double its revenues is not a cheap stock. A more attractive stock would sell for less than its revenues per share.

Price-to-Book Value—An Important Concept

Next, let's look at that price-to-book value. In this instance, the price is $51 and the book value is $21.03. Divide $51 by $21.03 and you get 2.43. Ideally, you would like to find a stock selling for less than its book value, but such stocks are few and far between. Here again, this does not appear to be a stock you would buy if you were a value investor.

The Price-to-Cash-Flow Ratio

One ratio that may seem strange to you is the price-to-cash-flow-per-share ratio. To be sure, it is well known to securities analysts and port-folio managers. But I am assuming you are neither.

Actually, it is not difficult to calculate if you have your *Value Line* handy. This ratio, incidentally, cannot be calculated for financial com-panies, such as banks and insurance companies because cash flow per share is not given.

To get things started, cash flow is arrived at by adding depreciation to earnings. Actually, it is a bit more complicated than this, but in any event, the number you want is given to you in each *Value Line* sheet. Let's look at an example. The December 18, 1992, issue contains a report on Bausch & Lomb. It gives the earnings per share for 1991 as $2.47.

In order to calculate the price/earnings (P/E) ratio, you would divide this number into the price at that time, which was $57. Thus, your P/E would be 23.08, which is a rather high multiple. It would discourage you from buying the stock. By contrast, the cash flow per share was $3.65—it's always higher than earnings because it contains the depreciation factor (plus some other items that we won't get into).

When you calculate the cash flow ratio, you divide $3.65 into $57, for a ratio of 15.62. This, too, is a high number and is indicative of a stock that might be overpriced. I could easily devote more space to this relationship, but I think I will refrain from trying to make you into a portfolio manager just yet.

The important point to be made is this: if you want to calculate this relationship, it is best to do it for several stocks in the same industry. This will give you a feel for what is high and what is low.

Another Way to Look at Value

Value Line is very helpful in providing you with data on how the company's P/E and yield looked in prior years. For instance, how does its current yield stack up historically? The yield is now 2.5 percent. Over the last 16 years, the yield has fluctuated from a high of 7.4 percent (in 1982) to a low of 2.6 percent (in 1988). If we average these yields from 1977 to 1992, it comes to 4.47 percent. Because the current yield is 2.5 percent, it seems obvious the stock is not exactly a bargain.

The same exercise can be performed using the P/E ratio. Over the period, the average annual P/E fluctuated from a high of 32 (in 1992 when earnings were severely depressed) to a low of 5.4 (in 1978). The average during these 16 years was 9.48 (if we leave out 1992's depressed figure). Once again, the stock does not exhibit any evidence that it is selling at an attractive price.

How about Growth?

Since Consolidated Papers has failed to impress us on the basis of value, it might be a good idea to see how it stacks up as a growth stock. There are several ways to evaluate growth:

- Compound growth of revenues per share
- Compound growth of cash flow per share
- Compound growth of earnings per share
- Compound growth of dividends per share
- Compound growth of book value per share

Some analysts would focus on the most recent five-year record. I usually look at the last 10 years.

This is the time to get out your calculator, preferably one that can calculate compound annual growth rates (such as the Hewlett-Packard 12C).

Let's work our way down the list, first examining the progress of revenues (or sales) per share. Consolidated Papers had revenues per share of $12.20 back in 1982, which had increased to $20.63 by 1992. According to my calculator, that works out to a compound annual growth rate of 5.39 percent, which is not anything to write home about. So far, at least, Consolidated Papers does not impress me.

A Free Lesson on How to Use the Hewlett-Packard 12C

Before we proceed any further, it might be a good idea to explain how I arrived at 5.39 percent using my Hewlett-Packard 12C. You can skip this explanation if you don't have such a calculator or if you don't want to get involved.

- *Step 1.* Enter the revenue figure for 1982, which was $12.20. Next, press the *CHS* button, followed by the *PV* (Present Value) button.

- *Step 2.* Enter the revenues per share for 1992, or $20.63. Press the *FV* (Future Value) button.

- *Step 3.* Enter the number of years, in this instance, it would be 10.

- *Step 4.* Press *n* (the number of years) and then *i* (the interest rate figure you are looking for).

As soon as you have completed this routine, the calculator will begin to whir into action. A few seconds later, the answer to the problem appears in the viewing screen.

Let's Return to Our Analysis of Consolidated Papers

Now, back to the procedure to determine if Consolidated Papers is exhibiting any signs of growth. We have already looked at growth of revenues. Let's next check cash flow. In 1982, cash flow per share was $1.56. (Cash flow, incidentally, is earnings with depreciation added back.) In 1992, it was $3.19, which works out to be a compound annual pace of 7.42 percent. Still not much to get enthusiastic over.

It should come as no surprise that we should look at the progress of earnings per share (EPS) in the 1982–1992 period. In 1982, the company had EPS of $1.04. Ten years later, the figure was $1.15, down from $2.10 the prior year. It doesn't take a rocket scientist to realize this is not an impressive showing. There is no need to bother with the calculator.

An Examination of Dividends

Now, let's see how dividends have done in this span. In 1982, the company paid 50 cents. In 1992, it paid $1.28, which looks impressive in so far as it works out to be a compound annual rate of 9.86 percent. Although this is quite acceptable, you still have to bear in mind that the company did not earn its dividend in 1992. Whenever the dividend grows faster than earnings, it means you should hesitate before buying the shares.

Perhaps the best way to judge growth is to look at what happened to book value per share during the 1982–1992 stretch. I like this approach because book value per share is less affected by what happened in any single year. In this case, book value was $7.74 in 1982 and $21.03 in 1992, for a compound annual growth rate of 9.98 percent. Although far from spectacular, it is at least above average.

If we were to summarize Consolidated's record as a growth stock, it would get a mixed reception.

Financial Strength

The final factor to look at is financial strength. Because *Value Line* gives the company an A+ rating, you can assume that it is well above average in this regard. Further confirmation comes from a look at the balance sheet. In 1992, Consolidated Papers had long-term debt of $171 million and common equity of $921.6 million. This is clearly an indication that the company is very sound financially.

This is further confirmed by looking at the box in the middle of the page on the left side, which is called Capital Structure. Total interest coverage is given as 9.3x. This refers to the company's ability to handle the interest payments on its debt. For a nonutility, anything better than six would indicate strength. Overall, there is no reason to be concerned with this company's ability to withstand adversity.

After you have massaged all the numbers, you will certainly want to read what *Value Line* has to say about the company. They devote several paragraphs to analyzing what is taking place. This is where your judgment comes into play. It is often helpful if you underline any statement that sounds favorable with a green felt-tip pen (but don't let the librarian catch you). Similarly, underline negative developments with a red pen. Here are the favorable statements:

- "Demand for Consolidated Papers' main product is picking up." The service goes on to point out that the company's plants are operating at capacity, or well above last year's pace.
- A price increase seems to be in the offing.

Despite all the favorable commentary, *Value Line* concludes with this statement: "But share price appreciation to mid-decade is unattractive."

Unfortunately, nothing is ever black or white. But, if we were to sum up the situation, it might run something like this:

Consolidated Papers is a strong company that seems to be doing well at the present. On the other hand, the growth rate historically is only fair, and the price of the stock is not indicative of a bargain. Decision: do not buy at present.

Westvaco Corporation

It's now time to move on to another company with a good financial strength rating, in this instance, A. Westvaco is a major paper company. Let's see how it looks when compared with Consolidated Papers.

If we look at *Value Line*'s timeliness rating, it is at the bottom of the heap, at 5. The safety rating is better but, at 2, is not as good as Consolidated, which was 1.

The beta coefficient is about the same, at 1.00. Insider selling, however, is clearly in evidence. In recent months, there have been six instances of insider selling and none of buying. This could be viewed as a negative.

Value Evaluation

Starting with dividend yield, Westvaco looks better, with a yield of 3.2 percent. The P/E ratio, on the other hand, is far too high, at 26.9. Price-to-revenues is much better than Consolidated, at $36 to $35.17. The price-to-book value is also an encouraging 1.35.

All told, Westvaco looks like a better value than Consolidated.

Value over the Last 16 Years

Before leaving the value sector, let's see how the company looks over the last 16 years. In that span, the yield has fluctuated from a high of 5.5 percent (in 1982) to a low of 2.3 percent (in 1987). The average yield during these years was 3.77 percent. This is modestly higher than the current yield of 3.2 percent, which would indicate that the stock is not grossly overvalued.

Next, let's go through the same exercise with the P/E ratio, which has fluctuated from a high of 17.8 (in 1992) to a low of 6.2 (in 1980). The average P/E during this 16-year span works out to be 10.11. By contrast, today's P/E ratio is 26.9. If you were to evaluate the stock's attractiveness based on this measure of value, you would quickly reject it.

A Glance at Growth

First, let's look at the progress of revenues per share. In 1982, revenues per share were $24.06 compared with $35.17 in 1992, for a compound annual growth rate of 3.87 percent. Not much to brag about here.

In the same 10-year span, cash flow per share moved ahead, from $2.46 to $4.80, for a growth rate of 6.91 percent.

Beware of Distortion

Earnings during this period were not very impressive, rising from $1.07 (down from $1.76 the prior year) to $2.06, a compound growth rate of 6.77 percent. On the surface, this might seem OK. On the other hand, this is an instance where the compound growth rate is distorted because the beginning year is depressed.

You can see how this distorts the results by using the prior year's figure as a starting point. If you calculate the 11-year compound growth rate, going from $1.76 (in 1981) to $2.06 in 1992, the rate is only 1.44 percent. Dividends during these years climbed from 53 cents to $1.10, a growth rate of 7.58 percent. Finally, book value per share rose from $12.54 in 1982 to $26.76, for a growth rate of 7.87 percent. Overall, growth was only fair, not much better than Consolidated Papers. In terms of financial strength, Westvaco is somewhat more leveraged. Its long-term debt is $1.06 billion, compared with equity of $1.78 billion. Coverage of bond interest is a very subnormal 2.

The final step is to read the evaluation given by *Value Line* at the bottom of the page. It starts out by saying, "Tough market conditions are hurting many of Westvaco's products."

Later on, the service says, "We are reducing our 1993 and 1994 earnings estimates."

Putting it all together, there doesn't seem to be much about Westvaco that would motivate an investor to buy it.

An Analysis of Bemis

Let's try one more company, to give you a better feel for fundamental analysis. Bemis is a major packaging company.

If we look in the upper left-hand corner, we see that *Value Line* rates Bemis a 3 for timeliness and a 2 for safety. The beta coefficient, however, is much higher than either Consolidated or Westvaco, at 1.20. This would indicate that Bemis is a bit more risky because it is more volatile.

Insiders have been selling rather than buying. But only two instances are recorded in recent months, which is probably not anything to be too concerned about.

A Look at Value

To start off with, Bemis has a yield of 2.3 percent, which quickly eliminates it for someone looking for liberal yield. Over the last 16 years, the yield has fluctuated from a high of 6.2 percent (in 1978) to a low of 1.9 percent (in 1992). The average yield during this span was 3.83 percent. From this exercise, you might decide that Bemis is not exactly a bargain at today's price.

Let's next examine the P/E ratio, which is 19.1, or about average in today's market. Historically, the company's multiple has fluctuated from a high of 21.5 (in 1992) to a low of 4.2 (in 1979). Here again, the P/E tells us that Bemis is currently on the high side.

Next, let's see how it stacks up when we calculate the price-to-revenue-per-share ratio. The price is $22 and the revenues per share figure is $23.09. I see nothing to be concerned about here.

Since the cash flow per share is $2.06, the price to cash flow works out to be 10.68, which does not seem to be an excessive figure. The book value per share is $7.06, which translates into a price-to-book value of 3.12, which is high if you are looking for a bargain.

In sum, Bemis cannot be regarded as a stock you would be attracted to for pure value.

How about Bemis as a Growth Stock?

In the 1982–1992 period, revenues per share advanced from $11.64 to $23.09, a compound annual growth rate of 7.09 percent. Thus far, it is above average for growth, although far from spectacular.

In this same 10-year period, cash flow per share grew from 56 cents to $2.06, a compound rate of 13.91 percent. This is more like it! Maybe we have a growth stock—at last.

In this period, earnings per share (EPS) climbed from 17 cents to $1.10. However, I would prefer to use the 11-year period because earnings dipped from 29 cents in 1981. If we use that number, the growth rate of EPS was 12.88 percent, which is certainly an indication the company is growing at a good clip.

Dividends during the 1982–1992 span also shot up nicely, rising from 10 cents to 47 cents, which works out to be a compound annual growth rate of 16.74 percent.

The last measure of growth—and the most reliable—is that of book value per share. In this instance, book value per share expanded from $2.98 in 1982 to $7.06 in 1992, a growth rate of 9.01 percent.

Overall, it is seems obvious that Bemis is growing at a far faster pace than either Consolidated Papers or Westvaco. It is worth further study.

How about Financial Strength?

To begin with, *Value Line* awards Bemis its highest rating for financial strength, at A++. Its balance sheet, while far from "clean," is not excessively leveraged. At the end of 1992, the company had long-term debt of $131.1 million, compared with equity of $361 million. Coverage of debt interest, moreover, is exceptionally strong, at 13.2 times.

What Does *Value Line* Say about the Company?

Value Line starts out with this statement: "We expect only modest earnings growth from Bemis this year." Later on, the service says, "Problems abroad continue." On the other hand, it offers a note of optimism: "Earnings should return to a growth track in 1994."

Over all, there is some reason to look at Bemis further. It is strong financially and has a solid record of growth, yet its P/E ratio is less than either Consolidated or Westvaco.

A Strategy to Consider

If you like this method of analyzing a stock, I have a suggestion. Pick out 15 or 20 stocks that you would like to analyze and make a photocopy of each *Value Line* sheet. Next, take the first two copies from your stack and look at each one carefully, looking for reasons to reject one or the other. Get your felt-tip pens and start underlying and circling in red and green.

These red and green marks should help you to decide which stock you like best. When you have made up your mind, throw the reject away, and place the winner at the bottom of the stack. Then, go through the same procedure with the next two, retaining the best one and tossing the other one in the wastebasket.

Although this elimination process may take two or three hours, the end result will be the selection of a stock that has withstood a lot of green and red markings.

Isn't There a Better Way?

As you get down to the end of your elimination process, it will become increasingly difficult. At this point, you may find it helpful to start calling the companies. You'll find the name of the investor contact on the back of the S&P tear sheet. How to interview this person is described in Chapter 2. The main thing to remember is this: don't be shy. You'll be surprised how eager the investor contact is to tell you everything you want to know.

When you have completed this exercise, you may begin to realize that sorting through all the positives and negatives, P/E ratios, growth rates, new products, possible acquisitions, new CEOs, and the like can drive you up a wall. It is for this reason that I developed a number of mechanical methods of stock selection.

Most of the remainder of this book will be devoted to them.

8
The Logic of Foreign Investing

Investors often ignore foreign securities because they don't normally receive information from their broker on these stocks. Although information is not as readily available on foreign stocks, it is not entirely lacking. *Value Line* and the Standard & Poor's tear sheets can be helpful.

Annual reports are also available, assuming you can find the address of the company. Quite often, these companies have a New York address and telephone number—as well as an investor contact (see the bottom of page 2 of the S&P tear sheet). *Value Line* and the tear sheets provide addresses and phone numbers.

How Much Should You Allocate to Foreign Stocks?

I believe that it makes sense to allocate 20 percent of your portfolio to foreign stocks. This can be accomplished through mutual funds, but my preference is for individual stocks. There are several hundred available through American Depositary Receipts (ADRs), which are traded exactly like any domestic stock and for the same commission.

Though traded like shares of stock, ADRs are receipts for stocks of specific foreign companies issued by American banks and trust companies. An ADR might represent a fifth of a share of a German stock or 10 shares of a Japanese stock. A U.S. bank or its foreign correspondent bank holds the stock, receives the dividends, pays foreign withholding taxes, converts the proceeds to dollars, and passes the shares on when investors sell their ADRs. The banks provide annual and quarterly reports and other materials in English.

An ADR is not exactly the same as the stock in the particular country, but it is much easier to trade. If you go directly to the country, you will have to open an account there and have the inconvenience of dealing with someone who may not speak English. In addition, the commission schedule and red tape may be onerous. Unless you have substantial means, don't get involved in a foreign stock that doesn't have an ADR.

Why Should You Buy Foreign Stocks?

Foreign stocks should be included in a well-diversified portfolio for two reasons:

- Including them reduces risk because these markets do not rise and fall at the same time and magnitude as the U.S. market. While our market is climbing 10 percent, for instance, the Hong Kong or French market may be advancing 20 percent or declining 15 percent. Each market is primarily dependent on conditions, legislation, political events, and the economy of that country.

- Because the U.S. market appears rather inflated at present, it makes sense to find securities in markets that are more reasonably priced, such as Britain, France, or Spain.

Although it is not difficult to buy and sell foreign stocks, because they are traded as ADRs, there are some extra risks to be considered.

Watch Out for Fluctuations in Foreign Currencies

Among these risks is the matter of foreign currencies. They are in a constant state of flux. For instance, the last time I was in Britain, two years ago, the pound sterling was worth $2. It is now (in 1994) about $1.50, which means the pound has declined in value in relation to the American dollar. This decline hurts American investors who own British stocks. By contrast, the value of the Japanese yen has increased in recent months, which means that American investors have fared better in that market.

Let's look at why I make these statements. Suppose you bought a British stock when the pound was worth $2 in U.S. currency. Let's further assume you bought 100 shares for 50 pounds, for a total of 5000 pounds. In order to buy the stock you would have to use U.S. dollars. Since the pound was worth $2, you would need $10,000.

Now, let's jump ahead six months, after the British stock has advanced 10 percent in price. If the pound were still worth $2, you would have increased your capital by 10 percent, to $11,000. But what would happen if the pound were now worth only $1? In that case, your shares would be worth only $5500. The exact reverse occurs if the value of the pound goes the other way.

What it all boils down to is this: when you buy stock in a foreign security, you want the currency of that country to remain firm or move up in relation to the American dollar. If it weakens, you stand to lose, unless the underlying security advances enough to offset the weak currency.

In Table 8-1 is a rundown of the performance of foreign stocks in 1993, as of late September. The impact of foreign currency fluctuations is easy to spot. For instance, Spanish stocks in local currency were up 34.8 percent, but because Spanish money declined in value relative to the American dollar your stocks advanced only 17.2 percent. Even so, this was better than you would have done in the average domestic stock because the U.S. index was up a modest 5.9 percent.

If you examine the Japanese market, the impact of currency was most heartening. In local currency, those stocks were up 23.7 percent,

Table 8-1

Performance of foreign stocks in 1993, as of late September. Because of changes in currency, U.S. investors did better than local investors when the local currency strengthened and worse when it declined in value relative to the U.S. dollar.

Country	Stock market change in U.S. dollars (%)	Stock market change in local currency (%)
Australia	15.1	22.3
Britain	8.0	8.6
France	14.2	17.6
Germany	22.3	23.2
Italy	33.1	43.7
Japan	45.7	23.7
Spain	17.2	34.8
United States	5.9	5.9

but because the yen was strong, a U.S. investor would have had a banner year, up 45.7 percent.

If you were to take time to read a book on foreign investing, you would learn that there are hedging strategies to protect you against a decline of a foreign currency. But unless you are a very large player in this sphere, such strategies are not practical. In fact, mutual funds don't normally protect their shareholders from this risk. Your only hope is that it will not happen too often. If you own stocks in half a dozen different countries, these shifts in foreign currencies tend to offset each other.

Taxes and Dividends

Still another shortcoming of foreign investing is the dividend. For starters, most foreign companies pay semiannually rather than quarterly. Worse yet, most countries deduct 15 percent—sometimes more—for taxes. The IRS, however, allows you a deduction for this, but you won't be able to take advantage of it if your stock is in an IRA.

Perhaps the worst part of investing abroad is the paucity of information. Although some brokerage houses have good coverage, it may be more available to institutions than individuals. Our firm, an investment advisor, for instance, gets a steady flow of these sophisticated reports.

Of course, Standard & Poor's has tear sheets on many companies, and *Value Line* also covers some. On the other hand, there are still hundreds that get very little coverage. For that reason, you may decide to invest via a mutual fund, and there are many to choose from.

In addition, there are a goodly number of country funds which are in the form of closed-end funds, traded either on the Big Board or over the counter. With these country funds, you can concentrate on Spain, Italy, or Germany among others. The trouble with country funds is expenses. Most of them charge at least 2 percent, which means you often get a much smaller dividend yield than if you owned an ADR. For those who would prefer to invest in individual stocks, this chapter may be helpful.

To give you a feel for this realm, I will discuss actual foreign stocks, such as Repsol (Spain), Hong Kong Telecomm, Ericsson Telecomm (Sweden), and Alcatel Alsthom (France) among others. What's more, I have devoted nearly a page to each one, describing its business and giving reasons why you should own that particular issue.

I realize, of course, that this information will be out of date by the time you read this book. Even so, it will introduce you to these important companies. In each instance, you can find additional information in *Value Line* or the S&P tear sheet.

Hanson PLC (HAN—NYSE)

Hanson PLC, headquartered in London, England, is one of the most successful diversified industrial management companies in the world. On August 31, 1993, Hanson was $19⅛ a share and had a dividend yield of 5.1 percent.

During the past three decades, Hanson has expanded by acquiring and revitalizing a succession of industrial, consumer, and building products companies in both the United States and the United Kingdom.

Hanson operates over 150 businesses—producing cranes, golf clubs, kitchenware, light fixtures, leisure products, and tobacco. It participates in such extractive industries as brick, cement, and aggregate production and coal mining. Except for chemicals (titanium dioxide), Hanson prefers simple, low-technology businesses in mature, low-growth industries.

Among the company's trade names are Jacuzzi, Tommy Armour (golf equipment), Ames tool, Bear Archery, Beazer Homes (the United Kingdom's third-largest house builder, with 5000 annual house sales), Farberware, Rexair, Grove Crane, SCM Chemicals (the number three producer of titanium dioxide and the second-largest producer to use the chloride process), Peabody Coal (Hanson's largest company and second-largest earner), Cavenham Forest Products, and Imperial Tobacco (the largest unit and Europe's lowest-cost cigarette producer).

Despite the cyclicality of many Hanson businesses, I believe Hanson's focus on cost controls and improved productivity will provide it with the needed leverage for its operating results to outperform the economic environment and its industry competition.

ENDESA (ELE—NYSE)

ENDESA (short for Empresa Nacional De Electricidad) is the largest electric utility in Spain, producing 35 percent of the power for that nation. A Spanish government agency, Instituto Nacional de Industria, owns 75.6 percent of ENDESA shares. At the end of August 1993, the ENDESA ADR was $42⅜ and had a dividend yield of 2 percent.

Annual revenues in 1992 were $6.3 billion. Unlike U.S. utilities, ENDESA does not pay out a large percentage of its earnings in dividends, which is a healthy sign. In 1992, earnings per share were $3.66, compared

Look at the table below. Notice that none of these four categories does well each and every year. Notice too that it would be impossible to predict a trend or pattern.

Annual Total Return, 1970–1991

Year	U.S. stocks (%)	U.S. bonds (%)	Foreign stocks (%)	Foreign bonds (%)
1970	+ 4	+ 18	− 10	+ 9
1971	+ 14	+ 11	+ 31	+ 23
1972	+ 19	+ 7	+ 37	+ 5
1973	− 15	+ 2	− 14	+ 6
1974	− 26	− 6	− 22	+ 5
1975	+ 37	+ 17	+ 37	+ 9
1976	+ 24	+ 19	+ 4	+ 11
1977	− 7	+ 3	+ 19	+ 39
1978	+ 6	+ 0	+ 34	+ 18
1979	+ 19	− 2	+ 6	− 5
1980	+ 32	+ 0	+ 24	+ 14
1981	− 5	+ 3	− 1	− 5
1982	+ 22	+ 39	− 1	+ 12
1983	+ 23	+ 9	+ 25	+ 4
1984	+ 6	+ 17	+ 8	− 2
1985	+ 32	+ 24	+ 57	+ 37
1986	+ 19	+ 16	+ 70	+ 34
1987	+ 5	+ 0	+ 25	+ 36
1988	+ 17	+ 8	+ 27	+ 3
1989	+ 32	+ 7	+ 11	+ 10
1990	− 1	+ 6	− 23	+ 15
1991	+ 31	+ 16	+ 13	+ 3
Number of times "best"	6	4	7	5

SOURCE: Gordon Williamson in *Low Risk Investing*, 1993, Bob Adams, Inc., page 7.

with a dividend of $1.05. Dividends have grown rapidly, from 34 cents a share in 1985. In the same span, earnings expanded from $1.74 to $3.66.

ENDESA has a strong balance sheet, with 52 percent of capitalization in common stock, which is much better than most U.S. electric utilities.

Power is generated mostly with fossil fuel (66.8 percent), with most of the rest being nuclear (23.9 percent) and hydro (9.3 percent). ENDESA is committed to increasing its market share, essentially by major investments in new generating capacity, which the company can fund internally.

Vodafone Group PLC (VOD—NYSE)

Vodafone Group PLC (formerly Racal Telecomm) operates a cellular telephone network in the United Kingdom; it serves about 57 percent of the country's cellular subscribers. At the end of August 1993, the price of the VOD ADR was $86¼, and the dividend yield was 1.3 percent.

International ventures include: a 30 percent stake in a cellular radio system operator in Hong Kong, an 80 percent interest in the Maltese cellular network operator, and an 18.9 percent stake in a company licensed to establish and operate one of three digital cellular networks in Sweden.

Vodafone has no long-term debt, sits on nearly $200 million in cash, and has a record of boosting its payout to stockholders every year.

Unlike the U.S. cellular firms that had to buy cellular rights at steep prices on the open market, Vodafone was one of the two U.K. companies that were granted the original franchise to build a British cellular network a decade or so ago. By contrast, American companies had to borrow heavily to buy franchises in the open market, where competition was intense.

Only two companies compete with Vodafone in the United Kingdom. The more formidable is Mercury One-2-One, which is co-owned by Cable & Wireless (a British firm) and US West (one of the regional Bell operating companies). Mercury is just getting started. Its principal advantage is low prices. On the other hand, it operates in a restricted area: London and its immediate suburbs, and it is not likely to expand outside its area for many years. By contrast, Vodafone's customers can use their equipment anywhere from Land's End in Cornwall to the far reaches of Scotland.

Societe Nationale Elf Aquitaine (ELF—NYSE)

Elf Aquitaine is the largest corporation in France and the sixth-largest integrated oil and gas company in the world. Elf operates worldwide. Annual revenues in 1992 were about $38 billion. By comparison,

Atlantic Richfield was $19 billion, Chevron was $41 billion, and Exxon was $116 billion. At the end of August 1993, Elf was $37¾ per ADR, with a dividend yield of 2.3 percent.

The company is an integrated producer, refiner, and marketer; it is self-sufficient in crude oil. Since 1989, between 50 and 63 percent of Elf's operating income has come from its exploration and production activities, while the overall contribution of the petroleum activities has varied between 64.4 and 74.5 percent.

Elf also conducts a specialty chemicals business, primarily in North America, which has withstood the economic decline of the early 1990s well. However, its large petrochemical business in Europe has been hurt by the weak economy.

After more than a decade of sinking wells in countries like Indonesia, Malaysia, the United States, and Australia—and spending more than a billion dollars for modest results—Elf has retreated to its proven fields in Africa and the North Sea and shifted its new ventures to Russia, Kazakhstan, and Venezuela.

Grand Metropolitan PLC (GRM—NYSE)

Grand Metropolitan, headquartered in London, England, is an international group that specializes in branded consumer businesses, which include food, drinks, and retailing. In the United States, GrandMet's operations include Pillsbury baked goods, Green Giant vegetables, Alpo pet foods, and Häagen-Dazs ice cream. On August 31, 1993, GrandMet ADRs were $27¼; its yield was 3 percent.

International Distillers & Vintners (IDV) is the company's worldwide wines and spirits business. IDV operates in 45 countries across four geographic regions: North America, Europe, Asia Pacific, and Africa with Latin America. It develops, produces, markets, and distributes more wines and spirits than any other company and owns 11 of the world's top 100 spirit brands. Leading brands include Smirnoff, the world's number one vodka and number two spirit brand; J&B Rare, the second-largest Scotch whisky in the world; and Baileys Original Irish Cream, the leading international liqueur brand.

GrandMet's branded retailing and pub activities incorporate the world's second-largest restaurant chain, Burger King; Pearle, the specialist eyewear and eyecare group; the Chef & Brewer group of pubs and pub restaurants; and GrandMet Estates, a specialist property management company, which is also the managing agent for 6850 pubs, owned by Inntrepreneur Estates.

Burger King operates in 44 countries worldwide and has over 6600 outlets, with systemwide sales in excess of $6.4 billion.

Repsol, S.A. (REP—NYSE)

Repsol is an integrated oil company engaged in all aspects of the petroleum industry, including exploration, development, and production of crude oil and natural gas; transportation of petroleum products and liquefied petroleum gas (LPG); petroleum refining, production of a wide range of petrochemicals and marketing of petroleum products, petroleum derivatives, petrochemicals, LPG, and natural gas. The price of Repsol ADRs at the end of August 1993 was $28¾; its yield was 2.2 percent.

In 1992, Repsol was the largest industrial company in Spain, in terms of revenues. With refining capacity of 740,000 barrels per day, Repsol serves about 60 percent of the country's rapidly growing oil product demand. Margins in this business are wide by world standards and could widen further when the company completes a major refinery upgrading program in several years. Growth will be fueled as well by Repsol's natural gas and exploration segment earnings.

A number of international economists and analysts expect the Spanish economy and petroleum demand to outpace the rest of Europe. Between 1985 and 1990, Spain's real GNP expanded at a 4.5 percent annual pace, compared with 3.1 percent for all of Europe.

Low car density in Spain remains a positive factor. In 1990, there were only 308 cars per 1000 people in Spain. Most other European countries have at least 400 cars per 1000 population.

British Telecommunications (BTY—NYSE)

London-based British Telecommunications is a large telephone company serving the United Kingdom. It has an 89 percent share of the market. Annual revenues are over $20 billion, thus making the company much larger than any of the U.S. Bell regional operating companies. At the end of August 1993, BTY was $65 a share and had a yield of 3.9 percent.

The company should benefit from the pickup in the economy that began in 1993. In addition, a reduction in headcount (down 18 percent in the fiscal year 1993) is improving margins. In the next two years, the workforce will be cut by another 18 percent. British Telecomm has an exceptionally strong balance sheet, even after a substantial investment in the American company MCI, a premier marketing organization. This partnership with MCI will enhance British Telecomm's global penetration. Dividends per share have climbed from 69 cents in 1984 to $3 in 1992, with further increases likely.

To enhance its share of corporate business, British Telecomm is investing $1 billion in an ultramodern worldwide network, Project Cyclone. It will feature facilities in 20 of the world's largest cities and will bypass existing telephone companies to provide intracompany services for multinationals.

Hong Kong
Telecommunications
(HKT—NYSE)

Hong Kong Telecomm holds a virtual monopoly position in Hong Kong's telecommunications industry and enjoys a return on equity of close to 50 percent. At the end of August 1993, Hong Tel had a yield of 3.4 percent, based on an ADR share price of $49¼. And since August 1993, the stock has split three-for-one.

Hong Kong Telecommunications Ltd. (HKT) is the holding company for Hong Kong Telephone Company Ltd. and Cable and Wireless (Hong Kong) Ltd., which have exclusive rights to provide Hong Kong's local and international telephone and telex services as well as its international facsimile and data transmission services. HKT also provides, without exclusive rights, a wide range of telecommunications products and services including mobile radio telephone and local data transmission.

Under its current franchise, HKT has the exclusive right to provide local public telephone facilities and basic telephone services in Hong Kong until June 30, 1995. The company has some 2.6 million telephone lines in operation serving Hong Kong's population of 5.7 million. The company also has exclusive right until 2006 to provide Hong Kong's international telecommunications facilities; voice, facsimile, and data services; and telex and telegram services.

On July 1, 1997, sovereignty over Hong Kong will be transferred from Great Britain to the People's Republic of China. Pursuant to the Sino-British Joint Declaration, current social and economic systems in Hong Kong will remain unchanged for a period of 50 years.

Unlike most utilities, Hong Kong Telephone is extremely strong financially, with virtually no long-term debt.

Alcatel Alsthom
(ALA—NYSE)

Alcatel Alsthom is the second-largest French company and ranks in the top 40 companies in the world. The ADR traded at $26⅛, with a dividend yield of 1.4 percent.

The company has a major stake in three businesses—telecommunications equipment, power company generators, and the manufacture of high-speed trains.

Alcatel Alsthom is enhancing its position among the preeminent telecommunications and engineering firms in the world. Sales are conducted in 100 countries, and manufacturing facilities are situated in 25 countries on five continents.

Alcatel has made a number of important acquisitions, including the purchase of 70 percent of ITT's telecommunications operations in 1986 and the remaining 30 percent in 1992. In addition, the company now has a joint venture with Sprint and has acquired the telephone transmission equipment units of Rockwell International and Fiat.

In research and development, Alcatel has a distinguished reputation in its industry for remaining at the leading edge of its core business technologies. Among its recent achievements: introduction of the broadband Alcatel 1000 switching system and the entire Alcatel 1000 Series of network products; a GSM-standard digital cellular radio communications system; advanced office switches and terminals; and high-capacity optical-fiber systems.

In December of 1992, a consortium headed by GEC-Alsthom was awarded a contract to supply a combined-cycle gas turbine power station in Hong Kong that could be worth up to $2.6 billion. The contract was the largest awarded anywhere in the world during 1992. The Hong Kong contract reinforces the importance of Asia to Alcatel for both telecommunications and power generation.

Telefónica de España, S.A. (TEF—NYSE)

Telefónica de España, Spain's largest listed company and the 10th-largest domestic telephone network in the world, is the only telephone company in Spain. In addition to domestic and international telephone services, the company holds an exclusive concession to provide mobile telephone communications and is Spain's sole supplier of data transmission services. On August 31, 1993, the stock had a yield of 3.9 percent and a price of $36\frac{3}{8}$.

Telefónica de España has 13.3 million phone lines in service (34 per 100 inhabitants). In the past three years, moreover, the company has installed over three million telephone lines, or nearly one-quarter of the total number now in operation.

Dividends have been paid since 1946. An initial dividend from each year's earnings is normally paid in February or March of the following year. A final dividend is paid in July or August. During 1991, the company changed its dividend policy so that dividend payments are now tied to profitability. Thus, the dividend can fluctuate from year to year.

Productivity, at 185 lines per employee, is superior to the European Community average of 166, and it is rising. Frozen payroll and new digital lines allow for very moderate increases in operating costs.

The stock is reasonably priced, compared to domestic telephone stocks. For instance, it is selling below its book value of $37. Comparable U.S. telephone companies often sell at twice book value.

Investing in Telefónica also provides the investor with an indirect stake in Latin American communications. Actual holdings of TEF, at $1.9 billion, are as follows: 8 percent of Telefónica de Argentina, 43 percent of CTC of Chile (one of the most prosperous South American countries), 80 percent of Puerto Rico Long-Distance Telephone, and 6 percent of CANTV in Venezuela.

One Last Word

If we were to sum up this chapter, it might go as follows: because common stocks tend to be more volatile than fixed-income instruments, you may want to reduce this risk by investing abroad. It is easy to do because there are scores of ADRs followed by *Value Line* and the S&P tear sheets. Your broker can buy and sell these stocks with ease. Although I don't normally recommend mutual funds, it might make sense to use them in this instance. You might also consider large U.S.-based companies that have significant international segments.

If you are curious about the author's conviction in foreign investing, here are the stocks my wife and I own: British Telecomm, British Gas, Hanson, Elf Aquitaine, Alcatel, Banco Bilbao, Banco Santander, Telefónica de España, ENDESA, Repsol, Royal Dutch Petroleum, and a mutual fund, Vanguard Index, Europe.

9
A Detective Story

A good friend of mine bluntly informed me that it was "obvious" that I did not have the talent to write a novel. In no uncertain terms, he told me, "By your own admission, you rarely read novels. And now you tell me you want to write a murder mystery. Slats, I think you're wasting your time."

Although his caustic remarks made some sense, my feelings were bruised. On the other hand, I realized that he was probably right. I rarely read novels, and I don't like murder mysteries. Still, I wanted desperately to prove him wrong.

But, how to do it?

The first thing I would have to do is get someone to help me—a detective on the local police force, for instance. That's how I met Succo D. Pomodoro, a man in his mid-forties who has been tracking down criminals for over twenty years.

He had been recommended to me by a lawyer friend of mine. I called the police station and asked to speak to Succo D. Pomodoro "if he's not tied up in solving a murder or something."

A few seconds later, the veteran detective came on the line. After explaining my mission, I was able to convince him to have lunch with me at The Gov'nor Pub, situated in the Huntington Building at the corner of East Ninth and Euclid.

Succo D. Pomodoro III

"Just call me Dan," the slightly built detective said when we introduced ourselves. I invited him to sit opposite me in the booth. "My father and grandfather are both named Succo D. Pomodoro, which makes me Succo D. Pomodoro III. To avoid confusion, they always called me Danny at home—that's my middle name."

After I explained to him that I wanted to write a murder mystery that was true to life, he said, "That's exactly why I consented to meet you." As he spoke, his countenance was serious. I could see that this conversation was not going to be jocular. Although not a particularly handsome man, Dan was well groomed and had a full head of black hair, with just of hint of gray. He continued: "Too many murder mysteries characterize the cops as a bunch of dummies—they always make the private eye the hero. Frankly, it disturbs me. I hope you don't have a slick private eye in your yarn."

I assured him that I would give the police an honest shake in my novel. It was up to him to provide me with the information that would make it possible. He volunteered to steer me in the right direction.

Dan explained to me that, in recent years, law enforcement has been given a clear advantage over the average criminal through developments in science.

Modern Methods of Crime Detection

"For instance," he said, "computers can now break fingerprints down into mathematical formulas. This makes it possible to scan thousands of fingerprints in an hour. It doesn't take long to find a match—it's a far cry from the old method of comparing smudgy cards by hand."

I gave him a moment to gulp down some coffee and whack off a tender morsel of prime rib.

"How about DNA?" I asked.

"Glad you asked," he replied. "DNA technology is one of the great advances of the age. It wasn't even dreamed about when I first became a patrolman. DNA can match a bit of blood, hair, or semen to a suspect with nearly 100 percent certainty. Not all judges, unfortunately, see it that way."

"This is exactly the type of information I need, Dan," I said. "Tell me more." At that point, he pulled out an ancient, gold pocket watch from the side pocket of his navy blue blazer. It seemed odd that he would stash it there although I suppose he deemed the weather too hot and humid to wear a vest. He looked at his wristwatch and then turned his attention to the pocket watch; he deftly flipped open the cover, wound the stem, and replaced it in his pocket.

More about Law Enforcement

Apparently oblivious to my attention to his eccentric activity, he made no reference to his watch routine but continued to tell me about law enforcement.

"A few of the richest and most sophisticated drug lords have adapted techniques like computer mail to avoid detection, but the truth of the matter is that the bulk of crime is random street violence by young punks—they seem younger every day. These wretches rarely make much effort to cover their tracks."

"I'm all ears, Dan." I said. I could see that he was beginning to neglect his food. "Go ahead and eat—your prime ribs will get cold."

He sliced into his thick, succulent beef strips (which I had recommended because I was paying the bill). He continued:

"Although the public is rarely aware of how we work, it is sometimes painstaking investigative work that leads us to the perpetrator. For example, one killer was found by tracing hundreds of parking tickets given out near the sites of his eight shootings; he had blocked a hydrant near one." He stopped momentarily to check his pocket watch. He pulled out the stem, made a minute shift, after comparing it with his Seiko quartz wristwatch. He returned to his story.

Crooks Are Rarely Perfectionists

"The vast majority of crimes are committed in the heat of the moment, with no thought of erasing fingerprints or witnesses. The fiction stories you see on TV often depict criminals as perfectionists who plot their crimes with precision. In the real world, criminals slip up by contacting their friends or family. Or, they run across a previous associate now cooperating with the authorities and will tell them what name they're living under."

"Keep up the good work, Dan. I'm taking notes, so I won't misquote you. And, of course, I'll let you read my manuscript before I send it to my agent."

He nodded, as if that would be a good idea; without a pause, he continued.

"Many fugitives have been lured from hiding by ruses that, in retrospect, seem ridiculously unsophisticated. I remember one case in which federal law enforcement officers duped several dozen criminals by mailing letters to their last known addresses telling them they'd won fancy color TV sets. When the fugitives called in from hiding to collect, they were told to await the truck from the United International Delivery Company. The truck arrived—with a police task force inside."

I looked up from my note taking and said, "I think I struck gold when I bumped into you, Dan. I hope you don't have to rush back to the precinct." He told me it was his day off and that he was prepared to spend as much time as needed to make sure my novel was authentic. After checking his pocket watch, to make sure it agreed with his wristwatch, he resumed his explanation of police methods. As he did so, I thought I caught sight of a bulge on the left side of his navy blue blazer. Could he have a weapon stashed there, I wondered?

"In another interesting case," Dan Pomodoro said, "police had even greater success by sending fugitives letters saying they had won hard-to-get tickets to a Cleveland Browns–Denver Broncos playoff game—plus a free pregame brunch with Bernie Kozar, Eric Metcalf, and Kevin Mack. Ninety-six showed up, produced identification, and were handcuffed."

"I'm almost out of space to take notes but don't stop now," I said.

The Art of Tracing a Phone Call

"Every once in a while criminals will slip up when they take seriously some of the propaganda they see in the movies. I remember a kidnapping case—back in 1978, I believe—when the thugs were trying to extract a $500,000 ransom. They were under the impression that to trace a phone call, police had to be on the line for a certain period of time. Don't believe it. You're a dead duck as soon as you dial the last digit."

As I munched on my last bit of prime rib, I said, "You have given me new respect for crime detection, Dan. I think I'll give up trying to plot the perfect crime."

He hastened to assure me that "There are plenty of perfect crimes committed every day of the year, Slats. In fact, I was reading the other day that, nationwide, there are 350,000 warrants outstanding for fugitives in felony cases. Unfortunately, there are criminals who have eluded arrest for years. We nail our share, of course, but entirely too many get away."

After we had talked for another half hour, he changed the direction of our discussion when he asked me if I was a full-time novelist.

"At the rate I'm going, I would have starved to death long ago writing novels, Dan. My main line of work is managing investments for people with substantial holdings. So far, none of my clients are policemen. I'm assuming that you and your colleagues are overworked and underpaid."

"There aren't many who need your services, Slats, but I may be an exception. My wife Polly teaches school, and we don't have any children. We live modestly and have saved up a few dollars over the years, but I doubt that it would put us in a class with your clients."

"If I can give you a few ideas, I would be happy to get you headed in the right direction—no charge, of course."

Money-Market Funds—Not Exactly the Road to Riches

"One of these days, I'll probably hand in my shoulder holster and let the younger men cope with the violence in the streets. Right now, our savings are in a money-market fund—not exactly the place to get rich these days."

"If you're looking for some good income stocks, I'd like to outline a method of picking stocks that has a good track record."

The idea of investing in stocks didn't strike a responsive chord in Dan Pomodoro. "No one in our family dabbles in the stock market, Slats. I guess we're too cautious. Can you believe I have never even read *The Wall Street Journal*?"

For the next several minutes, I explained to him the reason why common stocks are the best way to invest. He seemed to have an open mind. "Maybe I have missed the boat," he said. "Why don't you go ahead. If what you tell me makes sense, I'll have you over for some good Italian cooking. Polly will put some meat on those raw bones of yours." I think he was referring to my lanky, angular frame, devoid of muscle and excess adipose tissue.

I waited momentarily while he set his pocket watch so that it was synchronized with his Seiko. I was beginning to wonder if he was in a hurry to keep another appointment, but he assured me that we could continue talking until Eddie kicked us out of The Gov'nor Pub. "Eddie is a good buddy of mine, Dan. And besides, I'm his best customer. On the other hand, I don't have my tables and charts with me. Why don't we go back to my office—it's just a few doors from the Union Club. Otherwise, Eddie will start charging me rent."

The Scene Shifts to My Office in The Chesterfield

When we were seated comfortably on the sofa in my office, I pulled out some illustrations to show to Detective Pomodoro. When he took off his jacket, I saw for the first time his shoulder holster, replete with a menacing looking pistol.

I opened the conversation by explaining to him that good results can be obtained by investing in some of the stocks that make up the well-known Dow Jones Industrial Average.

"If you want a combination of income and capital gains, there is a simple way to achieve your objective. You first determine which of the 30 stocks have the best dividend yield. Then, you focus on the 12 with the highest yield. As a group, they will often do quite well. However, it seems to make sense to reject the one or two with the very highest yield. Let me show you how this idea worked back in 1975, for instance." I then told him about the results shown in Table 9-1.

I then explained to Dan Pomodoro that I used a statistical device called the "standard deviation" in order to remove one or two stocks

Table 9-1

Twelve stocks with the highest yield, selected from the Dow Jones Industrial Average. The two with the highest yield are excluded.

Stock	Dividend yield year-end 1975 (%)	Stock price change 12-31-75 to 12-31-76 (%)
AlliedSignal	5.4	+ 20.30
American Brands	6.9	+ 28.42
American Can	7.0	+ 24.30
AT&T	6.7	+ 24.82
Bethlehem Steel	6.1	+ 22.81
Chevron	6.8	+ 39.57
Exxon	5.6	+ 20.85
Inco	6.3	+ 29.21
International Harvester	7.6*	+ 47.49*
Texaco	8.6*	+ 18.72*
Westinghouse Electric	7.3	+ 31.78
Woolworth	5.5	+ 17.05
Average price change of remaining 10 stocks		+ 25.91
Average beginning yield of remaining 10 stocks		6.36
Total return of 10 stocks		+ 32.27
Dow Jones Industrial Average price change		+ 17.86
Beginning yield		4.81
Total return for Dow Jones Industrial Average		22.67

*Eliminated from consideration because they had yields that were too high.

that might be too speculative. (If you have forgotten how this idea works, you may want to review it in Chapter 6.) In brief, the standard deviation singles out the 16 percent that have a yield that is too high—which could be a sign that something is drastically wrong. Typically, in a group of 12, one or two stocks will fall in this category.

"In this illustration, Dan, two stocks are eliminated: International Harvester and Texaco. As it turned out, they would have been good stocks to own in the year that followed. However, later on International Harvester fell on hard times and ultimately changed its name to Navistar. As a long-term holding, it was a bust."

"I think I get the picture. You are trying to keep me from getting in trouble. Is that right?"

"Exactly," I told him. "I am a conservative investor, and I have tried to develop an approach that will enable you to do better than the general market. In this instance, the remaining 10 stocks outperformed the Dow Jones Industrial Average from year-end 1975 to year-end 1976. Whenever you outperform this well-known index, you should be satisfied. Not too many investors are able to accomplish this—even the professionals have trouble."

"Let me review what you have said, Slats. Remember, you're talking to a rank amateur. If I had bought these 10 stocks and held them for one year, my holdings would have increased in value by 25.91 percent. Then, if we add in the beginning dividend yield, the total return comes to 32.27 percent. Am I getting the hang of the lingo?"

While he adjusted the setting on his gold watch, I told him that you couldn't always expect to make 32.27 percent in one year.

Sinking Spells Must Be Endured

"Sometimes the market goes in reverse, Dan. On average, it goes up two years out of three. You have to be prepared for a sinking spell once in a while."

"That's what has kept me out of the stock market, Slats. I have enough to worry about trying to dodge bullets. What kind of 'sinking spell' are you referring to?"

"Let's move ahead one year, and you'll see what I mean." I flipped to a new page in my notebook to Table 9-2.

Using the standard deviation, I determined that two stocks should be eliminated: General Motors and Texaco. Even so, the rest of the list sank into minus territory in 1977. In fact, there were some major losers. I could see that Dan was getting nervous.

"The stock market may not be for me, Slats. One year I make 32 percent, and the next year I get torpedoed."

Table 9-2

Twelve stocks with the highest yield, selected from the Dow Jones Industrial Average. The two with the highest yield are excluded.

Stock	Dividend yield year-end 1976 (%)	Stock price change 12-31-76 to 12-31-77 (%)
American Brands	6.1	− 6.01
American Can	6.2	− 0.64
AT&T	6.0	− 4.72
Bethlehem Steel	5.0	− 47.68
Chevron	5.4	− 5.18
Exxon	5.2	− 10.26
General Foods	5.0	+ 4.13
General Motors	7.1*	− 19.90*
Inco	4.9	− 47.51
International Harvester	5.6	− 8.33
Texaco	7.2*	0.00*
Westinghouse Electric	5.5	+ 2.84
Average price change of remaining 10 stocks		− 12.34
Average beginning yield of remaining 10 stocks		5.49
Total return 10 stocks		− 6.85
Dow Jones Industrial Average price change		− 17.27
Beginning yield		4.40
Total return for Dow Jones Industrial Average		− 12.87

*Eliminated from consideration because yield is too high.

Let's Look at a Bear Market

"I wanted to show you what can happen in a bear market, Dan. Actually, my method of stock selection protected you to some extent. You can see that the 30-stock average plunged 17.27 percent in 1977. Even if you add in the beginning yield of 4.4 percent, the total return for the year was a minus 12.87 percent. Not a very pleasant experience, to be sure."

"How did the 10 stocks do?" he asked.

"They were down—as you would expect. But they were down less than the market, only 12.34 percent. Add in the beginning yield of 4.49 percent, and the loss was 6.85 percent. When you realize that you made over 30 percent the prior year, you are still ahead of the game."

Table 9-3

Twelve stocks with the highest yield, selected from the Dow Jones Industrial Average. The two with the highest yield are excluded.

Stock	Dividend yield year-end 1986 (%)	Stock price change 12-31-86 to 12-31-87 (%)
AlliedSignal	4.5	− 29.60
AT&T	4.8	+ 8.00
Chevron	5.3	− 12.67
Du Pont	3.8	+ 4.02
Exxon	5.1	+ 8.73
General Motors	7.6*	− 7.01*
Goodyear Tire	3.8	+ 43.28
Philip Morris	4.2	+ 18.78
Sears, Roebuck	4.4	− 15.72
Texaco	8.4*	+ 3.83*
Union Carbide	6.7	− 3.33
USX	5.5	+ 38.37
Average price change of remaining 10 stocks		+ 5.99
Average beginning yield of remaining 10 stocks		4.81
Total return of remaining 10 stocks		+ 10.80
Dow Jones Industrial Average price change		+ 2.26
Beginning yield		3.62
Total return for Dow Jones Industrial Average		+ 5.88

*Eliminated from consideration because yield was too high.

"I see what you mean. Maybe I should have started buying stocks earlier. Of course, what you have shown me is just ancient history. Do you have any charts that are more up to date?"

"I have all sorts of things in this notebook, Dan. Why don't we jump ahead to year-end 1986" (see Table 9-3).

"In Table 9-3 the market made only nominal progress. It barely inched ahead by 2.26 percent. Add in the beginning yield of 3.62, and your total return for the Dow Jones Industrial Average would have been a modest 5.88 percent."

"I hope you did better with your high-yield theory," he said as he reached into his jacket pocket to pull out his antique gold pocket watch. At no time, however, did he reach for his gun.

"Using the standard deviation maneuver, we would have set aside General Motors and Texaco because they both had extraordinarily high dividends that year. As it turned out, that was a good move. The other 10 stocks did considerably better than the index. Their average appreciation amounted to 5.99 percent. When we add in the beginning yield, the total return comes to 10.8 percent, which was much better than you could have done by buying all 30 stocks. Are you convinced yet, Dan, that this is a good method of stock selection?"

"You make a good case, Slats. On the other hand, 1986 was quite a few years ago. How did you do in 1992?"

I showed him Table 9-4.

Table 9-4

Twelve stocks with the highest yield, selected from the Dow Jones Industrial Average. The one stock with the highest yield was excluded.

Stock	Dividend yield year-end 1991 (%)	Stock price change 12-31-91 to 12-31-92 (%)
American Express	4.9	+ 21.34
Chevron	4.8	+ 0.72
Du Pont	3.6	+ 1.07
Eastman Kodak	4.1	− 16.06
Exxon	4.4	+ 0.41
General Motors	5.5	+ 11.69
IBM	5.4	− 43.40
Sears, Roebuck	5.3	+ 20.13
Texaco	5.2	− 2.45
Union Carbide	4.9	+ 64.81
Westinghouse Electric	7.8*	− 25.69*
Woolworth	4.1	+ 19.34
Average price change of remaining 11 stocks		+ 7.05
Average beginning yield or remaining 11 stocks		4.87
Total return of remaining 11 stocks		+ 11.92
Dow Jones Industrial Average price change		+ 4.17
Beginning yield		3.32
Total return for Dow Jones Industrial Average		+ 7.49

*Eliminated from consideration because yield was too high.

The Demise of IBM

"There were a couple stocks that hurt us in 1992: IBM and Westinghouse Electric. Both were sorry performers. Unfortunately, my system did not get rid of IBM. It plunged a sickening 43.4 percent. But it did get rid of Westinghouse since the yield on that stock was extremely high: 7.8 percent. The standard deviation would have kept you from losing 25.69 percent on that particular stock. And despite the IBM loss, the year was not a total disaster. What do you think of this idea, Dan?"

Table 9-5

Twelve stocks with the highest yield, selected from the Dow Jones Industrial Average. The one stock with the highest yield has been excluded.

Stock	Dividend yield year-end 1992 (%)	Stock price change 12-31-92 to 8-27-93 (%)
American Express	4.0	+ 31.16
Chevron	4.7	+ 32.37
Du Pont	3.7	+ 2.39
Eastman Kodak	4.9	+ 51.54
Exxon	4.7	+ 6.95
IBM	9.6*	− 12.41*
Morgan, J.P.	3.7	+ 14.26
Sears, Roebuck	4.4	+ 48.20
Texaco	5.4	+ 8.37
Union Carbide	4.5	+ 10.53
United Technologies	3.7	+ 19.74
Westinghouse Electric	5.4	+ 21.50
Average price change of remaining 11 stocks		+ 22.46
Average beginning yield of remaining 11 stocks		4.46
Total return of remaining 11 stocks		+ 26.92
Dow Jones Industrial Average price change		+ 10.29
Beginning yield		3.29
Total return for Dow Jones Industrial Average		+ 13.58

*Eliminated from consideration because yield was too high.

Table 9-6

Summary of five samples.

Years	High yield system (%)	Dow Jones Industrial Average (%)
1975–1976	+ 32.27	+ 22.67
1976–1977	− 6.85	− 12.87
1986–1987	+ 10.80	+ 5.88
1991–1992	+ 11.92	+ 7.49
1992–August 27, 1993	+ 26.92	+ 13.58
Average of five periods	+ 15.01	+ 7.35

At first, he didn't answer but got up from the sofa and wandered over to the window. Then, he returned and said, "I suppose it is too much to ask you how you've done so far in 1993."

"Not at all, Dan," I said. "Why don't we look at another table." I showed him Table 9-5.

He looked intently as I proceeded to show him how the high-yield strategy worked in the first eight months of 1993.

"In this instance, the standard deviation indicated that IBM had a dangerously high yield. Consequently, it was eliminated. The remaining 11 stocks have performed extremely well, as you can see. Even tired old Sears, Roebuck came to life. The total return for the 11 stocks, including dividends, was nearly double the Dow Jones Industrial Average: 26.92 percent compared with 13.58 percent for the Dow."

Almost Time for Pasta

"This has been a revelation, Slats. I think it's time I invited you over for some pasta. Polly will put some meat and muscle on your frame if it's the last thing she does. Frankly, I hope you can work your magic on her."

"Hold on, Dan, I'm not quite done. Let's look at this final table, which sums up all five years" (see Table 9-6).

"It's too bad you aren't a better shot, Slats. We could use you on the police force." He stood up, put on his blazer, and made one last check of his antique gold pocket watch.

10
How to Build a Portfolio for Growth and Income

The vast majority of investors are seeking stocks that provide above-average yield as well as some semblance of growth. Here is an approach that should prove valuable to this group.

Too many investors buy stocks without any effort and then wonder why they have poor results. Those same people would not buy a car or a house without expending some time and effort. If you spent $150,000 on a house, you would take a week or two and go out with several different real estate salespeople.

Is building a secure financial future any less important?

But getting back to the calculations that will be needed to build a portfolio of stocks for growth and income: step one is to get your Dow Jones list of 30 stocks and ascertain the six with the highest yield. Next, check the *Stock Guide* and write down the number of institutional owners next to each one. Buy the one with the fewest number of institutional owners.

Now, bring your list back to six by finding the stock with the highest yield from the 24 remaining Dow stocks. Continue this process until you have six stocks. Hold them for at least one year. At that point, you may want to go through the same routine again and make any needed changes.

To show you how this approach works, we will work with the 30 stocks that comprise the Dow Jones Industrial Average. It appears five days a week in *The Wall Street Journal* on page 3 of the third section. After the name of each stock, write down the number of institutional owners, which you will find in the *Standard & Poor's Stock Guide* available in any library or brokerage office. Table 10-1 gives you an idea of what you have to do.

In this exercise, you begin with the six stocks from the 30-stock list with the highest yield. They are denoted by a single asterisk in Table 10-1. Step one is to select the stock with the fewest number of institutional owners, namely, Westinghouse Electric, with 426 owners.

Because this reduces the number of candidates to five, it is necessary to add a new stock, the one with the highest yield from those remaining. It turns out to be Union Carbide, with a yield of 4.5 percent.

Now that we again have six stocks, we look for the one with the fewest number of institutional owners, which just happens to be Union Carbide with 315. Now we have two stocks in our quest to find a total of six.

As before, we look for a new high-yield stock, to bring our list of candidates back to six. Sears, Roebuck, with a yield at that time of 4.4 percent, is chosen. Once again, we scan the new list to see which one has the fewest institutional owners; we find that Sears is the one, with 605. The process continues until we end up with six stocks. They are listed in Table 10-2, along with their beginning prices and ending prices, as of September 9, 1993.

A word of explanation concerning Sears, Roebuck. In mid-1993, Sears divested some shares of Dean Witter, Discover & Co. This must be taken into account when we make our calculations. The price of Dean Witter has to be multiplied by 0.39031, which comes out to be $14.93. This figure must be added to the price of Sears, which was $54.62, giving us a total of $69.55, which is the price you will see in Table 10-2.

Nothing Short of Spectacular

In this first test of my idea, the results were nothing short of spectacular—although it is probably imprudent to use such a flamboyant term. Nevertheless, the six stocks selected had a total return that was more than double that of the Dow.

As noted earlier, no system, no matter how impressive, always works to your satisfaction. For instance, had you used this method of

Table 10-1

Thirty stocks that currently make up the Dow Jones Industrial Average, along with the number of institutional owners and the current dividend yield. Today's list has been the same since May of 1991, when three new stocks were added: Caterpillar (it was substituted for Navistar), Walt Disney (replacing USX), and J.P. Morgan (which knocked out Primerica). The price of the stock at the end of 1992 is also given.

Stock	Institutional owners	Dividend yield year-end 1992 (%)	Price year-end 1992 ($)
AlliedSignal	482	1.7	60.50
ALCOA	528	2.2	71.62
American Express	694	4.0**	24.88
AT&T	1080	2.6	51.00
Bethlehem Steel	215	Nil	16.00
Boeing	758	2.5	40.12
Caterpillar	459	1.1	53.62
Chevron	796	4.7*	69.50
Coca-Cola	897	1.3	41.88
Disney, Walt	736	0.5	43.00
Du Pont	836	3.7	47.12
Eastman Kodak	777	4.9*	40.50
Exxon	1077	4.7*	61.12
General Electric	1286	2.9	85.50
General Motors	790	2.5	32.25
Goodyear Tire	432	1.5	68.38
IBM	1189	9.6*	50.38
International Paper	612	2.5	66.62
McDonald's	812	0.8	48.75
Merck	1158	2.3	43.38
Minnesota Mining & Manufacturing	897	3.2	100.62
Morgan, J.P.	747	3.7**	65.75
Philip Morris	1445	3.4	77.12
Procter & Gamble	830	2.1	53.62
Sears, Roebuck	605	4.4**	45.50
Texaco	911	5.4*	59.75
Union Carbide	315	4.5**	16.62

Table 10-1 (*Continued*)

Thirty stocks that currently make up the Dow Jones Industrial Average, along with the number of institutional owners and the current dividend yield. Today's list has been the same since May of 1991, when three new stocks were added: Caterpillar (it was substituted for Navistar), Walt Disney (replacing USX), and J.P. Morgan (which knocked out Primerica). The price of the stock at the end of 1992 is also given.

Stock	Institutional owners	Dividend yield year-end 1992 (%)	Price year-end 1992 ($)
United Technologies	557	3.7**	48.12
Westinghouse Electric	426	5.4*	13.38
Woolworth	422	3.5	31.62

*The original six stocks with the highest yield.
**Stocks added as selections are made. Each time a selection is made, the next highest-yielding stock is added to the list. Once again, the stock with the fewest institutional owners is selected.

Table 10-2

Six stocks selected from Table 10-1, by using the dividend yield and the number of institutional owners as described in the text.

Stock	Price 12-31-92 ($)	Price 9-8-93 ($)	Stock price change 12-31-92 to 9-8-93 (%)
Westinghouse Electric	12.38	14.75	+ 10.28
Union Carbide	16.62	18.25	+ 9.77
Sears, Roebuck	45.50	69.55	+ 52.86
American Express	24.88	33.00	+ 32.66
United Technologies	48.12	55.62	+ 15.58
J.P. Morgan	65.75	75.88	+ 15.40
Average price change six stocks			+ 22.76
Average beginning yield			4.28
Total return			+ 27.04
Dow Jones Industrial Average 12-31-92			3301.11
Dow Jones Industrial Average 9-8-93			3588.93
Change in Dow Jones Industrial Average			+ 8.72
Beginning yield			3.18
Total return for Dow Jones Industrial Average			+ 11.90

Table 10-3

Six stocks selected from the Dow Jones Industrial Average at the end of 1979 using the dividend yield and the number of institutional owners as described in the text.

Order of selection	Stock	Dividend yield 12-31-79 (%)	Institutional owners	Stock price change 12-31-79 to 12-31-82 (%)
6	Goodyear Tire	9.1	177	+ 171.84
	General Motors	9.9	687	
3	US Steel	9.1	177	+ 20.00
	AT&T	9.6	895	
5	AmericanBrands	8.1	181	+ 35.17
1	American Can	8.1	120	− 13.33
	Supplemental list			
2	Johns Manville	8.0	147	− 57.51
	Exxon	8.0	867	
4	Bethlehem Steel	7.6	152	− 8.88
	Texaco	7.5	600	
	Union Carbide	7.1	416	
	Sears, Roebuck	7.1	506	
Average price appreciation of six stocks				+ 24.55
Beginning yield				8.50
Total return of six stocks				+ 33.05
Dow Jones Industrial Average price change				+ 24.78
Beginning yield				6.47
Total return				+ 31.25

stock selection at the end of 1979, you would have had indifferent results if you still held the stocks at the end of 1982. Table 10-3 shows the six stocks with the highest yield at that time, plus a supplemental list of six stocks with the next-highest yield.

Let's take another look at the Dow 30, this time at the end of May 1992 (see Table 10-4). This exercise will demonstrate that even a few months can make a difference in which stocks are selected. You will recall that our first illustration depicted the situation at the end of 1992.

In Table 10-4 the first stock selected would have been Sears,

Table 10-4

Six stocks selected from the Dow Jones Industrial Average at the end of May 31, 1992, using the dividend yield and the number of institutional owners, as described in the text.

Order of selection	Stock	Dividend yield 5-31-92 (%)	Institutional owners	Stock price change 5-31-92 to 8-25-93* (%)
	IBM	5.3	1214	
	Eastman Kodak	5.0	782	
	Texaco	5.0	895	
	Exxon	4.8	1045	
	Chevron	4.6	781	
1	Sears, Roebuck	4.6	597	+ 56.49
Supplemental list				
2	American Express	4.4	700	+ 47.80
3	Westinghouse Electric	4.2	481	− 6.02
4	Woolworth	4.1	414	− 8.18
5	General Motors	4.0	753	+ 17.24
6	J.P. Morgan	3.8	757	+ 30.50
	Union Carbide	3.5	305	
Average price appreciation of six stocks				+ 22.47
Beginning yield				4.18
Total return of six stocks				+ 26.65
Dow Jones Industrial Average price change				+ 7.51
Beginning yield				2.95
Total return for Dow Jones Industrial Average				+ 10.46

*Throughout this chapter, I have used different holding periods, some one year in duration, others more than that.

Roebuck. It was part of the original six high-yield stocks as of May 31, 1992. At that time, it had the fewest institutional owners within that six-stock group.

The next stock to be added would have been American Express, with only 700 institutional owners. The stock selection procedure would have continued until Westinghouse, Woolworth, General Motors, and J.P. Morgan had been added to the group. If these six stocks had been held until the cutoff date of August 25, 1993, their average price change would have been impressive, up 22.47 percent. Add in the beginning yield of 4.18 percent, and the total return adds up to 26.65 percent.

This performance was far better than the Dow Jones Industrial Average, which advanced from 3396.88 to 3652.09, a gain of only 7.51 percent. Even with the yield of 2.95 percent added in, the total return was only 10.46, which was not even half the action of the six stocks selected by this system.

A Look at the 50 Stocks of the Barron's List

Now that you have seen how this stock picking idea works, let's look at another illustration. In this instance, we will use the 50 stocks that make up the Barron's list. In the first three tests, you may recall that our goal was to find six stocks, which just happens to be 20 percent of the 30 stocks in the Dow Jones Industrial Average. Similarly, we will use 20 percent of the 50-stock list. Thus, step one is to find the 10 stocks in the Barron's list that had the highest dividend yield at the beginning of the test period, year-end 1984.

For the sake of brevity, I will list only the 20 stocks that had the highest dividend yield on that date. Initially, the first 10 will be considered. Once a selection has been made, a substitute will be chosen from the second 10, which appear in Table 10-5.

The selection process is identical to the one used on the 30 Dow stocks. After selecting Lone Star, the next stock added was Amoco, with a yield of 5.7 percent. At this point, Detroit Edison is selected because it had only 140 institutional owners at the end of 1984.

Next, we added CPC International, with a yield of 5.5 percent, which, incidentally, was the same yield as Norfolk Southern. However, the stock chosen was CPC because it had the lowest number of institutional owners.

Once again, the results were excellent: the average price appreciation of the 10 stocks during the period under study was 75.81 percent. (You may think it odd that I used the ending date of November 30, 1986. This is because the exercise was lifted from one of my notebooks, which just happened to have been calculated at that particular time.)

After the price appreciation is ascertained, we next add in the beginning yield, and the total return was 82.44 percent. In the same period,

Table 10-5

Twenty stocks with the highest yield from the Barron's 50. The first 10 are listed at the top of the table. The same procedure is used to denote the order of selection, with a number to the left of those selected. For instance, there is a *1* next to Lone Star because it was the first one chosen.

Order of selection	Stock	Dividend yield 12-31-84 (%)	Institutional owners	Stock price change 12-31-84 to 11-30-86 (%)
	AT&T	6.2	917	
2	Detroit Edison	10.5	140	+ 13.3
	Du Pont	6.1	609	
	General Motors	6.4	977	
8	Goodyear Tire	6.2	421	+ 65.4
1	Lone Star	7.3	90	+ 39.4
	Mobil Corporation	8.1	686	
6	SCEcorp	9.0	408	+ 54.9
	Union Carbide	9.3	479	
3	Wisconsin Energy	7.3	206	+ 83.1
	Norfolk Southern	5.5	436	
7	AlliedSignal	5.2	311	+ 20.3
5	American Standard	5.3	211	+ 42.4
	Amoco	5.7	759	
4	CPC International	5.5	298	+ 97.5
	Citicorp	5.3	539	
	Monsanto	5.2	466	
9	USG	5.1	188	+ 193.9
10	Wrigley	4.9	67	+ 147.9
	RJR	4.7	568	
Average price appreciation of 10 stocks				+ 75.81
Beginning yield				6.63
Total return of 10 stocks				+ 82.44
Average price appreciation of all 50				+ 51.20
Average beginning yield of 50 stocks				4.58
Total return of all 50 stocks				+ 55.78

Table 10-6

Nineteen stocks with the highest yield from the Barron's 50. The first 10 are listed at the top of the table. As in prior tables, I have put a number at the left of those selected. For instance, there is a *1* next to Detroit Edison because it was the first one chosen.

Order of selection	Stock	Dividend yield 7-31-87 (%)	Institutional owners	Stock price change 7-31-87 to 7-31-89 (%)
7	SCEcorp	7.7	520	+ 21.77
2	Wisconsin Energy	5.9	237	+ 23.08
	BellSouth	5.6	782	
1	Detroit Edison	11.0	196	+ 40.98
	General Motors	5.6	913	
	Citicorp	4.4	625	
3	American Brands	4.2	465	+ 54.66
	Mobil	4.2	847	
10	AlliedSignal	4.1	537	− 15.63
	Amoco	3.9	788	
Supplemental list				
	AT&T	3.7	761	
4	Norfolk Southern	3.4	503	+ 4.20
6	CSX	3.1	519	− 8.25
5	GATX	3.0	68	+ 39.56
	Monsanto	3.0	553	
	Procter & Gamble	2.9	672	
8	General Mills	2.8	413	+ 24.24
9	TRW	2.7	322	− 17.41
	Du Pont	2.7	764	
Average price appreciation of 10 stocks				+ 16.72
Beginning yield				4.79
Total return				+ 21.51
Dow Jones Industrial Average				+ 2.68
Beginning yield				2.88
Dow Jones Industrial Average total return				+ 5.56

Table 10-7

Performance of system stocks, compared to the Dow Jones Industrial Average in the same period.

Period	System (%)	Dow Jones Industrial Average (%)
12-31-92 to 9-8-93	+ 27.04	+ 8.72
12-31-79 to 12-31-82	+ 33.05	+ 31.25
5-31-92 to 8-25-93	+ 26.65	+ 10.46
12-31-84 to 11-30-86	+ 82.44	+ 55.78
7-31-87 to 7-31-89	+ 21.51	+ 5.56
Averages	+ 38.14	+ 22.35

the action of 50 stocks as a group was far less impressive: 51.20 percent. Add in the beginning yield, for a total return of 55.78 percent.

The Crash of 1987

In my next illustration (Table 10-6) of this idea, I picked a tough beginning date: July 31, 1987. You may recall that the market had surged to a very high level at that time and was later to fall apart, particularly in October. Thus, the results in this exercise will not be very impressive. Even so, the stocks selected beat the market handily. In this instance, I used the Dow Jones Industrial Average for comparison.

Although the performance of the 10 stocks did not make you a million dollars in this test, it was far better than you might have expected, in view of what happened to stocks in general. The Dow Jones Industrial Average was 2572.07 on July 31, 1987. It was modestly higher two years later, at 2641.12, a paltry gain of 2.68 percent. Add in the beginning yield of 2.88 percent, and the total return was 5.56 percent. By contrast, the 10 stocks selected by the system had a total return of 21.51 percent—almost four times as good.

The Final Tabulation

If we take these five exercises and present them together, we get the results shown in Table 10-7. It seems clear that this method of stock selection has considerable merit.

11
How to Reduce Risk

Unless you are extremely wealthy, you are probably concerned about keeping a lid on risk. This may explain why thousands of would-be investors avoid common stocks. Instead, they tie up their money in CDs, bank accounts, and bonds. Admittedly, risk of loss is less here. On the other hand, risk of purchasing power loss is increased.

Because this book is a guide to common stock investing, it's important that I provide you with some thoughts on how to invest in this realm and yet keep risk under control. Here are some brief ideas, followed by a more detailed discussion of dollar-cost averaging, which is one of the best ways to mitigate risk.

First, if you use the *Standard & Poor's Stock Guide,* you can use some of the information provided in that handy monthly publication to your advantage:

1. Stocks with a low price/earnings (P/E) ratio are normally less risky than those with a high multiple. In today's market, a P/E of 18 is about average. Whenever you buy a stock with a P/E in the mid- or high-20s, your risk is increased. In our portfolios, we concentrate on stocks with lower multiples. True, we may sacrifice some big gains, but we also protect our clients from huge losses. Before it collapsed in a heap, for instance, U.S. Surgical had a price/earnings multiple in the stratosphere.

Avoid Extremes in Yield

2. Pay attention to yield. Although some high-yield stocks are risky, it is generally true that the more volatile stocks are those with

extremely low yields or those that have no dividend. Perhaps the best course of action is to concentrate on stocks with above-average yields, while avoiding those with inordinately high or low yields.

3. Standard & Poor's grades most stocks with a letter, such as A+, B, or C. Here again, you may make a ton of money by buying stocks that are low quality (B+ is average), but you also increase your risk. For investors who are averse to risk, I recommend sticking with stocks rated A– or better.

4. The payout ratio is also important. Generally speaking, a very low payout ratio is an indication of a company that is aggressive and interested in growth. Such stocks are fine for younger investors who are willing to take on risk, but they may not be suitable for those who want to avoid this risk.

   At the other extreme are stocks with very high payout ratios, let's say 85 percent or above. These companies may have underlying problems; such stocks are best avoided. In sum, confine your investing to stocks with payout ratios that are somewhere near the mean rather than at one extreme or the other.

Don't Overlook Financial Strength

5. The *Stock Guide* also gives you a hint of the company's financial strength. On the right-hand page are the ingredients for calculating the current ratio. Divide the current assets by the current liabilities. A ratio of two-to-one or better is excellent. Those with a ratio of less than one-to-one are best avoided by risk-averse investors. You cannot use this measure on financial stocks such as banks or insurance companies. The *Stock Guide* does not provide the current assets and current liabilities for these industries. What's more, it may not give you these numbers for certain other companies that have a large financial subsidiary.

6. The number of institutional owners may also be worth examining. Although too many institutional owners can be a red flag, the opposite is also true. If a stock is being shunned by most mutual funds, pension plans, banks, and insurance companies, it is probably very small or speculative. To be sure, it may be fine for an aggressive investor, but it could be too volatile for someone who prefers to stick with stocks that are less venturesome.

Value Line Risk Measures

Value Line is your second important source of information that can be helpful in recognizing undue risk. Here are some hints that may be helpful:

1. The safety ranking can be found in the upper left-hand corner of every *Value Line* evaluation. The best score is *1*, while the worst is *5*. I have no idea how this number is arrived at, but it probably makes sense to avoid stocks rated below 3.

2. The beta coefficient is worthy of your attention. Beta is a measure of volatility. Stocks rated 1.00 tend to fluctuate in line with the market. When the market advances 10 percent, for instance, stocks with betas of 1.00 will do about the same. Those with a high beta, let's say 1.25 or above, are the more risky issues. At the other extreme are stocks with betas of 0.60, 0.70, or 0.80. Notable among the stocks with low betas are public utilities.

3. *Value Line* also has a financial strength rating. You'll find it in the lower right-hand corner of the page. The best rating is A++, which is comparable to the A+ rating found in the *Stock Guide.* Even so, you will note that these two services rarely agree. As an example, the *Stock Guide* gives Tektronix a rating of B−, while *Value Line* gives it a B+. Similarly, the *Stock Guide* rates Northeast Utilities as a B+ (which is average), while *Value Line* says it is worthy of a B (two notches below average).

Look for a Clean Balance Sheet

4. The balance sheet is a key to risk. If you want to keep risk within bounds, look for companies with low debt. For instance, Northeast Utilities had only 35.6 percent in common equity in 1991. At that time, *Value Line* estimated that this ratio would drop even further in 1992, to 28 percent. By contrast, Duke Power had an extremely strong balance sheet in 1991, with 51.1 percent in common equity. Public utilities are easier to analyze because the actual percentage of debt and equity is given in *Value Line.* This is not the case with most other industries. Instead, the dollar value is given. This means you must do your own calculating.

   As an example, EG&G had very little debt in 1991, only $2.2 million. Its common equity amounted to $420.7 million. It doesn't require much mental arithmetic to realize that EG&G had a "clean balance sheet."

In the same industry, Eastman Kodak had a great deal of debt in 1991, $7.6 billion. This exceeded its common equity, which was $6.1 billion. Although Eastman Kodak was a good stock to own in 1993, it was not without risk.

Examine Value Carefully

5. There are a number of value measures that have been discussed elsewhere in this book but are repeated here for emphasis:

   a. The *price-to-revenues ratio* is calculated by dividing the price of the stock by the revenues per share. For Eastman Kodak, you would have divided $41, its price in December of 1992, by $59.76, the revenues per share. As it turned out, this was a very favorable number. Whenever the price of the stock is much higher than the revenue figure, the risk is increased. As an example, Thermo Instrument had a much higher ratio, which you can see if you divide the price ($34) by the revenue-per-share figure of $11.77.

   b. The *price-to-cash-flow* number can also be helpful in determining value. (Cash flow is made up of earnings plus depreciation and other items.) For Eastman Kodak, the cash flow per share was $4.60 in 1991. However, this was a bit misleading because it had been $7.94 the prior year, and *Value Line* was expecting it to rebound to $7.65 in 1992, with a further improvement to $8.85 in 1993. Although I am not keen on such forecasts, this one might be an exception. The way to calculate this ratio is to divide the current price of the stock by the cash-flow-per-share figure. Thus, divide $41 by $7.65, and you get a ratio of 5.4 times. A more typical number would be 10. Thus, Eastman Kodak's number was a good one. By contrast, EG&G's number was much higher if you divide the price of the stock at that time ($19) by the cash flow per share in 1992 ($2.20), which gives you a ratio of 8.6. This is not especially high, but it was much higher than Eastman Kodak.

   c. The final important value measure is the *price-to-book ratio*. This is determined by dividing the price of the stock by the book value per share. (*Value Line* provides this figure, but the *Stock Guide* does not. Although the figure is given in *Value Line*, you should know that it is calculated by deducting the debt of the company from the equity and then dividing by the number of shares outstanding.) For Eastman Kodak, you would have divided $41 by $18.79, which means that Eastman Kodak was selling a bit above two times "book." At least in today's market, such a ratio is not excessive. A somewhat higher ratio was evident in EG&G. Its price ($19) compared with its $7.45 book value was nearly three times book. In the same industry, the ratio was much higher for Thermo Instrument. Divide $34 by $8.72 and you get a price-to-book ratio of 3.9 times. Such a ratio, although not extraordinarily high, is, nonetheless, more indicative of a risky stock.

How to Determine the Characteristics of Growth

6. Next, it makes sense to examine the company's history of earnings per share (EPS). The best companies increase their earnings steadily, year after year, with a minimum of deviations. An example of a company with problems is Eastman Kodak at the end of 1992. Its earnings per share had shown no sustained uptrend. Rather, EPS had fluctuated widely, with minuscule earnings in 1991 of 5 cents, down from $3.91 the prior year. A year or two earlier, the company had experienced a severe drop in earnings, from $4.31 in 1988 to $1.63 the following year.

7. In the same context, it makes sense to see how the company's dividend has been progressing. Here, too, you are looking for steady improvement, with no dividend cuts. Eastman Kodak passed one test because its dividend had not been reduced. On the other hand, it had stagnated at $2 per share for four successive years. In fact, it had failed to earn its dividend in two of those years. By contrast, EG&G had a splendid record: its dividend had climbed from 13 cents a share in 1981 to 42 cents 10 years later. Further, in none of those years had the company failed to earn its dividend, usually by a wide margin.

Research—The Key to New Products and Services

8. In some industries, such as pharmaceuticals, it pays to look at the percentage of sales devoted to research and development (R&D). In this realm, Eastman Kodak had a good record, with a 7.7 percent figure. By contrast, EG&G had only 0.9 percent devoted to R&D. With an even better score, Tektronix allocated 13 percent of sales to research. The rationale is that a company bringing out new

products is less risky than one that is merely copying the competition, or, even worse, dependent on commodity products.

9. There should also be less risk in investing in a company whose management has a high stake. *Value Line* normally provides this number. For Tektronix, the percentage is substantial: insiders own 9.3 percent of the common stock. By contrast, Polaroid management owns less than 1 percent. EG&G insiders own a modest amount, 2.7 percent; at Eastman Kodak, the number is low, at less than 1 percent. The thinking here is that high ownership by management makes you feel confident that its actions will be favorable to shareholders.

Cyclical Industries Can Add to Risk

10. Although there are times when cyclical industries are good performers, they are generally less stable, and the risk is greater. These industries include metals, airlines, chemicals, and paper among others. For investors looking for low risk, they are likely to be rewarded in such industries as drugs (although this has not been the case recently), food processors, tobacco, utilities, and petroleum.

Don't Forget Diversification and Asset Allocation

Although the above thoughts should be borne in mind, you should never forget that asset allocation is one of the keys to preservation of capital. If you want to survive a bear market, you will have to forgo the option of being 100 percent invested in common stocks.

At Hickory Investment Advisors, most of our accounts have the following asset allocation: 50 to 55 percent in common stocks; 35 to 40 percent in short-term bonds (long-term bonds are much more volatile) and 5 to 10 percent in money-market funds.

In addition, we endeavor to have 20 percent of the common stock portion invested in foreign stocks, mostly European, which are less risky than Latin American or Asian equities. Finally, try to spread your stocks among the 12 sectors discussed throughout this book, such as financial, basic industries, capital goods, and utilities. Invest at least 4 percent in each but refrain from investing more than 12 percent.

A Few More General Rules

If you have read this far, you are probably a diligent investor who reads annual and quarterly reports, subscribes to such publications as *The Wall Street Journal, Barron's, Forbes,* and *Business Week.* In other words, you are alert to any developments that might have an impact on your portfolio.

It goes without saying that risk can be reduced whenever you invest in a strong company. Here are some ways to recognize such an enterprise:

1. It should be a low-cost producer. This is not always easy to ascertain and may not be found in *Value Line* or other standard research literature. It may, however, be revealed in the company's annual report. In the automobile industry, for example, Ford is able to produce its domestic cars at a lower cost than General Motors. This allows the company to earn a better profit margin and to lower prices, if necessary, in order to increase market share.

2. Marketing is another key to success. It goes without saying that a good product is essential. But if there is a lack of advertising and sales push, the other guy may steal your markets. An excellent example of good marketing is Procter & Gamble. Coca-Cola, of course, is another superior outfit in this regard.

And, now, for my last idea, dollar cost averaging.

Dollar Cost Averaging

If you are new to the world of common stock investing, you may be fearful that you are investing at the wrong time. As this is being written, there are frequent comments by so-called experts that now is not a good time to invest. These same people were espousing equally dire and ominous warnings two or three years ago, which might indicate their forecasts are a bit tainted.

Then again, perhaps their prognostications will prove to be right on the mark. If you call "wolf" often enough, you will eventually be right. It's no secret that stocks have sinking spells every so often.

Investors with good memories may recall that stocks sank in the fall of 1987. Another year when stocks proved disappointing was 1990. Going back into history, 1973 and 1974 were especially rough on common stocks.

Although dyed-in-the-wool investors may tell you that common stocks are always a good investment, it must be admitted that you sometimes have to endure two or three consecutive years of unhappy fortunes.

One way to deal with these periodic ups and downs of the stock market is through a technique called "dollar cost averaging."

A Gift from Aunt Cordelia— 100,000 Big Ones

This method involves feeding your money into the market on a gradual, systematic basis, as opposed to investing all at once. Let's say that your Aunt Cordelia left you $100,000 in cash. If such an event had occurred in mid-1987, you would have been a rather unhappy investor by November because stocks slumped badly during that period.

By contrast, had you had elected to invest $5000 every three months, you would have taken five years to invest it all. Depending on what you invested in, the results would probably have been good because stocks performed well for most of the ensuing years.

Ordinarily, dollar cost averaging takes place over a period longer than five years, usually 10 or more. Because stocks fluctuate a good deal, some of your purchases take place when stocks are too high; some take place when stocks are at a low ebb; still others take place in between. Assuming that stocks are higher at the end of the period than at the beginning, you will be happy with the final results.

If you elect to dollar cost average with one stock, your ultimate results will depend to a large extent on the fortunes of that particular company rather than on the market as a whole.

For example, in recent years, IBM has been a disappointment, whereas General Electric has worked out quite well. Similarly, U.S. Surgical—a brilliant performer for many years—has been close to a disaster, compared with Intel, which has been a super growth stock. No amount of dollar cost averaging would have saved you from grief if you had purchased IBM or U.S. Surgical.

Typically, mutual funds are a good bet for dollar cost averaging. Barring the unforeseen, mutual funds follow the market. Consequently, if stocks do well, your program will be rewarding.

Don't Forget the Shortcomings

Although most articles on dollar cost averaging assure you that this strategy is sound, not enough has been written about the pitfalls of the idea.

When I was a neophyte in the investment business, we tried to convince investors to invest $100 a month in a mutual fund. Actually, just as many people preferred to invest even less, typically $25 or $50 a month.

As brokers, we assured them they would benefit from the ups and downs of the market and that there was no reason to worry about the occasional bear markets. To be sure, this was sound advice.

In hindsight, however, what we didn't realize at the time was that these small monthly payments would eventually be quite meaningless. Today, it is much easier to invest $1000 a month than it was to invest $100 a decade or two ago. In other words, those plans became obsolete as the investor's income increased—either because of inflation or because the person's income increased with the passage of time and promotions.

Thus, dollar cost averaging was no longer dollar cost averaging. If you later increased your monthly payment to $200, then to $500, and later to $1000, it is not a classic case of dollar cost averaging. Assuming the market was higher when you were putting in $500 or $1000 than when you were putting in $100 or $200, the end result will not be nearly as good.

Even a Blizzard of Resumes May Not Be the Answer

Let's move ahead to more recent times. Suppose you started a dollar cost averaging plan three years ago when your income was $100,000 a year. Then, your firm started restructuring and you lost your job at the age of 46. Despite sending out 1000 resumes, you are still unemployed. Finally, in desperation, you take a job that pays you only $32,000 a year. How are you going to keep up your dollar cost averaging program at the $1000-a-month level? You aren't.

These two examples may be extreme, but they are not entirely unrealistic. With this negative thought, let's look again at the concept and see whether it makes sense.

In order to be valid, dollar cost averaging involves investing the same amount of money on a regular and periodic basis, let's say $500 a month, $1000 quarterly, or $5000 every January when you receive your bonus. If you actually carried out this idea, the scheme would be successful. Practically no one does, for the reasons outlined above.

Even so, the idea has some merit because it does keep you from plunking down a huge sum of money at what could turn out to be a poor time. With stocks in 1994 yielding less than 3 percent and selling at about three times book, the time does not seem ideal for lump-sum investing.

Stocks Are Still the Best Game in Town

On the other hand, there are those who say that, given the alternatives, stocks are still the best game in town. They point to money-market funds that yield less than 3 percent and bonds that yield just over 6 percent. Unless you put your money in the proverbial mattress, you are forced to choose from among these imperfect alternatives. Looked at in this light, perhaps common stocks will continue their winning ways for another year or two. But, eventually, something will happen, and stocks will come tumbling down. Exactly when this will happen is impossible to predict. But it will happen.

And when it happens, it will probably come at a time when virtually none of the experts are bearish. The very fact that so many experts are skeptical may indicate that a plunge to lower levels is not exactly imminent.

But enough of this fatuous palaver. The fact remains that no one can predict what the market will do—at least not with any regularity or consistency. This argues in favor of something akin to dollar cost averaging.

Dollar cost averaging can take different forms. If you are a veteran investor, it is probable that you have been involved in the strategy since you first bought your first common stock. Like most people, you started modestly by buying 25 or 50 shares of a local utility or some other company in your vicinity. When that worked out OK, you put $1000 or $2000 in an oil stock or the bank on Main Street.

As time went on, your income increased and your boss gave you a Christmas bonus. Although part of it might have gone to pay off some debts, you may have used the rest to buy a third or fourth stock. During this period, the market was doing what it always has done: it was fluctuating. Thus, some of your purchases were made at an ideal time; others were made when stocks were too high.

If this process was carried out over 20, 25, or 30 years, you were dollar cost averaging. It worked just fine because stocks tend to rise—not every year but often enough to make the game a worthwhile venture. Assuming your job holds together and assuming you progress in your career and assuming you keep buying at least one stock a year, dollar cost averaging is bound to work out satisfactorily.

The problem arises when you obtain a huge sum of money at a very high point in the market. If you choose to invest it all at that time, it is possible that you will be an unhappy camper for a year or two.

It Was a Horrible Time to Buy
Common Stocks

In this regard, I also think of the anguish of investing a large sum of money at the end of 1972. In retrospect, it was a horrible time to buy stocks, with a devastating bear market rearing its ugly head. The Dow Jones Industrial Average ended 1972 at just over 1000, but it subsequently plummeted to about 600 before it bottomed out at the end of 1974. Then, it reversed directions and started a steep ascent to 850 a year later.

In retrospect, it would have been a better idea to invest that large sum of money over a three-year period. But, as it turned out, you eventually made a bundle of money because stocks are now close to 3800, as measured by the Dow Jones Industrial Average.

What it all amounts to is this: dollar cost averaging, or some variation, is a good way to buy stocks. Most people do it this way because their income and circumstances seem to guide them in this direction.

Why argue with success?

12
An Interview with a Middle-Aged Couple

My biggest fear when I visit London is the "lift" at Hampstead, a posh northern suburb. In my opinion, this "lift" is just a crowded elevator that transports you from the depths of the Underground (the Tube in British parlance).

At that particular point, the subway reaches its deepest penetration below ground. Which means you have to board a crowded lift in order to get up to the street level—you don't have the option of climbing up a flight of stairs.

For whatever reason, the lift is always packed. As it moves toward the surface, I always wonder what would happen if it stopped dead. I would be imprisoned with 25 or 30 strangers, waiting for someone to rescue me. Of course, my fears have always been groundless—so far.

This past October, we took our fourth trip to Britain, despite my brother's urging that we spend at least three days in France.

"Don't Tell Me You're Headed for the Sandringham"

As we emerged from the beastly lift, a middle-aged couple was right beside us and seemed to be moving up the same street we were. As it happens, the street is on a hill. The other couple was complaining, as were we. I said, "Don't tell me you're headed for the Sandringham."

With that comment, we struck up a conversation. "Anyone staying at the Sandringham must be civilized—we love it," said Bryce Glabrous Wicker, a husky, bald-headed, well-built man of above-average height. He had an erect posture and moved like an athlete. He wore brown corduroy trousers and a red check shirt under a light jacket.

His wife, Phoebe, a pleasant-looking woman of average height but modestly overweight, was attractive and well groomed. She was dressed in a gray jacket, matching her black hair and red slacks.

"We always stay at the same hotel when we're in London," Phoebe said. "I particularly like that hearty breakfast they serve. You need some nourishment when you have to spend the rest of the day tramping around the city."

As we headed north on Heath Street, we continued our conversation. We turned right onto Elm Row, a narrow, one-way street, which took us to Holford Road where the Sandringham is situated.

"Don't Forget Those Great Breakfasts"

The uphill climb was good exercise, I thought, but the two women were beginning to complain. "I'm never going to stay at the Sandringham again," someone said. "Life is too short."

"Yes, but don't forget those great breakfasts," I said. No one bothered to answer. It was then late afternoon and a long time before breakfast. They were probably thinking more about where they were going to have dinner.

When we arrived at the hotel, we spent a few minutes in the parlor, just off the lobby. There were several overstuffed, slightly old-fashioned chairs that felt good to sit in. While the others were chatting, I examined the books in the bookcase to see if there was anything worth "borrowing."

The Middle-Aged Farmer from Upstate New York

Of course, it wasn't long before we were discussing our occupations. Bryce and Phoebe own a farm just outside Johnson Creek, New York, a small, rural community not far from Lake Ontario. "Johnson's Crick is between Gasport and Middleport," volunteered the middle-aged farmer from upstate New York.

He didn't like to be called Bryce, he told us. He explained that his father—also a farmer—named him Bryce because he wanted his son to become a college professor, not a farmer. However, from the begin-ning, he didn't like a "fancy name like Bryce," he said. "A farmer with a name like that would be laughed out of Niagara County. He should have called me Angus or something manly ... certainly not Bryce. Just call me 'Wick,'" he insisted. I told him I preferred to be called "Slats."

"A Good Business If You Like Gambling"

"Farming is one occupation that never appealed to me," I said to Wick. "How to do you manage to make a living? I suppose farming is like anything else. You have to know what you're doing."

"It's also a good business if you like gambling," Wick said, as he took his glasses off for cleaning. "You never know from one year to the next which crops—if any—are going to do well. You might have a great harvest of wheat, but if everyone one else has a bumper crop, the prices will take a dive. The weather, of course, is always a big factor."

"I Don't Put All My Acres into One Crop"

I nodded my head as I listened. "Since you can afford to visit London, you must be doing all right. What's your secret?"

"The same as yours, Mr. Slatter ... er ... Slats," he said as he rubbed his hand over his bald cranium, as if the massage might stimulate a new growth of hair. "Diversification. I don't put all my acres into one crop. I have a large peach orchard, for instance, plus some cherries, red raspberries, hay, oats, corn, and wheat. In addition, I have a herd of beef cattle and a few hogs. In any given year, some of these will do well; some will be disappointments. Just about the same thing holds true for stocks, I've been told."

"I think I'll put you on the payroll, Wick. You have expressed my sentiments exactly."

At that point, my wife Beverly excused herself and announced that she was heading up to the room. "It's been a long day. If I have to climb that hill one more time, I'll have to order new feet from Sears, Roebuck. I think I'll leave you hardy folks to talk about crops and stocks."

"I think my feet need a rest too," agreed Phoebe. "Why don't we let the men solve the problems of the world?"

As the two ladies took their leave, we resumed the conversation and Wick said, "I suppose it might seem strange to you, Slats, but we have never bought any stocks—nothing more daring than a few CDs. I take lots of chances with my crops, but when it comes to my money, I play it safe. I'm probably too old to change my ways."

"That's a Long Time to Let Your Money Rot in CDs"

"From what I have observed, farmers usually live to a ripe old age. You'll be riding your tractor for another 30 years." He seemed to want to talk, so I went up to the room to get my trusty briefcase. In my business, you never know when you'll bump into someone who needs some professional counseling. I resumed the conversation: "That's a long time to let your money rot in CDs. Right now, the return is minuscule." I spent the next few minutes showing the farmer from Johnson Creek, New York, some exhibits to convince him that common stocks are the finest investment in the world.

"You're the first investment man we have ever talked with, Slats. I suppose you're a follower of Warren Buffett ... or some other guru."

"No, I'm afraid not. Obviously, he has done well—in fact, better than nearly anyone I can think of—but, somehow, his methods of stock selection don't quite mesh with mine."

"Warren Buffett is about the only stock expert I've heard of, but I suppose that's because I haven't been called on by any stock brokers, and I rarely read *The Wall Street Journal.*"

"I can understand that Johnson Creek is not big enough to have a brokerage firm. But there must be one in Buffalo ... that's not too far away, is it?"

He shook his head. "Actually, Lockport is closer ... we go there quite frequently. As I understand it, you're not a broker, is that right, Slats?"

"We Have to Extract Our Modest Annual Fee"

"No, I merely manage people's portfolios on a fee basis. On the other hand, I often give advice to people without charging them. If they want my firm to handle their portfolio on a continuing basis, then we have to extract our modest annual fee."

"Just for the sake of argument," he said, "suppose my bank certificates of deposit were worth $100,000. What stocks would you recommend?"

"I assume you are somewhat conservative and would like a diversified portfolio."

"You must understand that stocks are not something I understand—in fact, I rather doubt that you can convince me that stocks are better than CDs. In any event, if I decided to buy stocks, I think I would probably be conservative ... assuming I decide to do anything."

> If you (or more likely an ancestor) had invested $100 in the overall market each month during 1926–1991, your investment would have grown to $11,386,000, more than 140 times the total number of dollars you would have invested. Now admittedly, $100 a month was a lot of money back in the 1930s (worth about $800 in today's dollars), but so is $11 million today.
>
> SOURCE: Michael E. Edleson in *Value Investing*, Second Edition Revised, 1988, International Publishing Corporation, page 5.

"Nothing Works All the Time"

"I would like to show you a few tables that illustrate a method of investing that seems to work most of the time. Nothing works all the time—unfortunately. Let's see what would have happened to the seven Baby Bells if you had used this approach. You may recall that AT&T spun off these seven companies in the mid-eighties, close to ten years ago. Let's assume that at the end of 1990 you were faced with the decision of which two or three of these telephone stocks to buy."

"I'm with you so far," Wick said, as he eradicated the dust by rubbing his glasses with his shoe shining cloth, which he kept in his shirt pocket.

"If you had been faced with such a problem, Wick," I asked. "how would you make up your mind which stocks to buy?"

"If I can recall some things I learned at Cornell University, I would certainly look at the balance sheet and income statements. Beyond that, I would be stumped."

"Most people would, Wick. That's why they often consult a stock broker, an investment advisor, a trust officer, or someone who professes to know what Wall Street is all about."

My Magic System for Picking Stocks

"I assume that includes you, Slats."

"Let's hope so. But, getting back to my magic system for picking stocks. It's incredibly simple ... assuming you can add and divide, using a calculator."

"I've forgotten how to do simple arithmetic," he said, as he smoothed the skin on his hairless skull. "My Hewlett-Packard 12C is right on my desk ... at home, of course. But I see you have one in your brief case. Anyone who uses a Hewlett-Packard 12C must be trustworthy."

"At least my boss thinks so. Well, here goes, Wick. The way to pick stocks is to first consult the *Standard & Poor's Stock Guide*."

"The what?" he said. I could see that he was puzzled.

After I explained to him about the *Stock Guide,* I proceeded to discuss my stock selection concept. "We need the *Stock Guide* to tell us how many institutional owners each stock has. At that time, for instance, Ameritech had 558 institutional owners, such as pension funds, banks, and insurance companies. In my opinion, the stock with the fewest big owners is a better bet than one that is widely owned."

It Pays to Shun Stocks That Are Too Popular

"It seems to me that these people are experts and should know which stocks to own...and yet you're telling me to *avoid* stocks that are popular with institutional managers. Did I hear you correctly?"

"You did. My research shows that it pays to shun stocks that are too popular. Next, I check the dividend yield on each stock—such as 3 percent, 4 percent, 5 percent and so forth. A stock with an above-average yield is probably unpopular. Generally, there are one or more reasons why the stock is being ignored. There's something about the stock that makes investors shy away from it. It could be poor earnings; it could be an out-of-favor industry (such as drugs), tough competition, a weak balance sheet, a poor return on equity ... any number of problems that make investors wary of the stock."

"Obviously, then, it's not a good idea to buy these wounded beasts—or is it?" Wick asked.

"It seems to pay off," I replied. "But I'll admit that it's often tough to convince yourself that you should invest in a stock that is bleeding from the mouth. Sometimes, you have to shut your eyes and pray. In most instances, you would rather buy a stock that is free of blemishes. Unfortunately, this is a good way to pay too much for a stock."

"What's next?" Wick asked. "Now that we know the yield and the institutional ownership, how do we zero in on the best stocks?"

"We get our trusty Hewlett-Packard 12C and average up the two sets of numbers," I said. "I have placed two asterisks," I said, showing him Table 12-1, "next to each telephone stock that at that time (the end of 1990) had a below-average number of institutional owners. Similarly, I have put one asterisk next to the yield of each stock that is above the average for the group."

Table 12-1

Seven regional Bell telephone stocks and how they performed from the end of 1990 to June 30, 1993.

Stock	Institutional owners	Dividend yield year-end 1990 (%)	Stock price change 12-31-90 to 6-30-93 (%)
Ameritech	558**	5.09*	+ 20.41
BellSouth	739	4.89	+ 1.37
Bell Atlantic	651	4.40*	+ 10.72
NYNEX	660**	6.41*	+ 27.24
Southwestern Bell	723	4.93	+ 38.39
Pacific Telesis	754	4.46	+ 7.45
US West	636**	5.14*	+ 18.01
Mean	674	5.05	

*Above mean (or average) yield.
**Below mean institutional owners.

After glancing at the numbers, Wick said, "I suspect that you're going to tell me to buy any stock with an asterisk next to it."

"Not exactly, Wick," I said. "The stocks we buy are the ones that are on *both* lists. In other words, they must be both unpopular and have a high yield. As it turned out, three stocks fell into this category. If we look at a more recent *Stock Guide,* we can see how the seven stocks performed from the end of 1990 to the present."

"I can't wait for the results."

"Ameritech, NYNEX, and US West had an average appreciation of 21.89 percent for two and a half years. Add in the average beginning yield of 5.55 percent, and the total return for each of the three stocks is +27.44 percent. The other four telephone stocks appreciated much less, only 14.49 percent, plus an average beginning yield of 4.67 percent, for a total return of +19.16 percent."

"It's Incredibly Simple"

"So far, I think I understand how your system works. Is there anything more to it?"

"Not really. It's incredibly simple. That's why I don't tell my boss how I do it. If he knew my secret, he would immediately sack me and go ahead on his own."

"Is he really that much of an ogre?" Wick asked.

"It Could Be the End of My Career"

"Not so far. But I don't want to put him to the test. You can see that I must keep this system absolutely secret. You can understand that. You'll have to promise not to come to Cleveland and tell my clients—and especially my boss—what I am doing ... it could be the end of my career. I might have to move to Johnson Creek to work for you as a cherry picker ... or something."

"Why not. We pay top wages. If you really want to earn our highest pay, you'll have to pick red raspberries."

"Let's hope it doesn't come to that," I said. I could just imagine bleeding to death from all the scratches I would get from those pesky raspberry bushes. No wonder the pay was good, I thought.

"Now that you have confided your innermost secrets of stock picking, I suppose we should get ready for dinner. Can you and Bev join us at one of the local pubs? It'll be our treat."

"I would feel guilty sponging off you, Wick. Besides, I haven't really shown you enough illustrations to demonstrate to you that this method really works. Do you have a few minutes to look at some additional tables?"

More Proof

"I thought you said that's all there was to it. Now, you're going to make it more complicated."

"Not at all," I assured him. "I merely want to show you some more proof that it works on a consistent basis. For instance, let's look at the Dow Jones Industrial Average at the end of 1987. I'm sure you've heard of the 30 stocks that make up this well-known average."

"Oh, yes. But I was never sure which stocks were used." He glanced at Table 12-2. "I've heard of most of them. I suppose you're going to use your system on this group of stocks ..."

"Exactly. In fact, it makes more sense to test the system on a diversified group of stocks. After all, the seven Baby Bells were all in one industry. The Dow Jones list, on the other hand, includes stocks from several industries, such as aluminum, steel, oil, drugs, autos, and so forth. Of course, they're all big companies. On the other hand, you said you wanted a conservative way to invest."

"If I were to buy stocks from this list, that would classify me as conservative. Is that what you're saying, Slats?"

"Most of them would fall into that category, with a few exceptions, such as Bethlehem Steel."

Table 12-2

Stock	Institutional owners	Dividend yield year-end 1987 (%)	Stock price change 12-31-87 to 6-30-93 (%)
AlliedSignal	529	6.4	+ 138.39
AT&T	826	4.4	+ 133.33
Chevron	790	6.1	+ 121.45
Philip Morris	1029	4.2	+ 127.23
Primerica	290	6.6	+ 227.20
General Motors	928	8.1	+ 45.01
Sears, Roebuck	786	6.0	+ 64.18
Union Carbide	359	6.9	+ 59.77
United Technologies	630	4.1	+ 59.41
Average performance of 9 stocks			+ 108.44
Average beginning yield			5.87
Total return			+ 114.31
Dow Jones Industrial Average in same period			+ 81.35
Average beginning yield of 30 stocks			4.12
Total return of Dow Jones Industrial Average			+ 85.47

"I thought you said the list had 30 stocks. There are only nine stocks here."

Accused of Juggling the Numbers

"I was hoping you wouldn't notice. Actually, for the sake of simplicity, I have listed only those that passed both tests: they all had a below-average number of institutional owners; and all had above-average dividend yields."

"How do I know you didn't juggle the numbers?"

"After all the years we've known each other, Wick, you still don't trust me. I am incensed." There was a smile on my face, of course.

"OK ... OK ... I trust you. Now, how did these nine stocks perform? Or, is that a stupid question?"

"According to my calculations, these nine stocks did quite well. From the end of 1987, the group climbed an average of 108.44 percent, as of June 30, 1993. In addition, they had good initial dividend yields.

This is neither good nor bad until you compare this performance with the entire list of 30 stocks. In that particular period, the Dow Jones Index advanced 81.35 percent, which is well below the performance of the nine stocks selected by my system. None of the nine declined during the period."

"Are you sure your boss doesn't know about this system?"

"Not yet ... unless you plan to call him before supper."

"If you'll pay for the call."

Bryce Glabrous Wicker stood up as if to return to his room. "You've convinced me, Slats. Let's put on the feed bag."

"Don't be in such a hurry, Wick. I can't let you get away without proving my system really works."

"But I'm hungry. Farm boys like to eat, you know."

"Calm down for a minute," I said. "I would feel guilty if I didn't show you my complete case—lock, stock, and barrel."

"Just One More Table"

He sat down and glanced at Table 12-3. "Just to humor you, I'll look at one more table." He paused and then blurted out, "But that's all. Is it agreed?"

I looked away, not wanting to let him know that I had more than one table left in my kit bag. "This won't take long, Wick. After all, you're going to get rich if you start using my system."

"I'm *already* rich. Right now, I am trying to keep from getting poor. But go ahead. I'm listening."

"In this instance, I started with a list that often appears in *Barron's Financial Weekly*. It stays pretty much the same, but there are occasional changes from time to time. This is really an excellent list on which to test my theory because it contains a more diverse group of stocks, including transportation and utility stocks."

"You're sure you wouldn't like to wash up and go eat?"

"I couldn't eat, knowing I had failed to convince you that my theory holds water."

"I think I studied something about a guilt complex at Cornell, but that was a long time ago." He took his glasses off and cleaned them thoroughly with his hotel shoe shining cloth.

"Don't worry, Wick. The girls are tired. They will thank us for letting them recover from today's sightseeing. In this table," I said, showing him Table 12-3, "are the survivors of my elimination system. You will note that 13 stocks survived out of the 50. In this test, I assumed that we made our calculations at the end of June 1992 and then checked them a year later, on June 30, 1993. Since that was a shorter

Table 12-3

Stocks taken from the Barron's 50. The average beginning yield was 2.92 percent. The average number of institutional owners was 600.8.

Stock	Institutional owners	Dividend yield 6-30-92 (%)	Stock price change 6-30-92 to 6-30-93 (%)
American Brands	566	3.9	− 25.28
Detroit Edison	330	6.3	+ 11.20
GATX	133	5.0	+ 42.38
Inco	263	3.3	− 26.53
James River	272	2.9	− 3.66
Raytheon	574	3.0	+ 39.49
SCEcorp	519	6.3	+ 9.60
Timken	203	3.7	+ 21.46
TRW	319	3.3	+ 17.44
United Technologies	547	3.4	+ 3.35
Westinghouse Electric	477	4.1	− 9.93
Weyerhaeuser	561	3.5	+ 24.45
Wisconsin Energy	265	4.9	+ 3.92
Average performance of 13 stocks			+ 8.30
Average beginning yield			4.12
Total return			+ 12.42
Dow Jones Industrial Average in same period			+ 5.95
Average beginning yield of 30 stocks			2.92
Total return of Dow Jones Industrial Average			+ 8.87

period than the one we looked at earlier, you would expect that most of the stocks didn't move up too much."

"In other words, your system is not a get-rich-quick scheme."

"Precisely. All I hope to do is beat the market on a consistent basis. In this particular instance, the market—as measured by the Dow 30—made only modest progress. It was up less then 6 percent, or 5.95 percent. By contrast, the 13 stocks singled out by my system were up 8.3 percent. And, of course, the dividends were also higher. Which means that the total return was 12.42 percent for the 13 stocks, compared with 8.87 percent for the full Dow."

Enough Is Enough

At this point, I could see that he was getting even more impatient. He stood up and looked me in the eye and said, "What do you say we saddle up and head out of here, Slats."

"Not so fast, Wick. Remember my guilt complex. I simply have to show you Table 12-4."

"I'm getting faint from hunger," Wick said. "I'll be so famished that I'll have to order two dinners to stay alive."

"I know what you're saying, Wick. I'm half-starved myself, but I simply must go on. This next table is a real eye-popper. It assumes that

Table 12-4

Stocks taken from the Barron's 50. This table takes the 13 stocks that were the most popular with institutions at the beginning of this period.

Stock	Institutional owners	Dividend yield 6-30-92 (%)	Stock price change from 6-30-92 to 6-30-93 (%)
General Electric	1317	2.8	+ 23.15
IBM	1210	4.9	− 49.55
Merck	1189	1.9	− 27.18
Pfizer	964	2.0	− 8.22
Mobil	997	5.2	+ 21.54
AT&T	1014	3.1	+ 46.51
Amoco	894	4.6	+ 14.92
Boeing	847	2.5	− 7.21
Coca-Cola	900	1.4	+ 7.50
Schlumberger	944	1.9	+ 0.80
Minnesota Mining & Manufacturing	899	3.3	+ 11.34
Du Pont	833	3.5	− 6.68
Hewlett-Packard	835	1.2	+ 17.60
Average performance of 13 stocks			+ 3.42
Average beginning yield			2.95
Total return			+ 6.37
Dow Jones Industrial Average in same period			+ 5.95
Average beginning yield of 30 stocks			2.92
Total return of Dow Jones Industrial Average			+ 8.87

you used the same list of 50 stocks from *Barron's* but picked the ones *preferred* by institutions."

"I have a feeling you don't like these institutions, Slats. What if they find out how much you hate them?"

"Sometimes I wake up in the middle of the night in a cold sweat, thinking they're pounding on my front door, demanding revenge. At any rate, I picked the 13 stocks from the list of 50, those with the *most* institutional owners. As you can see," I said, showing him Table 12-4, "the performance of these stocks was not very impressive. For starters, it included a few real disappointments, such as IBM and Merck. Even though it also included AT&T, which was a huge winner, the group as a whole was up only 3.42 percent. Adding in the beginning yield, the total return was only 6.37 percent, which was even less than the Dow 30, and far less than the 13 stocks chosen by my crazy system. What do you think of that?"

Wick Was about to Collapse

"One more table and I'll fall on the floor from lack of nourishment. That will mean I won't be able to honor my pledge to Cornell University. They are counting on me to help fund their endowment drive. You wouldn't want Cornell on your conscience, would you, Slats?"

"I see what you mean, Wick, but I'll have to chance it. Only one more horrible table, and you can be on your way. How's that?"

He sat down and whipped out his shoe shining cloth to clean his glasses. He said, "If you keep showing me tables, I'll tell your boss how your system works."

I shuddered at the thought. I said, "I promise not to. Let's look at this table," showing him Table 12-5.

"My eyes are getting bloodshot," the upstate farmer said. "I'm not sure I can see the numbers."

"Once again, I used the 50 stocks in the Barron's list of 50. In this instance, I went back to year-end 1990. After eliminating all the stocks that had above-average numbers of institutional owners and below-average yields, I came up with the 11 stocks in this table" (see Table 12-5). "Then I checked to see how they performed if you held on to them until our cut-off date, June 30, 1993."

Wick Grows Ever Weaker from Lack of Food

"My eyes have gone bad, Slats. You'll have to tell me. I'm too weak to see the page."

"I always thought farmers were hardy. You disappoint me."

Table 12-5

Stocks taken from the Barron's 50. The average beginning yield was
4.11 percent. The average number of institutional owners was 570.

Stock*	Institutional owners	Dividend yield year-end 1990 (%)	Stock price change 12-31-90 to 6-30-93 (%)
AlliedSignal	426	6.7	+ 147.22
CSX	398	4.4	+ 125.20
Detroit Edison	291	6.3	+ 23.01
GATX	147	4.3	+ 44.44
Goodyear Tire	301	9.5	+ 350.33
Inland Steel	199	5.7	+ 16.16
SCEcorp	489	7.0	+ 28.05
Timken	196	4.7	+ 52.40
TRW	319	4.8	+ 66.67
Weyerhaeuser	499	5.5	+ 94.86
Wisconsin Energy	261	5.6	+ 31.03
Average performance of 11 stocks			+ 89.49
Average beginning yield			5.86
Total return			+ 95.35
Dow Jones Industrial Average in same period			+ 33.51
Average beginning yield of 30 stocks			4.11
Total return of Dow Jones Industrial Average			+ 37.62

*Stocks excluded because of high number of institutional owners were General Electric
(1312), IBM (1748), and Exxon (1050). Stocks with yields less than 4.1 percent were also
excluded.

"Farmers are hardy because they eat hearty. You're deliberately trying to starve me into submission."

"Calm down. We're almost done. At any rate, the 11 stocks performed
admirably. As a group, the 11 stocks shot up 89.49 percent. Add in the
beginning yield, and the total performance was 95.35 percent. Does that
impress you?"

He didn't answer. He was staring blankly off into space.

"In that same period, the Dow rose only 33.51 percent. Add back the
beginning dividend yield of 4.11 percent, and the total performance
was a pathetic 37.62 percent. You'll have to admit that's pretty good
proof that my system is a world-beater. Right, Wick?"

At that moment, there was a terrible thud, as Bryce Glabrous Wicker fell off his chair onto the floor.

"Wick ... Wick ... Wick ... speak to me ..."

I wondered whether dialing 911 in London would do any good.

13

How to Combine Quality, Income, and Growth in One Portfolio

If you are new to the world of common stock investing, it's probable that you would like your portfolio to have three features:

- Quality and financial strength
- Above-average dividend income
- Growth of capital

Some investment pundits would tell you that you can have any *one* of the three but not all three in one package. Let's see if we can prove these experts wrong.

First, let's refresh your memory a bit and define what is meant by quality and financial strength. There are a number of signs that indicate that a company is endowed with this feature.

The easiest way to determine quality is to look at each stock in the *Standard & Poor's Stock Guide*. If the stock is rated A+, A, or A−, it can be considered above average, since B+ is an average quality rating.

You could also look at the ratio of current assets to current liabilities. A two-to-one ratio would certainly be an indication of above-average financial strength.

If you wanted to make the chore a little more complicated, you could check *Value Line*. This statistical service also has a rating similar to Standard & Poor's. Its best financial strength rating is A++. An average rating would be B++.

Finally, *Value Line* would give you the figures to determine whether the company in question has a strong balance sheet—one with considerably more common equity than long-term debt.

A Simple Measure of Financial Strength

Although all of these approaches to quality and financial strength have their merits, I have chosen the simplest one for use in the system that I will describe in this chapter. It is the letter rating used in the *Stock Guide*. In order for a stock to be included in your portfolio, it must be rated A+. Normally, if you were to use the 30 stocks in the Dow Jones Industrial Average, you would find six or seven that were rated A+.

So much for quality.

Next, we want to pick some stocks that have an attractive yield. This is necessary because most stocks rated A+ have relatively low yields.

The best way to pick these stocks is to use the standard deviation statistical tool. Although I have mentioned this in previous chapters, it might bear repeating. If you are examining the yields of the 30 Dow Industrials, the standard deviation helps you select those that have extraordinarily high yields, normally the highest 16 percent in the group. Typically, there will be five or six stocks that qualify as high yield among the 30 industrials. For a more detailed discussion of the standard deviation, refer to Chapter 6, "A Simple Way to Play the Stock Market."

As you might expect, these high-yield stocks are much more speculative than the ones rated A+. In other words, they have a high yield because of problems. These problems are sometimes solved, and the stock moves up smartly. At other times, the problems get worse, and the stock sinks even lower.

To summarize, then, there are two criteria to consider in selecting a stock for your portfolio:

- Buy all stocks in the Dow 30 that are rated A+
- Buy all stocks in the Dow 30 that have a yield that is more than one standard deviation from the mean (or average). In a typical period, the mean yield for the 30 Dow stocks might be 3.4 percent, with a standard deviation of 1.6 percent. If you add 3.4 percent to 1.6 per-

cent, you get 5 percent. Thus, any stock with a 5 percent yield is included in the portfolio.

Proof in the Pudding

To make this method of stock selection a little more believable, let's look at several examples taken from my notebooks. Table 13-1 shows the 30 stocks in the Dow Jones Industrial Average, as of August 31, 1992. You may recall that *The Wall Street Journal* makes changes in this list of stocks from time to time.

Spin-Offs Must Be Considered
When You Calculate Performance

A few words of explanation are in order. During this period, Sears, Roebuck spun off Dean Witter, Discover. To calculate the return on Sears, this stock must be added back because an investor who bought the stock would have been given these shares during 1993.

Similarly, Union Carbide spun off shares of Praxair. If you owned 100 shares of Union Carbide, you would have received 100 shares of Praxair. This, too, must be considered when the performance numbers are crunched.

If you examine Table 13-1 again, you will see that several stocks performed well; several others were big losers, including such blue chips as IBM, Merck, and Philip Morris. Even so, the overall performance was much better than the Dow Jones Industrial Average itself. During this one-year period, the Dow climbed from 3257.35 to 3651.25, a gain of 12.08 percent. Because the average beginning yield was 3.13 percent, the total return was 15.21 percent.

By contrast, had you constructed a portfolio using my two criteria, you would have fared considerably better. Despite some obvious losers, the total performance of the 10 stocks was much better than the Dow. The average gain was 18.03 percent. If we add in the average beginning yield of the 11 stocks of 3.55 percent, the total return was 21.58 percent.

The Reason This System Works

Because the A+ stocks were rather dismal performers, you might wonder why I have included them. The answer is simple: there are times when high-quality stocks perform well; there are times when high-yield stocks perform well. By combining them in one portfolio, your

Table 13-1

The 30 stocks in the Dow Jones Industrial Average are listed below, along with three factors: the S&P quality rating, the yield as of August 31, 1992, and the percentage change in price one year later.

Stock	S&P rating	Yield 8-31-92 (%)	Price 8-31-92 ($)	Price 8-31-93 ($)	Change (%)
AlliedSignal	B −	1.9	52.38		
ALCOA	B	2.5	64.62		
American Express	B +	4.8	20.88	32.50	+ 55.69
AT&T	A −	3.1	42.25		
Bethlehem Steel	C	Nil	12.00		
Boeing	A +	2.7	37.25	39.62	+ 6.38
Caterpillar	B −	1.2	48.25		
Chevron	B	4.5	73.50		
Coca-Cola	A +	1.3	43.00		
Disney, Walt	A −	0.6	34.50		
Du Pont	A	3.6	49.38		
Eastman Kodak	B	4.5	44.25		
Exxon	A −	4.5	64.25		
General Electric	A +	3.0	74.00		
General Motors	B −	4.6	34.62		
Goodyear Tire	B	0.6	63.12		
IBM	A −	5.6	86.62	45.75	− 47.19
International Paper	B +	2.7	62.25		
McDonald's	A +	0.9	42.50	63.75	+ 26.47
Merck	A +	2.1	48.62	31.88	− 34.45
Minnesota Mining & Manufacturing	A +	3.2	98.50	109.62	+ 11.29
Morgan, J.P.	B +	3.7	59.50		
Philip Morris	A +	3.2	82.00	48.75	− 40.55
Procter & Gamble	A	2.3	46.88		
Sears, Roebuck	B +	4.8	41.50	69.67	+ 67.88
Texaco	B −	4.9	65.75	64.88	− 1.33
Union Carbide	NR	5.6	13.38	33.88	+ 153.31
United Technologies	B +	3.3	55.00		
Westinghouse	B +	4.4	16.38		

Table 13-1 (*Continued*)

The 30 stocks in the Dow Jones Industrial Average are listed below, along with three factors: the S&P quality rating, the yield as of August 31, 1992, and the percentage change in price one year later.

Stock	S&P rating	Yield 8-31-92 (%)	Price 8-31-92 ($)	Price 8-31-93 ($)	Change (%)
Woolworth	A	3.7	30.25		
Mean		3.13			
Standard deviation		1.55			
Buy level		4.68			
Average performance of 10 stocks that qualified					+ 18.03
Average beginning yield					3.55
Total return for period					+ 21.58
Dow Jones Industrial Average for same period					+ 12.08
Average beginning yield for 30 stocks					3.13
Total return for Dow Jones Industrial Average					+ 15.21

overall performance is consistently above average. By contrast, if you included only one of these groups, your performance might also be good, but it would be far less consistent. I will treat this idea in more detail later.

Back-Checking to Prove the Concept

One example, to be sure, doesn't prove that the idea has merit. It is necessary to back-test the concept in order to see how often it produces good results. To do this back-testing, I consulted old copies of the *Standard & Poor's Stock Guide.* I have been saving *Stock Guides* for over 30 years, which facilitates this back-testing. For you to do this back-testing yourself might be quite difficult. I am not aware of any public libraries that keep back copies of the *Stock Guide.* Nor is it likely that you will find old *Stock Guides* in most brokerage house branch offices.

Now that you have an idea of what this portfolio building idea involves, let's look at some more historic examples.

For the next example, let's go back into ancient history. Suppose we selected year-end 1975 for our beginning point. Table 13-2 shows the 30 stocks that made up the Dow Jones Industrial Average at that time.

Table 13-2

The 30 stocks in the Dow Jones Industrial Average are listed below, along with three factors: the S&P quality rating, the yield as of December 31, 1975, and the percentage change in price one year later.

Stock	S&P rating	Yield 12-31-75 (%)	Price 12-31-75 ($)	Price 12-31-76 ($)	Change (%)
AlliedSignal	B +	5.4	$33.25		
ALCOA	B +	3.5	33.62		
Johns-Manville	A −	5.2	23.25		
AT&T	A +	6.7	50.88	63.50	+ 24.82
Bethlehem Steel	B +	6.1	32.88		
INCO	B +	6.3	25.25		
International Harvester	B +	7.6	22.38	33.00	+ 47.49
Chevron	A +	6.8	29.38	41.00	+ 39.57
Owens-Illinois	A	3.3	51.88		
USX	B +	4.3	65.00		
Du Pont	A −	3.4	126.50		
Eastman Kodak	A +	1.9	106.12	86.00	− 18.96
Exxon (2-for-1)*	A +	5.6	88.75	53.62	+ 20.85
General Electric	A +	3.5	46.12	55.38	+ 20.05
General Motors	A −	4.2	57.62		
Goodyear Tire	A	5.1	21.75		
Chrysler	B −	Nil	10.12		
International Paper	A −	3.5	57.75		
American Brands	A +	6.9	35.62	45.75	+ 28.42
Esmark	B +	4.8	31.62		
Anaconda	B	3.5	17.12		
American Can	A −	7.0	31.38	39.00	+ 24.30
General Foods	A	5.1	27.62		
Procter & Gamble	A +	2.2	89.00	93.62	+ 5.20
Sears, Roebuck	A +	2.9	64.50	69.00	+ 6.98
Texaco	A +	8.6	23.38	27.75	+ 18.72
Union Carbide	A	3.9	61.12		
United Technologies	B +	4.3	46.38		
Westinghouse	B +	7.3	13.38	17.62	+ 31.78

Table 13-2 (*Continued*)
The 30 stocks in the Dow Jones Industrial Average are listed below, along with three factors: the S&P quality rating, the yield as of December 31, 1975, and the percentage change in price one year later.

Stock	S&P rating	Yield 12-31-75 (%)	Price 12-31-75 ($)	Price 12-31-76 ($)	Change (%)
Woolworth	A −	5.5	22.00		
Mean		4.81			
Standard deviation		1.91			
Buy level		6.72			
Average performance of 12 stocks that qualified					+ 20.77
Average beginning yield					5.58
Total return for period					+ 26.35
Dow Jones Industrial Average for same period					+ 17.86
Average beginning yield for 30 stocks					4.81
Total return for Dow Jones Industrial Average					+ 22.67

*Stock split two-for-one.

You will notice quite a few names that are no longer in the index, such as American Brands, Esmark, and General Foods. Even so, it is necessary to use the stocks that were in the Average at that time.

Once again, by combining these two disparate groups, we are able to develop a portfolio with above-average yield, coupled with above-average price appreciation. One word of explanation: you will notice that Exxon appears to have declined in price. However, the stock was split two-for-one during the year, which means you must divide the earlier price by two before making your calculation.

The System Does Not Always Work

As you might expect, no method of picking stocks is infallible. This method is no exception. For instance, it didn't work in the two-year period ending August 31, 1993. See Table 13-3.

As you can see, the results of the 13 stocks were close to those of the Dow Jones Industrial Average. Even so, the system failed to beat the Dow in this particular period.

Table 13-3

The 30 stocks in the Dow Jones Industrial Average are listed below, along with three factors: the S&P quality rating, the yield as of August 31, 1991, and the percentage change in price two years later.

Stock	S&P rating	Yield 8-31-91 (%)	Price 8-31-91 ($)	Price 8-31-93 ($)	Change (%)
AlliedSignal	B	4.7	38.38	74.75	+ 94.79
ALCOA	B	2.6	69.25		
American Express	B +	3.5	26.50		
Bethlehem Steel	B −	2.2	17.88		
Boeing	A	2.0	49.75		
Caterpillar	B −	2.5	47.50		
Coca-Cola (2-for-1)*	A +	1.5	65.75	43.38	+ 31.94
Disney, Walt	A −	0.6	118.75		
Du Pont	A	3.5	48.25		
Eastman Kodak	B +	4.6	43.12		
Exxon	A −	4.6	58.25		
General Electric	A +	2.7	74.88	98.25	+ 31.22
General Motors	B	4.2	38.00		
Goodyear	B	1.0	38.25		
IBM	A	5.0	96.88	45.75	− 52.77
International Paper	B +	3.4	69.62		
McDonald's	A +	1.1	32.62	53.75	+ 64.75
Merck (3-for-1)**	A +	2.0	126.88	31.88	− 24.63
Minnesota Mining & Manufacturing	A +	3.6	86.88	109.62	+ 26.19
Morgan, J.P.	B +	3.6	55.75		
Philip Morris	A +	2.8	74.12	48.75	− 34.23
Procter & Gamble	A	2.4	83.50		
Sears	B +	4.8	41.50	69.67	+ 67.88
Texaco	B −	5.0	64.12	64.88	+ 1.17
Union Carbide	B −	4.7	21.50	33.88	+ 57.58
United Technologies	A −	3.8	47.88		
Westinghouse	A −	5.8	24.00	15.38	− 35.94
Woolworth	A +	3.5	30.62	25.75	− 15.92
Mean		3.32			

Table 13-3 (*Continued*)

The 30 stocks in the Dow Jones Industrial Average are listed below, along with three factors: the S&P quality rating, the yield as of August 31, 1991, and the percentage change in price two years later.

Stock	S&P rating	Yield 8-31-91 (%)	Price 8-31-91 ($)	Price 8-31-93 ($)	Change (%)
Standard deviation		1.34			
Buy level		4.66			
Average performance of 13 stocks that qualified					+ 16.31
Average beginning yield					3.63
Total return for period					+ 19.94
Dow Jones Industrial Average for same period					+ 19.96
Average beginning yield for 30 stocks					3.32
Total return for Dow Jones Industrial Average					+ 23.28

*Stock split two-for-one.
**Stock split three-for-one.

Now that you have an idea what I am trying to demonstrate, let's look at two or three more illustrations. To save space, however, I have elected to show only those stocks that qualified rather than the full list of 30.

Next, let's look at an illustration that is nothing short of spectacular (see Table 13-4). This involves the period from the end of 1990 to June 30, 1992.

Now that you have an idea how this method of stock selection can work, it is probably best to summarize the results obtained in other periods. In all instances, the yield for the selected stocks was better than the Dow as an entity. What's more, in all but one of these instances, capital gains were also better. Thus, in Table 13-5, I have not listed the yield separately. Rather, I have shown only the total return of the selected stocks and how they compared with the Dow. I have also shown the dates of each illustration.

Because it is well known that very few investors do as well as the general market (or such indexes as the Dow Jones Industrial Average or the Standard & Poor's 500), it's interesting that this simple method of selecting stocks did 43 percent better than the Dow Jones Industrial Average. (I arrived at this figure by dividing 32.64 percent by 22.85 percent.)

Table 13-4

An abbreviated list of the 30 stocks in the Dow Jones Industrial Average, along with three factors: the S&P quality rating, the yield as of December 31, 1990, and the percentage change in price, as of June 30, 1992.

Stock	S&P rating	Yield 12-31-90 (%)	Price 12-31-90 ($)	Price 6-30-92 ($)	Change (%)
AlliedSignal	B	6.7	27.00	53.75	+ 99.07
Coca-Cola (2-for-1)*	A +	1.7	46.50	40.00	+ 72.04
General Electric	A +	3.6	57.38	77.75	+ 35.51
General Motors	B +	8.7	34.38	44.00	+ 28.00
Goodyear Tire	B +	9.5	18.88	68.62	+ 263.58
McDonald's	A +	1.2	29.12	46.00	+ 57.94
Merck (3-for-1)**	A +	2.5	89.88	48.75	+ 62.73
Philip Morris	A +	3.3	51.75	73.50	+ 42.02
Sears, Roebuck	A −	7.9	25.38	39.75	+ 56.65
Westinghouse	A +	4.9	28.50	17.62	− 38.16
Mean		4.20			
Standard deviation		2.13			
Buy level		6.33			
Average performance of 10 stocks that qualified					+ 67.94
Average beginning yield					5.00
Total return for period					+ 72.94
Dow Jones Industrial Average for same period					+ 26.00
Average beginning yield for 30 stocks					4.20
Total return for Dow Jones Industrial Average					+ 30.20

*Stock spit two-for-one.
**Stock split three-for-one.

The Theory behind the Figures

A few pages back, I mentioned that the reason this idea works so well is that the portfolio created is made up of two disparate parts: A group of high-quality stocks and a group of cats and dogs that have sunk so low they are ripe for overhauling. In any given period, one group may

Table 13-5

This table summarizes 11 different periods, giving the total return of
the selected stocks, compared with the Dow Jones Industrial Average in
each period.

Period	Selected stocks (%)	Dow Jones Industrial Average (%)
12-31-75 to 12-31-76	+ 26.35	+ 22.67
12-31-86 to 12-31-87	+ 12.26	+ 5.88
12-31-87 to 12-31-88	+ 17.24	+ 15.56
12-31-87 to 5-31-92	+ 103.33	+ 79.32
12-31-88 to 12-31-89	+ 35.72	+ 30.49
12-31-89 to 12-31-90	+ 0.71	− 0.98
5-31-90 to 5-31-92	+ 39.13	+ 21.65
12-31-90 to 6-30-92	+ 72.94	+ 30.20
12-31-91 to 6-30-92	+ 9.82	+ 8.04
8-31-91 to 8-31-93	+ 19.94	+ 23.28
8-31-92 to 8-31-93	+ 21.58	+ 15.22
Totals	+ 32.64	+ 22.85

do well while the other languishes. The trouble is that you don't know
ahead of time which is which. By combining the two, you normally
create a portfolio that outpaces the general market.

Let me be more specific.

Let's look at an example of what happened to the portfolio constructed at the end of 1975. Table 13-6 shows the low-yield (A+) stocks
and how they performed in 1976.

This was not impressive because the Dow Jones Industrial Average
climbed 17.86 percent in the same period.

By contrast, the high-yield segment performed much better. See
Table 13-7.

By examining the performance of the two segments, it is clear that
the portfolio was helped by the inclusion of the stocks with high yields
because the high-quality stocks were only average performers.

As you might guess, this same type of lackluster performance happened recently. For instance, let's look at the two-year period from
August 31, 1991, to August 31, 1993. Table 13-8 shows what happened
to the low-yield (A+) stocks.

Table 13-6
Performance of the low-yield (A+) segment stocks.

Stock	Price action 12-31-75 to 12-31-76 (%)
AT&T	+ 24.82
Chevron	+ 39.57
Eastman Kodak	− 18.96
Exxon	+ 20.85
General Electric	+ 20.05
American Brands	+ 28.42
Procter & Gamble	+ 5.20
Sears, Roebuck	+ 6.98
Texaco	+ 18.72
Average performance	+ 16.18

Table 13-7
Performance of the high-yield segment stocks.

Stock	Price action 12-31-75 to 12-31-76 (%)
AT&T	+ 24.82
International Harvester	+ 47.49
Chevron	+ 39.57
American Brands	+ 28.42
American Can	+ 24.30
Texaco	+ 18.72
Westinghouse	+ 31.78
Average performance	+ 30.73

During the same span, the high-yield group was destined to outperform the A+ stocks. See Table 13-9.

Here again, the high-yield stocks were much better investments. Now, let's look at another example to see whether the A+ stocks did better than their high-yield counterparts. In this instance, our starting date is the end of 1990. As of June 30, 1992, this is how the A+ stocks performed (see Table 13-10).

Table 13-8

Performance of the low-yield (A+) segment stocks.

Stock	Price action from 8-31-91 to 8-31-93 (%)
Coca-Cola	+ 31.94
General Electric	+ 31.22
McDonald's	+ 64.75
Merck	− 24.63
Minnesota Mining & Manufacturing	+ 26.19
Philip Morris	− 34.23
Woolworth	− 15.92
Average performance	+ 11.33

Table 13-9

Performance of the high-yield segment stocks.

Stock	Price action from 8-31-91 to 8-31-93 (%)
AlliedSignal	+ 94.79
IBM	− 52.77
Sears, Roebuck	+ 67.88
Texaco	+ 1.17
Union Carbide	+ 57.58
Westinghouse	− 35.94
Average performance	+ 22.12

Table 13-10

Performance of the low-yield (A+) segment stocks.

Stock	Price action from 12-31-90 to 6-30-92 (%)
Coca-Cola	+ 72.04
General Electric	+ 35.51
McDonald's	+ 57.94
Merck	+ 62.73
Philip Morris	+ 42.03
Westinghouse	− 38.16
Average performance	+ 38.68

This performance may seem heartening, but it was not as good as that turned in by the stocks with high yields at the end of 1990. Table 13-11 shows how they acted, as of June 30, 1992.

High-Yield Stocks Sometimes Falter

You must admit, it wasn't even close—the high-yield segment walked away with the honors.

By now, you might be convinced that it is the high-yield stocks that make my system tick. Not necessarily. Let's go back to that fateful year 1987. Suppose you were building a portfolio at the end of 1987 and were going to hold the stocks until May 31, 1992. Table 13-12 is what the low-yield segment looked like.

Table 13-11
Performance of the high-yield segment stocks.

Stock	Price action from 12-31-90 to 6-30-92 (%)
AlliedSignal	+ 99.07
General Motors	+ 28.00
Goodyear	+ 263.58
Sears, Roebuck	+ 56.65
Average performance	+ 111.83

Table 13-12
Performance of the low-yield (A+) segment stocks.

Stock	Price action from 12-31-87 to 5-31-92 (%)
Coca-Cola	+ 361.6
General Electric	+ 73.1
IBM	− 21.4
McDonald's	+ 113.1
Merck	+ 186.0
Philip Morris	+ 263.1
Westinghouse	− 31.7
Average performance	+ 134.8

Contrast this with the action of the high-yield group in the same period shown in Table 13-13.

In this sharp reversal, the A+ stocks were clearly the ones to own.

Next, let's see what happened to the two disparate groups, as of December 31, 1989. Table 13-14 shows how the A+ stocks acted if held for one year.

The market that year did even worse, down 4.34 percent. But the high-yield stocks sagged even more, as you can see in Table 13-15.

Let's look at still another illustration in which it was better to concentrate on stocks rated A+. The time period in this instance begins May 31, 1990, and ends two years later. This is the performance of stocks rated A+ on May 31, 1992. See Table 13-16.

See Table 13-17 for how the high-yield stocks performed during the same period (5-31-90 through 5-31-92).

Table 13-13
Performance of the high-yield segment stocks.

Stock	Price action from 12-31-87 to 5-31-92 (%)
AlliedSignal	+ 107.1
Chevron	+ 80.1
General Motors	+ 29.9
Primerica	+ 59.1
Sears, Roebuck	+ 30.2
Union Carbide	+ 32.2
Average performance	+ 56.4

Table 13-14
Performance of the low-yield (A+) segment stocks.

Stock	Price action from 12-31-89 to 12-31-90 (%)
Coca-Cola	+ 20.39
General Electric	− 11.05
IBM	+ 20.05
McDonald's	− 15.58
Merck	+ 15.97
Philip Morris	+ 24.32
Westinghouse	− 22.97
Average performance	+ 4.45

Table 13-15
Performance of the high-yield segment stocks.

Stock	Price action from 12-31-89 to 12-30-90 (%)
AlliedSignal	− 22.58
Eastman Kodak	+ 1.22
General Motors	− 18.64
IBM	+ 20.05
Sears, Roebuck	− 33.44
Texaco	+ 2.76
Average performance	− 8.44

Table 13-16
Performance of the low-yield (A+) segment stocks.

Stock	Price action from 5-31-90 to 5-31-92 (%)
Coca-Cola	+ 95.0
General Electric	+ 10.9
McDonald's	+ 35.4
Merck	+ 82.6
Philip Morris	+ 84.0
Westinghouse	− 53.3
Average performance	+ 42.4

Table 13-17
Performance of the high-yield segment stocks.

Stock	Price action from 5-31-90 to 5-31-92 (%)
AlliedSignal	+ 58.9
Eastman Kodak	− 0.9
Exxon	+ 25.8
General Motors	− 18.0
Goodyear	+ 98.6
Sears, Roebuck	+ 20.3
Texaco	+ 8.2
Union Carbide	+ 43.8
Average performance	+ 29.6

With this evidence, it seems logical that combining the A+ stocks with the high-yield segment makes a good deal of sense.

Summary

Just in case this method of stock selection is still fuzzy, here is all it entails.

- Make a list of the 30 Dow Industrials. You can find the list on the third page of the third section of *The Wall Street Journal.*
- Check the dividend yield of each stock.
- Using a sophisticated calculator, determine the mean (or average) of these yields, as well as the standard deviation. Buy all stocks whose yield is at least one standard deviation better than the mean. If you don't have a good calculator, use the five stocks with the highest yield.
- Check the latest monthly *Standard & Poor's Stock Guide.* Buy any stock rated A+ among the 30 Dow stocks.
- If you buy the stocks as described in this chapter, you will be investing in about a dozen stocks.
- Hold these stocks for at least one year. Do the calculations again, making any needed adjustments to your list.

14
An Interview with a Widow from Vermont

One of the reasons I don't attend reunions of my high school class is distance. It takes several hours to fly from Cleveland to Baton Rouge, rent a car, and drive to Natchez, Mississippi.

The other reason is August. I have never understood why the committee always insists on having the reunion in August. Why not February? That's when I get fed up living in Cleveland. Not August. Natchez is a place to visit in the winter. In the summer, you need a portable air conditioner every time you leave a building.

Last summer, I decided to go anyway. It had been several decades since I had last seen most of my classmates. Quite a few, unfortunately, were no longer alive. It had been so many years since I had driven a car in Natchez that I had to ask my brother Bill how to get from Baton Rouge to his house on South Union Street.

My Brother and His Wife Are Not Sharecroppers

Because my brother doesn't have a garage, I had to leave my car on the street. The heat of Natchez is doubly disturbing when you emerge from an air-conditioned home and hop into your car at midday. You shouldn't get the idea, incidentally, that Bill and Denver (his charming wife) are deprived sharecroppers for not having a garage. It is quite common in

Natchez because many of the homes are packed closely together. It's also a blessing in disguise because they don't have huge lawns to mow.

At any rate, I was looking forward to a gala round of social events in which I would meet my former classmates. Many of them are still denizens of Natchez ("where the Old South still lives") but quite a few, like myself, had to fly in from far-off cities. None would admit, of course, that they had been transformed into "Damn Yankees."

Despite my obvious—and wretched—Yankee twang, everyone treated me like a long-lost friend. Were they just being polite, I wondered, or had they forgiven me for such gauche remarks as referring to "the War Between the States" as the "Civil War"?

My Odious Northern Accent

Above all else, people from Natchez are affable, genial, and gregarious. And they love parties. It was quite a change for me when I moved there from Buffalo at the beginning of my sophomore year of high school. Being stubborn, I made no effort to get rid of my odious northern accent. On the other hand, a good deal of this southern geniality and warmth rubbed off on my younger brother. I suspect he became a southern gentleman partly because he married a native of Natchez—a gorgeous southern belle, no less.

Looking back, it was my own fault that I didn't marry a southern belle. For two years, I sat next to one of the most beautiful girls in the school, Mimi Brown, in French I and II.

One reason I went to Natchez in August was in hopes that some of my classmates had earned huge sums of money and would now need my firm to untangle their portfolios. So far, none of them have forgotten that I still have an "inhuman" Yankee accent—and thus am not fit to touch their portfolios. Of course, they didn't actually tell me this in so many words, but I knew that this hostility must be burning deep in their psyches. Not that I am paranoid, of course.

Rendezvous with a Widow at Natchez Under the Hill

But, all was not lost. By chance, I bumped into a wealthy widow one day. It was just after lunch when I took a walk to Natchez Under the Hill. (The city proper is situated high above the Mississippi on a bluff.) Despite the August heat—the townspeople told me that the weather that week was unseasonably hot—I found it only mildly uncomfortable. Maybe I should take my brother's advice and move back to Natchez, I said to myself.

I stopped at a shop, in full view of the mighty Mississippi River. I am not sure whether natives trade there or not, but it appealed to me as a good place to pick up a memento from my trip. At any rate, I overheard one of the customers, a woman in her early seventies. She was tastefully dressed in a print dress and was wearing low-heeled shoes to mitigate her above-average height.

Her accent was clearly not southern. Being an outspoken sort, I commented to her, "You are in for trouble in this town with a northern accent. If they catch you, they'll have you tarred and feathered and banished to some godforsaken place like Cleveland."

"How Have You Avoided Capture?"

She could see that I was kidding. "Anyplace but Cleveland," she gasped. "Even Detroit or Chicago—but not Cleveland. What about you? How have you avoided capture?"

That brief encounter with Olivia Terpsichorean—a long-time resident of Burlington, Vermont—developed into a discussion of where we were from, what we did for a living, why we were visiting Natchez and so forth. For an "uncouth Yankee," she had a most ingratiating personality. When she asked me my line of work, I hastened to inform her that I was a senior portfolio strategist with Hickory Investment Advisors.

"I wish my husband had known something about the stock market," she said. "All he ever bought was pharmaceutical stocks. That strategy worked well up until recently. Every day, my stocks fall to new lows. Even Merck and Pfizer have not been immune. It's getting so I don't dare look at *The Wall Street Journal* anymore."

Retirement and the accelerating costs of old age should be provided for. Friends in their 80s advise that old age and its costs and threats are profoundly different from what most people mean by "retirement"—and require separate consideration. In retirement, you have less income. In old age, the costs of health care increase rapidly and can be "exploding." A daunting rule of thumb is worth considering: 95% of the lifetime cost of medical care is incurred in the last 5% of a typical individual's life—and 50% in the last 1%.

Source: Charles D. Ellis in *Investment Policy, How to Win the Loser's Game*, Second Edition, 1993, Business One Irwin

"I know what you mean," I said, trying to show some empathy for her plight. "I own two drug stocks myself. Fortunately, I have about 45 other stocks that are not being hurt by the Clinton Administration's anti-health-care industry bias."

"Do you think I should sell my drug stocks?" Olivia asked.

"Before I answer your question, Mrs. Terpsichorean ..."

"Please, call me Olivia ..."

"You Could Be Bound and Gagged and Held for Ransom"

"Fine. Before I answer your question, Olivia, perhaps it would be more private if you stopped over at my brother's house on South Union. That way, the natives won't find out how rich you are. You could be bound and gagged and held for ransom."

"I never thought of that. My friends in Vermont would be forced to order out the National Guard. My car is just outside. Shall I follow you?"

"I'm afraid I can't afford a car." I told her. "I walked down here for some exercise—and to get a little sun. As you can see, all those years in Cleveland have given me a pale, sallow complexion."

When we got to the air-conditioned comfort of Bill and Denver's house, we enjoyed a glass of iced tea and sat down in the living room to discuss Olivia's portfolio. Her husband had left her with a portfolio worth $450,000, of which $200,000 was invested in bonds and money-market funds, leaving $250,000 devoted to common stocks. Dr. Terpsichorean was convinced that medical stocks were the wave of the future.

She asked, "Now that you have some idea of my situation, what do you think I should do?"

"Well, to begin with, I should confess that I'm not a miracle worker. In fact, almost no one is. Professional investment managers are constantly being judged by how well they do when compared to the general market. For instance, our aim is to beat the Dow Jones Industrial Average or the Standard & Poor's 500. If you can do that consistently, you are a success."

"I think you are being modest, Mr. Slatter," Olivia said. "Surely an expert like you should be able to do better than the general market."

"Someone Has to Be on the Wrong End of Every Trade"

"Most experts *don't*," I said. "And, please ... call me Slats. Only my wife calls me Mr. Slatter." She nodded, and I continued. "Since most of the action in the stock market involves one expert selling to another, someone has to be on the wrong end of every trade. Studies show that two-thirds of mutual funds, for instance, do not even equal the market, much less beat it. The same holds true for other professional money-managers and institutions, such as pension plans, investment advisors, bank trust departments, and insurance companies."

"That's rather discouraging," Olivia said. "How can you charge a fee for managing a portfolio if you can't assure people that you will help them make money?"

"Now, you're giving me an inferiority complex, Olivia. And a guilt complex, as well. Do you want me to refund your money?" I smiled. I didn't want her to think I was serious.

"Fortunately, I haven't paid you a fee, so I guess you're spared the embarrassment of having to refund it. But, seriously, do you have any advice I can carry back to Burlington? If it makes sense, I might even hire Hickory Investment Advisors to manage my portfolio. That's assuming, of course, that you don't get captured by a regiment of crazed Confederates before you can make it back to Cleveland." I was thankful that she didn't refer to my adopted hometown as "the Mistake on the Lake."

"They won't harm me as long as Bill and Denver are here to watch over me, " I told her. "One strategy that will assure you of good results is to buy most of the 30 stocks that make up the Dow Jones Industrial Average. In other words, if you own the Average, you probably won't do much worse than the overall market. How does that sound?"

"I have been reading *The Wall Street Journal* ever since my husband died three years ago. So far, that idea has never been mentioned. On second thought ... that rather sounds like an index fund."

"Index funds have gained some adherents. There are quite a few of them. For instance, you can buy index funds that include all 500 stocks in the S&P 500. But my idea goes one step further ..."

"One step further?"

An Incredibly Simple Idea

"Yes. I have created a new wrinkle. It enables you to do a bit better than the market. Would you like me to explain how it works?"

"Well, yes, why not."

"This idea is incredibly simple. If I tell you how to use it, you might decide that it wouldn't be necessary to pay me a fee to manage your portfolio ... and I need the money desperately."

"I suppose you would take the money and move out of Cleveland ..."

"Most people think we should," I confessed. "Actually, my wife and I enjoy living in Cleveland and have no desire to leave. Promise you won't tell anyone—it could lead to overpopulation. Getting back to business, here's how my ingenious scheme works. Are you taking notes?"

"This pen you loaned me doesn't write. Maybe you should borrow some money from your brother and get a refill."

"I've tried that before, but he refuses until I pay back what I already owe him. But, let's not talk about *my* problems. It's more important to concentrate on extricating you from *your* predicament."

"You're stalling, Slats. You are deliberately trying to withhold this strategy from me."

"It Would Ruin My Business"

"No … no … no. I'm going to tell you. But first … you must promise not to reveal this secret to anyone in Cleveland. It would ruin my business."

"Fear not. When I visit Cleveland, I will honor your secret."

"OK. Here goes. You invest about 5 percent of your money in each of the six or seven best stocks in the Dow 30. Avoid the half dozen that are the worst … and then put about 4 percent in each of the rest."

"And, pray, how do you determine which are the best and the worst?"

"If I knew that, I would be rich," I said.

"Is that the end of your system? What a letdown …"

"Patience, Olivia. The best is yet to come. Step number one is to make a list of the 30 Dow Jones stocks, along with the dividend yield on each one. That's easy to determine; just check the stock pages of *The Wall Street Journal*."

"It sounds easy enough … is that all there is to it?"

"Oh, no. To illustrate how my idea worked in 1992, here is a list of the 30 stocks—which I just happen to have with me—along with their dividend yields at the end of 1991" (see Table 14-1).

"I assume those asterisks have some significance," Olivia said.

"Pick the Ones That Are Not the Favorites of the Institutions"

"Right. By using a calculator, I determined which stocks had at least an average dividend yield. Anything from 3.3 percent or above is at least average. My next step is to pick the ones that are *not* the favorites of the institutions."

Table 14-1

The 30 Dow stocks with yields at the end of 1991. Stocks with yields that are at least average are denoted by an asterisk.

Stock	Yield year-end 1991 (%)
AlliedSignal	2.3
ALCOA	2.8
American Express	4.9*
AT&T	3.4*
Bethlehem Steel	Nil
Boeing	2.1
Caterpillar	1.4
Chevron	4.8*
Coca-Cola	1.2
Disney, Walt	0.6
Du Pont	3.6*
Eastman Kodak	4.1*
Exxon	4.4*
General Electric	2.9
General Motors	5.5*
Goodyear Tire	0.7
IBM	5.4*
International Paper	2.4
McDonald's	1.0
Merck	1.5
Minnesota Mining & Manufacturing	3.3*
J.P. Morgan	3.2*
Philip Morris	2.6
Procter & Gamble	2.1
Sears, Roebuck	5.3*
Texaco	5.2*
Union Carbide	4.9*
United Technologies	3.3*
Westinghouse Electric	7.8*
Woolworth	4.1*
The average yield	3.2

"In other words, you don't have a high regard for what the institutions like. Is that what you're saying?"

"Well ... I suppose you could say that. At any rate, it seems that if a stock gets too popular with the institutions, it becomes vulnerable. Let's look at the stocks that have been singled out because they have attractive yields (see Table 14-2). In the column to the right of the yield column is a column denoting the number of institutional owners, as of the end of 1991.

"It looks like the asterisks are indicating the stocks that are *the best*," Olivia said.

"You seem to be getting the idea. By adding up the column of institutional owners, we find that the average is 743. Any stock that has fewer institutional owners is to be purchased. You invest 5 percent in each. Table 14-3 shows how these six stocks performed in 1992.

"Shall I continue?" I asked. She nodded. "Now, we have to determine if an average gain of 14.77 percent was better than the market in the year 1992. As it turned out, it was exceptional because the Dow Jones Industrial Average was up only 4.2 percent, not counting dividends. Nor did the S&P 500 do much better. That index gained 4.5 percent in 1992. Obviously, a gain of 14.77 percent was far better than either."

"How Do You Determine Which Are the Worst?"

"I'm impressed," the widow from Vermont said. "I'm beginning to think you may have a good idea. You mentioned something about avoiding the worst stocks. How do you determine which are the worst?"

"I take all the stocks that have a below-average yield, normally about 15. Then, I average up the number of institutional owners and exclude those stocks that are overowned by the professionals. Here is a list of stocks with below-average yields, along with the number of institutional owners, as of year-end 1991" (see Table 14-4).

"As you can see," I said. "These seven stocks did quite poorly. On average, they gained only 2.42 percent during 1992. Thus, it was wise to avoid them and invest more heavily in the stocks selected as 'the best.'"

"It's beginning to make some sense. Can you calculate how well the restructured portfolio performed in 1992, compared with the general market?"

"The Dow Jones Industrial Average did not perform very well that year, advancing a modest 4.2 percent. The S&P 500 did only slightly better, up 4.5 percent in 1992."

Table 14-2

Stocks with at least average yields.

Stock	Yield year-end 1991 (%)	Institutional owners year-end 1991
American Express	4.9	732*
AT&T	3.4	891
Chevron	4.8	793
Du Pont	3.6	808
Eastman Kodak	4.1	760
Exxon	4.4	1003
General Motors	5.5	782
IBM	5.4	1254
Minnesota Mining & Manufacturing	3.3	860
Sears, Roebuck	5.3	561*
Texaco	5.2	907
Union Carbide	4.9	285*
United Technologies	3.3	527*
Westinghouse Electric	7.8	568*
Woolworth	4.1	419*

*Stocks with below-average number of institutional investors.

Table 14-3

Stocks in 1992, purchased at end of 1991.

Stock	Stock price change 12-31-91 to 12-31-92 (%)
American Express	+ 21.34
Sears, Roebuck	+ 20.13
Union Carbide	+ 64.81
United Technologies	− 11.29
Westinghouse Electric	− 25.69
Woolworth	+ 19.34
Average performance of six stocks	+ 14.77

Table 14-4

Stocks to be avoided, based on low yield and excessive ownership by institutions.

Stock	Yield year-end 1991 (%)	Institutional owners year-end 1991	Stock price change 1992 (%)
Boeing	2.1	837	− 15.97
Coca-Cola	1.2	832	+ 4.36
General Electric	2.9	1246	+ 11.76
McDonald's	1.0	733	+ 28.29
Merck	1.5	1081	− 21.85
Philip Morris	2.6	1334	− 3.89
Procter & Gamble	2.1	769	+ 14.25
Average price change			+ 2.42

"I assume the other 24 Dow stocks did not do as well," Olivia said.

"On average, they appreciated 6.61 percent. Thus, if you had a portfolio of $100,000, you would have invested $3000 in each of the 24 stocks, for a total of $72,000. If they advanced an average of 6.61 percent, that portion of your list would now be worth $76,759.

"Now let's add in what the other six Dow stocks did," I suggested. "Instead of investing 3 percent in each, we actually invest 3 percent plus 1.67 percent (divide six into 10 percent). This works out to an average investment of $4670. Since these stocks climbed an average of 14.77 percent, each holding would be worth $5360 at the end of 1992. Multiply by six, because we had six stocks, and you have another $32,159 to be added to the $76,759, for a grand total of $108,918." Commissions and taxes are not included in this illustration.

"How does that compare with a person whose performance was the same as the Dow?" Olivia asked.

"Since the Dow advanced 4.2 percent that year, a $100,000 portfolio would be worth $104,200, or $4718 less. Of course, if my firm had been handling your affairs, we would have deducted our fee, which is 1 percent. That amounts to $1000 per year, not including brokerage commissions. Thus, to get a true picture, you should deduct this fee from the $4718 extra that we made for you, bringing your next extra gain to $3718."

Table 14-5

Stocks with above-average yields.

Stock	Yield year-end 1992 (%)	Institutional owners year-end 1992
American Express	4.0	694*
Chevron	4.7	796
Du Pont	3.7	836
Eastman Kodak	4.9	777
Exxon	4.7	1077
IBM	9.6	1189
J.P. Morgan	3.7	747*
Philip Morris	3.4	1445
Sears, Roebuck	4.4	605*
Texaco	5.4	911
Union Carbide	4.5	315*
United Technologies	3.7	557*
Westinghouse Electric	5.4	426*
Woolworth	3.5	422*
Average		771

Action on Stocks Purchased	
Stock	First half 1993 (%)
American Express	+ 29.65
J.P. Morgan	+ 3.23
Sears, Roebuck	+ 20.88
Union Carbide	+ 23.20
United Technologies	+ 12.21
Westinghouse Electric	+ 18.69
Woolworth	− 14.23
Average performance	+ 13.38

*Stock to be purchased.

Table 14-6
Stocks to be avoided.

Stock	Yield year-end 1992 (%)	Institutional owners year-end 1992	Price change 1993 (%)
AT&T	2.6	837	+ 23.53
Boeing	1.2	832	− 7.79
Coca-Cola	2.9	1246	+ 2.69
General Electric	1.0	733	+ 11.99
General Motors	1.5	1081	+ 37.98
McDonald's	2.6	1334	+ 0.77
Merck	2.1	769	− 18.16
Minnesota Mining & Manufacturing	3.2	897	+ 7.33
Procter & Gamble	2.1	830	− 3.03
Average price change			+ 6.15

"Can We Look at Some Additional Evidence?"

"That sounds OK to me," Olivia said. "I thought you said it was difficult to outperform the market. Yet, your simple idea appears to be able to do it. Can we look at some additional evidence that your idea works consistently?"

"I think I have something that might help convince you. Why don't we see how the idea worked since the beginning of 1993. Let's assume the period under study ended in mid-1993. Again, we use the 30 stocks from the Dow Jones Industrial Average.

"The following stocks should be avoided since they had below-average yields and had more than the average number of institutional owners. Look at this table" (see Table 14-5). "This is a list of the stocks that had at least an average yield at the end of 1992. I have indicated the number of institutional owners at that time. The ones that were least popular with the institutions are marked with an asterisk."

"It looks as though you picked a good list, Slats. The only loser was Woolworth. How does that compare with what the market did during that six-month period?"

"The difference was quite startling," I answered. "At the end of 1992, the Dow Jones Industrial Average was 3301.11. By June 30,

1993—just six months later—it had risen to 3516.08. In percentage terms, the Dow Jones Industrial Average was up only 6.51 percent. Are you impressed, Olivia?"

"Maybe it's time to sell my pharmaceutical stocks. Oh, by the way, how did the rejects do in this same period?"

"They did reasonably well, advancing about the same as the Dow itself." (See Table 14-6.) "The average gain was 6.15 percent—but, of course, not nearly as well as the stocks with high yields and low institutional ownership."

"You have really opened my eyes about investing, Slats. Have you ever considered writing a book? I'll bet a lot of people would thank you for telling them how to pick stocks. What do you think?"

"It would ruin my business. If the whole world knew how I pick stocks, they wouldn't need my firm to manage their money. No, there's no chance I will ever reveal my secrets to those people."

"Not even your friends in Natchez?"

"Well … I must admit they're wonderful people … but I just don't think I could trust them. They go to parties every night of the week. You can see what would happen. In two weeks, the whole state of Mississippi would be buying stocks using my system."

"I see what you mean, Slats. I guess it would be suicide to write a book like that. We'll just share the secret between us."

"Just you and me, Olivia."

15

How to Achieve Income and Growth in One Portfolio

When I ask investors to describe their investment objectives, they often tell me they want dependable income and steady growth—and, of course, no risk!

Guaranteeing no risk is a little difficult.

However, I do have a formula for achieving above-average income, along with above-average growth of principal.

Two factors are involved:

- The dividend yield
- The payout ratio

The Dividend Yield

By now you should be aware how to calculate the yield: simply divide the price of the stock into its annual dividend. If you don't like calculating, you can obtain the current yield (as of last month's end) by consulting the *Standard & Poor's Stock Guide.* If you want the latest yield (as of yesterday), you will find it in the stock tables in the third section of *The Wall Street Journal.*

The Payout Ratio

The payout ratio is calculated by dividing the indicated dividend by the latest 12-month's earnings per share. The best place to find this number is in the *Stock Guide*. Using the November 1993 *Stock Guide*, the payout ratio for General Electric would be calculated by dividing $2.52 (the indicated annual dividend) by $5.89 (the earnings per share in the 12 months ended September 30, 1983). That works out to a payout ratio of 42.8 percent.

Although that was easy, there are times when you will run into difficulty. For instance, you will not be able to calculate IBM's payout ratio. The dividend is $1.00, but there are no earnings because IBM suffered a deficit in the most recent 12 months.

You will also get an odd figure if the earnings are not high enough to pay the dividend. To be sure, in this instance you can make a calculation, but the payout ratio will exceed 100 percent.

How the System
Works

But more about these problems later. Meanwhile, let me describe how this approach to stock selection works.

- First, you want to confine your selection to stocks with an above-average yield.
- Next, you want to select any stock from this group that has a below-average payout ratio.

The logic behind the system is twofold.

1. A stock with an above-average yield is less likely to be overpriced than one with a low yield.
2. A company that pays out less of its earnings in the form of dividends is more apt to be growth-oriented. By retaining a large percentage of its earnings, the company can expand its horizons because it will be able to use that extra cash for acquisitions, research, a better marketing program, or new facilities.

Once you have determined which stocks have a good yield, your second step is to select those that have a below-average payout ratio. When you go through this exercise, you develop a list of stocks with good yield that are growth-oriented.

The Proof of the Pudding

So much for the logic. Does it really work?

Let's look at some examples. The first list is made up of stocks that are part of the S&P 500. All are rated A- or better, and all have earnings that are higher than their dividends. This means we won't have any trouble calculating the payout ratio. Table 15-1 shows a list of stocks, as of year-end 1987.

Step one is to calculate the average yield of these 15 stocks. It turns out to be 3.43 percent. Step two is to single out any stock with a yield of 3.4 percent or higher, along with its payout ratio. This list is presented in Table 15-2.

I have marked with an asterisk the three stocks that qualify because all have a payout ratio of less than 64.8 percent. The average price change of these three stocks during 1988 was 28.46 percent. Because the group as a whole appreciated only 16.9 percent, this test would indicate that the system was a success.

Table 15-1

Stock	Yield 12-31-87 (%)	Payout 12-31-87 (%)	Price 12-31-87 ($)	Price 12-31-88 ($)	One year price change (%)
Abbott Labs	2.1	37.9	48.25	48.12	− 0.26
Air Products	2.5	35.3	40.75	41.25	+ 1.23
Alberto Culver	1.2	18.8	20.75	36.75	+ 77.11
Albertson's	1.9	27.8	25.38	37.88	+ 49.26
American Brands	4.9	51.8	44.50	65.50	+ 47.19
American Cyanamid	2.5	36.1	41.25	46.75	+ 13.33
American Electric Power	8.9	80.1	26.25	27.25	+ 3.81
American Home Products	4.6	59.6	72.75	83.25	+ 14.43
American Medical International	5.7	57.1	12.62	15.62	+ 23.76
American Stores	1.7	18.9	50.50	57.88	+ 14.60
Ameritech	6.4	66.9	84.62	95.75	+ 13.15
Amoco	4.8	73.5	69.00	75.00	+ 8.70
AMP	1.9	43.1	46.75	44.50	− 4.81
Anheuser-Busch	1.8	30.3	33.38	31.50	− 5.62
Archer-Daniels	0.5	6.1	21.25	20.88	− 1.76
Averages	3.43				+ 16.90

Table 15-2

Stock	Yield 12-31-87 (%)	Payout 12-31-87 (%)	Price 12-31-87 ($)	Price 12-31-88 ($)	One year price change (%)
American Brands	4.9	51.8*	44.50	65.50	+ 47.19
American Electric Power	8.9	80.1	26.25	27.25	+ 3.81
American Home Products	4.6	59.6*	72.75	83.25	+ 14.43
American Medical International	5.7	57.1*	12.62	15.62	+ 23.76
Ameritech	6.4	66.9	84.62	95.75	+ 13.15
Amoco	4.8	73.5	69.00	75.00	+ 8.70
Average payout ratio		64.8			

*Stocks with below-average payout ratio.

Let's try another group of 15 stocks selected in exactly the same way and from the same copy of the *Stock Guide*. I arbitrarily picked the first 15 stocks in the alphabetical list. The first list is made up of stocks that are part of the S&P 500. They are easy to spot because there is a paragraph sign in front of each one. In both instances, stocks were selected without using hindsight. I simply ran my finger down the page and picked every stock that met my minimum requirements (that are rated A- or better and have earnings higher than their dividend) regardless of any prior knowledge. See Table 15-3.

As before, the next step is to segregate all stocks with a yield of 3.4 percent or higher. They appear in Table 15-4.

Only two stocks have a payout ratio below 61.93: Baltimore Gas & Electric and Boeing. Their average appreciation during 1988 was 34.68 percent, which is more than triple the 10 percent turned in by the 15 stocks as a group. Once again, the two-part system has been vindicated.

At this point, you may be curious as to how well this concept has been working lately. To demonstrate this, I resorted to the year-end 1992 *Stock Guide*. I opened up the *Stock Guide* to a random page and wrote down all stocks rated at least A- that were also part of the Standard & Poor's 500. They are easy to spot because there is a paragraph sign in front of each one. When I had recorded these stocks, I flipped ahead 10 pages and continued to add to my list. This procedure was followed until I had 15 stocks. See Table 15-5.

As before, the next step is to segregate all stocks with a yield of 3.1 percent or higher. See Table 15-6.

Table 15-3

Stock	Yield 12-31-87 (%)	Payout 12-31-87 (%)	Price 12-31-87 ($)	Price 12-31-88 ($)	One year price change (%)
Atlantic Richfield	5.8	77.4	69.00	80.62	+ 16.85
Automatic Data	1.0	23.9	44.88	38.75	− 13.65
Ball Corporation	2.7	34.5	35.38	27.88	− 21.20
Baltimore G&E	6.4	55.6	29.50	31.12	+ 5.51
Bard, C.R.	1.4	23.6	17.25	23.00	+ 33.33
Bausch & Lomb	2.5	31.8	34.62	43.38	+ 25.27
Baxter-Travenol	1.9	40.4	22.75	17.62	− 22.53
Becton, Dickinson	1.7	25.2	51.00	52.00	+ 1.96
Bell Atlantic	5.9	62.2	65.00	71.12	+ 9.42
BellSouth	6.0	65.3	36.38	39.88	+ 9.62
Bemis	1.9	32.7	19.19	23.25	+ 21.17
H. & R. Block	2.8	59.5	31.00	28.38	− 8.47
Boeing	3.8	41.1	37.00	60.62	+ 63.85
Borden	2.6	37.1	49.50	59.25	+ 19.70
Bristol-Myers	4.0	70.0	41.62	45.25	+ 8.71
Averages	3.36				+ 10.00

Table 15-4

Stock	Yield 12-31-87 (%)	Payout 12-31-87 (%)	Price 12-31-87 ($)	Price 12-31-88 ($)	One year price change (%)
Atlantic Richfield	5.8	77.4	69.00	80.62	+ 16.85
Baltimore G&E	6.4	55.6*	29.50	31.12	+ 5.51
Bell Atlantic	5.9	62.2	65.00	71.12	+ 9.42
BellSouth	6.0	65.3	36.38	39.88	+ 9.62
Boeing	3.8	41.1*	37.00	60.62	+ 63.85
Bristol-Myers	4.0	70.0	41.62	45.25	+ 8.71
Average payout ratio		61.93			

*Stocks with below-average payout ratio.

Table 15-5

Stock	Yield 12-31-92 (%)	Payout 12-31-92 (%)	Price 12-31-92 ($)	Price 10-31-93 ($)	10-month price change (%)
Quaker Oats	2.9	52.9	59.75	71.00	+ 18.83
Ralston Purina	2.6	36.1	45.88	41.62	− 9.26
Sara Lee	1.8	32.5	27.94	26.50	− 5.15
SCEcorp	6.0	90.9	23.50	21.12	− 10.11
Schering-Plough	2.7	46.8	58.50	68.12	+ 16.45
Schlumberger	1.7	34.4	68.88	63.12	− 8.35
Southwestern Bell	4.4	70.4	33.25	44.25	+ 33.08
U.S. Bancorp	3.4	36.4	22.38	24.62	+ 10.06
Air Products	2.0	36.6	42.25	41.75	− 1.18
Ameritech	5.1	74.7	68.50	84.75	+ 23.72
Bankers Trust	4.6	34.4	60.50	79.25	+ 30.99
Bard, C.R.	1.7	43.0	29.88	25.25	− 15.48
Barnett Banks	3.7	72.6	35.38	41.88	+ 18.37
Bausch & Lomb	1.6	51.0	50.00	51.88	+ 3.75
Browning-Ferris	2.6	61.3	26.12	22.62	− 13.40
Averages	3.12				+ 6.15

After eliminating all stocks with yields below 3.1 percent, I calculated the average payout ratio of those remaining. It turned out to be 63.23 percent. Only two stocks had a low enough payout ratio to qualify for purchase. They are marked with an asterisk. Their average price change was 20.53 percent, which exceeds the 6.15 percent for the whole group by a wide margin.

Leaving Out the Bank Stocks

In the next test, I decided to leave out all bank stocks because two bank stocks were the winners in the last example. For no particularly good reason, I also omitted all public utilities. Otherwise, I proceeded as before, selecting all stocks rated A- or better from among those in the S&P 500. See Table 15-7.

Table 15-6

Stock	Yield 12-31-92 (%)	Payout 12-31-92 (%)	Price 12-31-92 ($)	Price 10-31-93 ($)	10-month price change (%)
SCEcorp	6.0	90.9	23.50	21.12	− 10.11
Southwestern Bell	4.4	70.4	33.25	44.25	+ 33.08
U.S. Bancorp	3.4	36.4*	22.38	24.62	+ 10.06
Ameritech	5.1	74.7	68.50	84.75	+ 23.72
Bankers Trust	4.6	34.4*	60.50	79.25	+ 30.99
Barnett Banks	3.7	72.6	35.38	41.88	+ 18.37
Average payout ratio		63.23			

*Stock with below-average payout ratio.

Table 15-7

Stock	Yield 12-31-91 (%)	Payout 12-31-91 (%)	Price 12-31-91 ($)	Price 10-31-92 ($)	10-month price change (%)
Medtronic	0.5	19.2	94.00	95.25	+ 1.33
Melville	3.2	44.7	44.50	53.12	+ 19.38
Merck	1.5	47.9	55.50	43.38	− 21.85
Meredith	2.4	43.0	27.12	27.00	− 0.46
National Medical Enterprises	2.7	26.0	16.88	12.38	− 26.67
Pall	1.1	31.5	18.08	20.12	+ 11.29
Paramount	1.8	55.6	38.75	45.00	+ 16.13
Parker-Hanifin	3.0	85.2	30.62	29.62	− 3.27
Procter & Gamble	2.1	41.1	46.94	53.62	+ 14.25
Rohm & Haas	2.9	48.6	43.50	53.50	+ 22.99
Royal Dutch Petroleum	4.1	48.6	86.25	81.00	− 6.09
Rubbermaid	0.9	34.7	38.25	31.75	− 16.99
Russell	0.9	26.2	35.62	31.38	− 11.93
Snap-On Tools	3.3	61.0	32.38	31.38	− 3.09
Sysco	0.9	23.4	23.31	26.38	+ 13.14
Averages	2.09				+ 0.54

Table 15-8

Stock	Yield 12-31-91 (%)	Payout 12-31-91 (%)	Price 12-31-91 ($)	Price 10-31-92 ($)	10-month price change (%)
Melville	3.2	44.7*	44.50	53.12	+ 19.38
Meredith	2.4	43.0*	27.12	27.00	− 0.46
National Medical Enterprises	2.7	26.0*	16.88	12.38	− 26.67
Parker-Hanifin	3.0	85.2	30.62	29.62	− 3.27
Procter & Gamble	2.1	41.1*	46.94	53.62	+ 14.25
Rohm & Haas	2.9	48.6*	43.50	53.50	+ 22.99
Royal Dutch Petroleum	4.1	48.6*	86.25	81.00	− 6.09
Snap-On Tools	3.3	61.0	32.38	31.38	− 3.09
Average payout ratio		49.8			

*Stock with below-average payout ratio.

After eliminating all stocks with above-average dividend yields, you end up with the stocks in Table 15-8.

The next step is to select those with below-average payout ratios, the ones marked with an asterisk. Their average performance during 1992 was a plus 3.9 percent. This may not seem impressive, but it was much better than the group as a whole, which advanced a modest 0.54 percent during the same period.

A Ridiculous Assumption

Let's make one more test, just to be sure the system never fails— which, of course, is a ridiculous assumption. In fact, it fails about one-third of the time, as I will show you later.

Meanwhile, let's look at one more example—one that proves the rule because my fancy system failed to do its job. See Table 15-9.

As before, I separated out the stocks with an above-average yield and placed them in Table 15-10.

The average price change of the five selected stocks was 15.67 percent. This was well below the action of the full 15, which advanced 24.50 percent during this one-year span.

Table 15-9

Stock	Yield 12-31-90 (%)	Payout 12-31-90 (%)	Price 12-31-90 ($)	Price 12-31-91 ($)	One year price change (%)
Stride Rite	1.4	19.8	14.31	29.12	+ 103.49
Torchmark	2.9	32.3	48.88	57.88	+ 18.41
UST	3.6	71.0	36.50	65.50	+ 79.45
Winn-Dixie	3.3	56.0	32.38	37.50	+ 15.83
Woolworth	3.4	39.1	30.25	26.50	− 12.40
Worthington Inc.	2.6	43.5	15.25	23.38	+ 53.28
Alberto Culver	0.6	15.4	33.25	31.62	− 4.89
Albertson's	1.3	29.3	36.50	39.25	+ 7.53
Alco Standard	2.7	34.4	33.12	34.25	+ 3.40
Anheuser-Busch	2.3	34.4	43.00	61.50	+ 43.02
Archer-Daniels	0.4	6.3	22.75	33.12	+ 45.60
Becton, Dickinson	1.6	24.8	74.50	68.50	− 8.05
Bell Atlantic	4.4	82.2	53.62	48.25	− 10.02
BellSouth	4.9	74.2	54.75	51.75	− 5.48
Bemis	2.4	37.1	29.62	41.00	+ 38.40
Averages	2.52				+ 24.50

Table 15-10

Stock	Yield 12-31-90 (%)	Payout 12-31-90 (%)	Price 12-31-90 ($)	Price 12-31-91 ($)	One year price change (%)
Torchmark	2.9	32.3*	48.88	57.88	+ 18.41
UST	3.6	71.0	36.50	65.50	+ 79.45
Winn-Dixie	3.3	56.0	32.38	37.50	+ 15.83
Woolworth	3.4	39.1*	30.25	26.50	− 12.40
Worthington Inc.	2.6	43.5*	15.25	23.38	+ 53.28
Alco Standard	2.7	34.4*	33.12	34.25	+ 3.40
Bell Atlantic	4.4	82.2	53.62	48.25	− 10.02
BellSouth	4.9	74.2	54.75	51.75	− 5.48
Bemis	2.4	37.1	29.62	41.00	+ 38.40
Average payout ratio		54.09			

*Stocks with below-average payout ratio.

Table 15-11

The stock group results below have been selected by calculating the average dividend yield in each sample. Those survivors are then measured for their payout ratio. Those with a payout that is less than the other high-yield stocks are selected and their average performance compared to the group as a whole. I have marked with an asterisk the winner in each instance. In the first group, for instance, the selected stocks had an appreciation of 9.74 percent, compared with the group as a whole, which was up only 6.55 percent.

Performance of selected groups (%)	Performance of group as a whole (%)
*+ 9.74	+ 6.55
*+ 20.14	+ 7.02
*+ 1.98	− 3.74
*+ 21.62	+ 6.58
+ 12.89	*+ 23.82
*− 12.15	− 16.58
*+ 14.77	+ 13.19
+ 9.20	*+ 11.61
+ 9.13	*+ 18.12
*+ 76.17	+ 19.70
*+ 28.46	+ 16.90
*+ 26.26	+ 10.00
*+ 63.48	+ 13.70
*+ 23.52	+ 10.20
*+ 32.00	+ 22.10
*+ 25.49	+ 19.60
+ 22.69	*+ 35.60
*+ 14.41	− 1.14
+ 26.45	*+ 45.40
+ 13.95	*+ 16.00
*+ 67.59	+ 21.40
*+ 39.30	+ 13.90
*+ 35.74	+ 22.21
+ 4.20	*+ 11.32
*+ 78.60	+ 32.93
+ 21.80	*+ 22.62
+ 15.67	*+ 24.50
*+ 3.90	+ 0.54
*+ 20.53	I 6.15
*+ 34.68	+ 10.03
*+ 25.41	+ 14.67

Exceptional Overall Results

As noted above, no system works all the time. In fact, some systems don't work even half the time. This one works about two-thirds of the time and produces exceptional overall results. Using my notebooks, I picked out 30 tests, which are summarized in Table 15-11.

73.2 Percent Better Than the Market Is Tough to Beat

If you count the asterisks, you will see that this system outperforms the group 21 times out of 30, or 70 percent of the time. More than that, the average gain of these miniportfolios was 25.41 percent, compared with the group portfolios of 14.67 percent. If you divide 14.67 percent into 25.41 percent, it would appear that the system stock did 73.2 percent better than the control groups. Do you know of any mutual fund that has average performance that is 73.2 percent better than the market? Hardly.

Of course, if you are a negative thinker, you might be fearful of using this method of stock selecting—because it fails almost a third of the time!

Here's an answer to your fears. Use this system on only a third of your portfolio, using two entirely different systems—such as those described in other chapters—on the other two-thirds. The chances of all three systems failing at the same time is rather remote. It is more likely that all three will be successful.

16
When
to Sell

Typically a nervous lot, investors seem to be convinced that you must be prepared to sell the day after you invest in a common stock.

These quivering blobs of jelly may feel this way because they have read articles that advise them to set a target price whenever they invest in a common stock. Apparently, someone has told them, "Once the stock reaches that level, call your broker and bail out."

Perhaps this admonition may have some logic to it, but, for my part, I have never bothered to set a sell price. In most instances, I hang onto my stocks for many years. In fact, most stocks that I sold turned out to be a mistake.

Home Runs Are Better
Than Doubles

Basically, my strategy is to hold winners and sell losers. If you sell your winners too soon, your overall results will be mediocre. If you are going to overcome the inevitable losses, you need some home runs and triples. Whenever you sell a stock simply because it has doubled, you are robbing your portfolio of a potential home run.

The best way to make money in the stock market is to buy common stocks and hold them a long time. Trading, by contrast, will never lead to riches. The trouble with trading is twofold:

1. Commissions
2. Taxes

To be sure, if you actually knew which stocks to buy and sell, trading would be a great strategy. But you don't.

Because this little piece of advice probably won't make you happy, I will endeavor to placate your wrath (the British pronounce it "rawth") by pointing out some instances where selling a stock might make some sense.

What about Merck, Philip Morris, and IBM?

In hindsight, you can always point out times when selling a stock would have been a great idea. At the beginning of 1993, for instance, it would have been a stroke of genius to sell Merck and Philip Morris. The year before that, you would have become a hero had you sold IBM before it collapsed in a heap.

All three of these stocks are the bluest of blue chips. I sincerely doubt that many portfolio managers had the foresight to sell any of these issues. On the other hand, *somebody* must have been selling them, or they wouldn't have plunged to lower levels.

At Hickory Investment Advisors, it is my job to restructure portfolios. This means that I must be on the lookout for stocks that have outlived their usefulness. Along with Paul Abbey, the president of the firm, it is my aim to be right more often than I am wrong.

As you might guess, this is not always easy. I am guilty of telling Paul to sell Boeing in early 1993, when it was in the low $30s. By the end of the year, Boeing was over $40. I also suggested to him that we sell Tenneco. He ignored my suggestion, and the stock rewarded our clients, as it recovered smartly. Now that you are aware that I have feet of clay, let me discuss some reasons why you might decide to sell a stock.

Beware of High-P/E Stocks

Studies have been conducted on the efficacy of buying stocks with a low price/earnings (P/E) ratio. It follows, then, that stocks with high P/Es are to be avoided. Suppose you owned the following 20 stocks, which I selected from the *Standard & Poor's Stock Guide* on a random basis, as of year-end 1990. All stocks have significant earnings, so the P/E can be calculated. All are stocks in the S&P 500. See Table 16-1.

In this particular illustration, the high-P/E stocks did not distinguish themselves because they climbed only 20.4 percent, compared with 40 percent for the group as a whole. The low-P/E stocks acted better, climbing an average of 38.6 percent.

Table 16-1

Stock	Price 12-31-90 ($)	P/E ratio	Price 11-31-93 ($)	Price action to 11-31-93 (%)
Exxon	51.75	16.7	62.75	+ 21.3
Fedders	6.88	8.4	5.75	− 16.4
Federal Express	33.88	14.0	71.50	+ 111.0
Federal National Mortgage	35.62	8.5	75.50	+ 112.0
Federal Paper Board	18.38	5.0	22.12	+ 20.3
Gannett	36.12	15.0	55.62	+ 54.0
Gap, Inc. (2-for-1)*	33.12	19.3	40.00	+ 141.5
General Electric	57.38	12.1	96.38	+ 68.0
General Mills	49.00	19.0	60.75	+ 24.0
Heinz, H.J.	34.88	17.4	37.62	+ 7.9
Hilton Hotels	37.25	16.1	45.75	+ 22.8
Home Depot (4-for-3)**	38.62	30.7	41.50	+ 43.3
Homestake Mining	19.25	25.0	18.75	− 2.6
Kellogg (2-for-1)*	75.88	20.3	60.38	+ 59.1
Kerr-McGee	44.88	16.3	46.75	+ 4.2
Kimberly-Clark (2-for-1)*	84.00	15.6	52.88	+ 25.9
King World Products	24.50	11.4	40.75	+ 66.3
Monarch Machine Tool	10.25	19.7	11.25	+ 9.8
Monsanto	48.25	10.4	68.00	+ 40.9
Moore Corporation	22.75	14.0	19.50	− 14.3
Average price change				+ 40.0
Mean P/E		15.7		
Standard deviation		5.9		
Eliminate level		21.6		
Buy level		9.8		
Price action of two stocks at 21.6 or above				+ 20.4
Price action of three stocks at 9.8 or below				+ 38.6

*Stock split two-for-one.
**Stock split four-for-three.

Beware of High-Payout Ratios

As you may recall, I am opposed to stocks with a high dividend pay-out ratio. A low payout ratio gives the company additional funds to reinvest in expansion. In this instance, one stock (Exxon) had a payout ratio that was more than one standard deviation above the mean. Exxon underperformed the group, rising only 21.3 percent. By sharp contrast, the three stocks with extremely low payout ratios were stunning performers, shooting up 73.5 percent, from the end of 1990 to November 30, 1993. Thus, it would have paid to avoid Exxon and concentrate on the three stocks with extremely low payout ratios. See Table 16-2.

Is It Time to Adjust Asset Allocation?

Now, let's shift gears and examine another reason to sell stocks. This refers to asset allocation. Table 16-3 shows a breakdown of these 20 stocks, according to their industry sectors. You may recall that in my chapter on diversification, I suggested that you should not concentrate your assets in any one of the 12 sectors, such as utilities, financial, transportation, or capital goods. Oddly, even though these 20 stocks were selected on a random basis, they ended up not conforming at all to my sector guideline thesis. Entirely too many are concentrated in consumer growth, consumer staples, and basic industries. At the same time, there were no stocks in such sectors as capital goods-technology, conglomerates, and utilities.

You recall that my guidelines caution against investing more than 12 percent in any one sector. At the same time, it is best to have some assets—at least 4 percent—in sectors you may feel unenthusiastic about. In this portfolio, it is obvious that some changes should be considered. However, it would not make sense to effect a wholesale change in one year. But at least some effort should be made to correct the imbalance.

Additional Sell Candidates

If none of the above sell ideas appeal to you, here is another one that you may like to consider. It is much more complicated and requires a good bit of judgment. If you have some extra time, I recommend it.

First, make a copy of each stock's *Value Line* sheet. Next, have at

Table 16-2

Stock	Price 12-31-90 ($)	Payout ratio (%)	Price 11-31-93 ($)	Price action to 11-31-93 (%)
Exxon	51.75	86.5	62.75	+ 21.3
Fedders	6.88	58.5	5.75	− 16.4
Federal Express	33.88	0.0	71.50	+ 111.0
Federal National Mortgage	35.62	20.9	75.50	+ 112.0
Federal Paper Board	18.38	27.5	22.12	+ 20.3
Gannett	36.12	51.5	55.62	+ 54.0
Gap, Inc. (2-for-1)*	33.12	29.1	40.00	+ 141.5
General Electric	57.38	43.0	96.38	+ 68.0
General Mills	49.00	49.6	60.75	+ 24.0
Heinz, H.J.	34.88	47.8	37.62	+ 7.9
Hilton Hotels	37.25	51.9	45.75	+ 22.8
Home Depot (4-for-3)**	38.62	9.5	41.50	+ 43.3
Homestake Mining	19.25	26.0	18.75	− 2.6
Kellogg (2-for-1)*	75.88	51.5	60.38	+ 59.1
Kerr-McGee	44.88	52.4	46.75	+ 4.2
Kimberly-Clark (2-for-1)*	84.00	50.6	52.88	+ 25.9
King World Products	24.50	0.0	40.75	+ 66.3
Monarch Machine Tool	10.25	38.5	11.25	+ 9.8
Monsanto	48.25	41.8	68.00	+ 40.9
Moore Corporation	22.75	58.0	19.50	− 14.3
Average price change				+ 40.0
Mean payout ratio		39.7		
Standard deviation		21.3		
Eliminate level		61.0		
Buy level		18.4		
Price action of one stock at 61.0 or above				+ 21.3
Price action of three stocks at 18.4 or below				+ 73.5

*Stock split two-for-one.
**Stock split four-for-three.

hand two felt-tip pens, one red, one green. Place your *Value Line* sheets in a neat stack in front of you. Take the first two stocks, and begin a detailed comparison of the following factors.

Table 16-3

Credit Cyclical	Capital Goods–Technology
Fedders	None
Consumer Growth	**Energy**
Gannett	Exxon
Gap, Inc.	Kerr-McGee
Home Depot	**Basic Industries**
King World Products	Federal Paper Board
Moore Corporation	Homestake Mining
Consumer Cyclical	Kimberly-Clark
Hilton Hotels	Monsanto
Consumer Staples	**Financial**
General Mills	Federal National Mortgage
Heinz, H.J.	**Transportation**
Kellogg (2-for-1)	Federal Express
Capital Goods	**Conglomerates**
General Electric	None
Monarch Machine Tool	**Utilities**
	None

- Examine the P/E ratio of each stock. If one P/E seems too high, circle it in red. If either one seems quite reasonable, circle it in green.

- If you are looking for better-than-average income, go through the same exercise with the yield on each stock. All the way through this exercise, red is an unfavorable mark, and green is favorable.

- Go through the same process by examining other value factors, such as the price-to-revenue per share, the price-to-cash flow, and the price-to-book value. Always be ready to wield your red and green pens.

- Look at the payout ratio, again using your two felt-tip pens, if there is a significant difference.

- Using your calculator, ascertain the compound growth rate of (1) cash value, (2) earnings per share, (3) dividends, (4) revenues per share, and (5) book value per share. Once again, underline or circle favorable items in green and unfavorable ones in red.

- Examine the balance sheet to see how much debt the company has, relative to shareholders' equity. More red and green markings.

- Have there been any significant purchases or sales by insiders? Ignore one or two, but be on the lookout for three or more in the last month or two.

- Check to see if the return on equity is too high or too low. A fairly normal return is 15 percent. A company with 20 percent return on equity probably has better prospects than one with 11 or 12 percent.

- Read *Value Line*'s comments on each stock, underlining in red unfavorable comments and in green those that are favorable.

As you can see, your judgment comes into play here. Even so, it is a good exercise for someone with an analytical mind. When you have completed your analysis of these two stocks, ask yourself which one you would sell if someone held a gun to your head. Place that one at the bottom of the pile, and discard the one you would retain. Continue this procedure by examining the next two *Value Line* sheets. After each analysis, place the loser at the bottom of the pack.

When you are down to one stock, that's the one to sell. If it goes up, shoot yourself for having no analytical ability.

17

The Ultimate Road to Wealth

This chapter is devoted to a more complicated method of stock selection. I have saved it for now for two reasons:

1. I didn't introduce it earlier because I am certain it would have frightened off lethargic louts who might be intimidated by excessive calculations. Because you have persevered to the bitter end, I can only assume you are made of sterner stuff.

2. I wanted to finish with a flourish—leave you "gasping," so to speak. Without question, this is my best system of stock selection—assuming you are interested primarily in growth rather than income.

The Four Factors Used

This method should only be used on good quality stocks. Thus, I restrict its use to stocks which are rated at least A– by the *Standard & Poor's Stock Guide.* Preferably, the stocks used should be from the S&P 500. Here are the four factors I use:

1. The price/earnings (P/E) ratio, based on the most recent 12-month's earnings.

2. The price/earnings ratio, based on the median earnings during the last four years. This means that the two worst earnings-per-share figures should be eliminated and the calculation based on the next worst. For example, let's assume the earnings in the last five years

were as follows: $3.50, $2.92, $1.78, $3.12, and $2.04. You would eliminate the two worst ($1.78 and $2.04), and base your P/E calculation on $2.92.

3. The payout ratio, based on the most recent 12-month's earnings and the indicated annual dividend.

4. The payout ratio based on the median earnings per share—the same one described in the normalized P/E step.

It May Seem Complicated at First

So far, this is not too complicated, but it gets a little sticky in the next step. In effect, it gives more weight to the payout numbers. That's why this method produces stocks with extraordinary growth potential.

To give you an idea of how it has worked in the past, I went through my notebooks of previous test portfolios and picked out 10 samples at random. The stocks with the best scores (the top 16 percent—using the standard deviation) were pitted against the group as a whole. See Table 17-1.

Table 17-1

An unbiased sample of tests taken at various times and for periods of varying length. On the left are the stocks selected by the system. On the right is the performance of the entire group from which these selections were taken.

	Best scorers (top 16 percent) (%)	Group as a whole (%)
	+ 23.7	+ 7.4
	+ 23.3	+ 16.3
	+ 43.9	+ 0.7
	+ 22.7	+ 11.3
	+ 53.6	+ 21.5
	+ 14.7	+ 43.1
	+ 59.4	+ 39.1
	+ 37.9	+ 23.1
	+ 47.2	+ 18.0
	+ 78.7	+ 31.2
Averages	+ 40.5	+ 21.2

It should not be assumed that these are the results for one year. The periods vary in length but are at least one year in duration.

With this brief overview, let me tell you in exact detail how to use this system, which I call "The Ultimate Road to Wealth."

How I Came to Develop This System

Some 15 years ago—I can't precisely tell you when—I wondered if there was some way I could grade stocks so you could tell instantly how attractive they were.

Prior to that time, I had always used my grid system, giving points to each factor, adding up the points, and picking those with the fewest points. The trouble with that approach is that you can't single out one stock and determine how it ranks. In other words, you have to pit it against 15 or 20 others before you can make this determination.

The method described here does not require this step.

In addition, I wanted a scoring system that was somewhat similar to the grading system used in school, where 90 and over is excellent and 80 and over is above average.

Here's How I Went about It

In order to accomplish this task, I first had to determine which factors to use. I decided that the two most important were the P/E ratio (to ensure value) and the payout ratio (a growth factor). By combining these two key ratios, I would have a stock that was not overpriced and yet had growth potential.

But how to put this into a classroom-type scoring system?

The First Breakthrough

It suddenly dawned on me. Let's first look at the P/E ratio. As you may know, a typical price/earnings ratio is somewhere between 15 and 25. As it stands, however, using the P/E ratio would not make much sense because whoever heard of a grade in school of 15, 18, or 23?

This was solved by deducting the P/E from 100. Thus, a P/E of 21 becomes 79, which is beginning to look more like a grade Miss Abernathy might award you on your solid geometry paper.

Because a low P/E ratio is considered good, and a high P/E is considered bad, this approach sounded quite logical. A P/E of 12 translates into a score of 88, and one of 34 translates into a score of 66—obviously a failing grade.

I sensed that I was onto something important—but I had no idea then that this was a revolutionary idea. No one in the entire world of investments had ever concocted such an idea. Or, if they did, it does not appear in any book I have ever read.

What about the Payout Ratio?

Next, I wondered if I could use the same approach on the payout ratio. You may recall that the payout ratio is the percentage of earnings paid out to shareholders in the form of dividends. If a company earns $3.50 and pays out $1.75, that's a typical payout ratio of 50 percent. If, instead, they pay out $2.50, that is a payout ratio of 71.4 percent and is not characteristic of a growth company. By contrast, if the company had a $1 annual dividend, that would be a payout of 28.6 percent. Such a stock might not appeal to an income-oriented investor, but it would certainly be a good bet for an investor seeking maximum growth of capital.

I decided that the payout ratio could be treated in the same fashion as the P/E ratio. In the first instance, you would deduct 71.4 from 100 and get a score of 28.60. Miss Abernathy, I am sure, would consider that a flunking grade. On the other hand, the score of 28.6, if deducted from 100, becomes a much more acceptable score of 71.4.

If you are still with me, you have the essence of my breathtaking system.

Making It a Bit More Complicated

Nothing, of course, is ever that simple. The P/E ratio, for instance, can be difficult to calculate if the company has had a bad year and earns only 25 cents, down from $2.75 the prior year. If you try to divide 25 cents into a stock selling for $32, the P/E is an astronomical 128.

The same thing holds true for the payout ratio. If the same company had a dividend of $1 and earnings per share (EPS) of 25 cents, the payout ratio would be impossible to calculate.

Thus, in order to qualify for inclusion in this system, the company's dividend must be less than its earnings per share. When you check the stock in the *Standard & Poor's Stock Guide,* you can quickly determine if this is the case. All you do is look at the indicated dividend and the earnings per share for the most recent 12 months. Reject any stock whose dividend is greater than the EPS in the most recent 12 months.

The Normalized P/E and Payout Ratios

This next concept is a bit sticky. I call it the normalized P/E and pay-out ratio. In your *Stock Guide* are the earnings per share for the past four years. In order to calculate the normalized figure, eliminate the two worst years and then take the next one. Let's look at an example.

At the end of August 1991, Ball Corporation had yearly earnings as follows: $2.80 (for 1987), $1.40, $1.44, and $2.03 (for 1990). The latest 12-month EPS number was $2.10.

In order to determine the normalized EPS, we delete the two worst years: $1.40 and $1.44. That means that $2.03 is the number we want because it is the next lowest—in other words, a sort of median figure.

The price of the stock on that date was $34.62. If you divide $2.03 into $34.62, the normalized P/E ratio is 17.55. Deduct this from 100, and you get a score for this factor of 82.45.

The same approach is used to calculate the normalized payout ratio. In this instance, Ball had an annual dividend of $1.20. If you divide $2.03 into $1.20, you get 59.1 percent (after multiplying by 100). Deduct that from 100, and you get a final answer of 40.9.

To arrive at the final score for Ball Corporation, these four num-bers—the two P/E scores and the two payout scores—are added up and divided by four. Now, you can see why I left this chapter until last. Only a devoted investor, bent on maximizing her results, would be still reading the book.

Although this method of stock selection sounds intimidating, it is actually not quite as bad as it appears. Once you do a few stocks, you will experience only a modest amount of trauma.

Believe me, the trauma is worth it because the results are nothing short of breathtaking. No other system works as well or as consis-tently.

Another Example

Now that you are swimming in a sea of confusion and bewilderment, it's time to tackle another example. This time, you had better get out your calculator and work along with me.

Let's look at Bristol-Myers (BMY) as of August 31, 1991. Here are the numbers you will need:

- The price of the stock: $87
- The indicated dividend: $2.40
- 1987 earnings per share: $2.47

- 1988 earnings per share: $2.39
- 1989 earnings per share: $1.43
- 1990 earnings per share: $3.33
- Most recent 12-month's earnings per share: $3.64

With these numbers in front of you—and your calculator in hand—you are ready to solve the problem.

Step One. Calculate the P/E ratio by dividing $87 by $3.64, which gives you 23.90. Subtract from 100, which gives you a score of 76.10.

Step Two. Calculate the normalized P/E ratio by first determining what the normalized figure is. This is accomplished by eliminating the two lowest EPS figures, which are $1.43 and $2.39. The next lowest number is $2.47. You divide this into $87 and get 35.22. Deduct from 100, giving you a score of 64.78.

Step Three. Calculate the payout ratio by dividing the indicated dividend ($2.40) by the most recent 12-month's earnings per share ($3.64). The answer is 65.9 percent. This may mystify you because your figure is 0.659. That means you have to multiply by 100 to get 65.9 percent. Now, deduct this from 100 to obtain the answer you are looking for, which is 34.1.

Step Four. Calculating the normalized payout ratio is almost impossible because the dividend is nearly the same as the normalized earnings of $2.47. You shouldn't be too surprised when BMY gets a very poor score. You divide the dividend ($2.40) by the normalized EPS ($2.47) and get 0.972. Multiply by 100 to get 97.2. Deduct from 100 to obtain your final score for this factor: 2.83.

Step Five. The last step is simple: add up the four individual scores and divide by four:

    76.10
    64.75
    34.07
     2.83

177.75 divided by four gives you 44.44

With a score like this, Miss Abernathy would immediately call your father and order him to whip your gluteus maximus with a stout leather strap. It would have been justified because Bristol-Myers turned out to be a bummer, declining from $87 to $56.12 in the two-year period from August 31, 1991, to the same date in 1993.

One More for the Road

If you are still a bit shaky on how to proceed, let's try another example; this time we'll use Walt Disney.

Here are the numbers you will need:

- The price of the stock: $118.75
- The indicated dividend: $0.70
- 1987 earnings per share: $3.23
- 1988 earnings per share: $3.80
- 1989 earnings per share: $5.10
- 1990 earnings per share: $6.00
- Most recent 12-month's earnings per share: $5.19

With these numbers in front of you—and your calculator in hand—you are ready to deal with the second problem.

Step One. Calculate the P/E ratio by dividing $118.75 by $5.19, which gives you 22.88. Subtract from 100, which gives you a score of 77.12.

Step Two. Calculate the normalized P/E ratio by first determining what the normalized figure is. Next, eliminate the two lowest EPS figures, which are $3.23 and $3.80. The next lowest number is $5.10. You divide this into $118.75 and get 23.28. Deduct from 100, giving you a score of 76.72.

Step Three. Calculate the payout ratio by dividing the indicated dividend ($.70) by the most recent 12-month's earnings per share ($5.19). The answer is 13.49 percent. Now, deduct this from 100 to find the answer you are looking for, which is 86.51. This is not the number you use, however because I prefer to keep this score to a maximum of 80. The reason: I don't want the payout ratio to overshadow the P/E ratio any more than it already does.

Step Four. Calculate the normalized payout ratio. You divide the dividend ($.70) by the normalized EPS ($5.10) and get 13.73—after making sure you multiply by 100. Next, deduct 13.73 from 100 to obtain your final score for this factor: 86.27. Finally, reduce it to 80.

Step Five. The last step is simple: add up the four individual scores and divide by four.

77.12

76.72

80.00

80.00

313.84 divided by four gives you 78.46.

This is an excellent score, as you will see later. In most instances, it is best to buy stocks that score close to 80.

Assuming you have done everything right so far, you can hold your head high. Miss Abernathy would be proud of you.

The Proof of the Pudding

Now that you have a grasp of the fundamentals, my next objective is to convince you to use this stock selection system whenever you are seeking three or four stocks for maximum capital gains.

In order to demonstrate how effective this method of stock selection is, I dusted off an old copy of the *Standard & Poor's Stock Guide,* in this case the September 1991 issue.

I opened the book at random and selected the first stock rated at least A– that was also designated as part of the S&P 500. Also important, the dividend had to be smaller than the earnings per share for the most recent 12 months. Table 17-2 shows 20 stocks selected in this way.

In order to test the validity of this sample, we must resort to the standard deviation. If you don't have a sophisticated calculator, you can simply pick the 16 percent with the highest score. If you multiply 16 percent by 20, you get a figure of 3.2, which means there are three winning stocks, which, in this illustration, is precisely the number the standard deviation will give you.

For those who care to make the calculation, the mean (or average) score is 66.45. Add in the standard deviation of 9.95 and you get a buying level of 76.40. Table 17-3 shows the three stocks you should buy.

If you compare the price appreciation of the three stocks, it compares very favorably with the average price change of the whole list, which was only 16.07 percent.

I have made no attempt to figure in dividends. Because most of these stocks will have low dividends, total return would not be materially affected.

Table 17-2

Stocks selected on August 31, 1991, and held for two years.

Stock	P/E	N-P/E	Payout	N-Payout	Final score	Two-year price change (%)
			Factor Scores			
Ball Corporation	83.51	82.94	40.89	41.00	62.07	+ 3.62
Baltimore G&E	83.72	89.75	Nil	31.15	51.16	+ 32.00
Banc One	84.22	81.10	60.00	52.07	69.35	+ 56.28
Bristol-Myers	76.10	64.75	34.07	2.83	44.44	− 35.49
Brown-Forman	84.83	77.04	54.57	30.86	61.83	+ 6.53
Brown. Ferris	81.20	81.20	50.36	50.36	65.78	− 3.88
Bruno's	80.64	73.09	75.61	66.10	73.86	− 33.07
Charming Shoppes	78.91	74.37	80.00	80.00	78.32	+ 19.76
Cooper Industries	80.91	77.79	60.27	53.78	68.19	− 7.17
Cooper Tire	77.80	74.21	80.00	80.00	78.00	+ 46.08
CoreStates	73.95	88.08	Nil	49.10	52.78	+ 24.13
Corning	77.79	77.00	65.55	67.43	71.94	− 11.50
Dillards	75.56	69.90	80.00	80.00	76.37	− 18.00
Disney, Walt	77.12	76.72	80.00	80.00	78.46	+ 32.21
Dominion Resources	88.04	88.70	16.91	21.46	53.78	+ 45.08
Donnelley, R.R.	82.05	83.08	62.12	64.29	73.14	+ 29.82
Dover	83.62	83.11	64.26	63.16	73.54	+ 36.04
Dow Jones	73.36	87.44	23.23	63.81	61.96	+ 18.96
Exxon	87.76	85.25	43.70	32.15	62.22	+ 12.23
First Union	88.90	89.38	53.53	55.56	71.84	+ 67.76
Mean score					66.45	
Standard deviation					9.95	
Buy level					76.40	
Average price change for all 20 stocks						+ 16.07

Another Example

One test, to be sure, does not prove very much. Let's look at a more recent group, as of June 30, 1992. The ending date will be October 31, 1993.

In Table 17-4, I spare your bloodshot eyes by omitting the individual factor scores, giving you only the final score.

Table 17-3

Stock	Two-year price change (%)
Charming Shoppes	+ 19.76
Cooper Tire	+ 46.08
Disney, Walt	+ 32.21
Average price appreciation	+ 32.68

Table 17-4

Stock	Final score	Price change 6-30-92 to 10-31-93 (%)
Walgreen	72.44	+ 25.46
Wal-Mart	69.07	− 1.86
Air Products	70.64	− 1.76
Ameritech	54.71	+ 34.79
Anheuser-Busch	73.28	− 14.19
Bankers Trust	78.45	+ 34.89
Bard, C.R.	68.09	+ 2.02
Barnett Banks	57.29	+ 12.79
Bausch & Lomb	58.83	+ 8.64
Capital Cities	79.54	+ 33.47
Capital Holding	82.11	+ 38.49
Carolina Power	58.27	+ 25.25
Coastal Corporation	64.40	+ 10.05
Coca-Cola	61.59	+ 8.44
Dayton Hudson	71.71	+ 3.73
Deluxe	60.23	− 15.88
Detroit Edison	67.34	+ 7.60
Emerson Electric	66.81	+ 17.69
Fleming	65.56	− 10.55
Grainger	76.09	+ 18.40
Mean score	67.82	
Standard deviation	7.84	
Buy level	75.66	
Average price change for all 20 stocks		+ 11.88

For those who care to make the calculation, the mean (or average) score is 67.82. Add in the standard deviation of 7.84, and you get a buying level of 75.66. Table 17-5 shows the four stocks you should buy.

If you examine the price appreciation of the four stocks, it compares very favorably with the average price change of the whole list, which was only 11.88 percent.

What about Income?

As noted earlier, this method of picking big winners is best used by investors who are seeking capital gains, not income. Most of the best stocks selected in this manner have low yields.

Table 17-5

Stock	Price change 6-30-92 to 10-31-93 (%)
Bankers Trust	+ 34.89
Capital Cities	+ 33.47
Capital Holding	+ 38.49
Grainger	+ 18.43
Average price appreciation	+ 31.32

Table 17-6

Stock	Final score	Price change 6-30-92 to 10-31-93 (%)
Ameritech	54.71	+ 34.79
Bankers Trust	78.45	+ 34.89
Barnett Banks	57.29	+ 12.79
Carolina Power	58.27	+ 25.25
Deluxe	60.23	− 15.88
Detroit Edison	67.34	+ 7.60
Emerson Electric	66.81	+ 17.69
Mean score	63.58	
Standard deviation	7.63	
Buy level	71.21	

On the other hand, I believe that you could adapt this system to income stocks. For instance, if we calculate the yields on the stocks in Table 17-2, the average yield is 2.7 percent.

Table 17-6 shows the stocks with at least a 2.7 percent yield, listed in alphabetical order.

You will note that only one stock has a score that qualifies it for purchase: Bankers Trust, which was a big winner.

Let's go back to the first example (see Table 17-2) and see if the same pattern exists.

Here are the stocks with at least a 2.8 percent yield, listed in alphabetical order. See Table 17-7.

You will note that only one stock has a score that qualifies it for purchase: First Union, which was a big winner.

How about Some Ancient History?

So far, I have shown you two examples of how this unique system has worked recently. Now, let's go back and look at some ancient history. Table 17-8 shows how some Dow Jones stocks performed from 1978 to April 30, 1985. It assumes that stocks purchased were not disturbed during this long period.

Table 17-7

Stock	Final score	Two-year price change (%)
Ball Corporation	62.07	+ 3.62
Baltimore Gas & Electric	51.16	+ 32.00
Bristol-Myers	44.44	− 35.49
Brown-Forman	61.83	+ 6.53
CoreStates	52.78	+ 24.13
Dominion Resources	53.78	+ 45.08
Dow Jones	61.96	+ 18.96
Exxon	62.22	+ 12.23
First Union	71.84	+ 67.76
Mean score	58.01	
Standard deviation	8.15	
Buy level	66.16	

Table 17-8

Stock	Final score	Price change 12-31-78 to 4-30-85 (%)
Allied Corporation	75.20	+ 136.3
American Brands	62.62	+ 155.6
American Can	72.10	+ 48.1
AT&T	61.62	+ 35.5
Chevron	73.85	+ 58.4
Du Pont	62.00	+ 32.1
Eastman Kodak	65.02	+ 13.5
Exxon	65.10	+ 109.7
General Electric	66.78	+ 150.9
General Foods	70.95	+ 96.1
General Motors	70.18	+ 25.8
Goodyear Tire	70.32	+ 60.5
IBM	52.52	+ 69.5
Merck	64.60	+ 61.2
Minnesota Mining & Manufacturing	63.02	+ 22.0
Owens-Illinois	78.90	+ 146.9
Procter & Gamble	64.78	+ 17.3
Sears, Roebuck	72.30	+ 71.5
Texaco	62.58	+ 68.1
Union Carbide	73.82	+ 12.9
United Technologies	77.25	+ 96.1
Woolworth	78.00	+ 123.2
Mean score	68.34	
Standard deviation	6.60	
Buy level	74.94	
Average price change for all 20 stocks		+ 73.2

For those who care to make the calculation, the mean (or average) score is 68.34. Add in the standard deviation of 6.60 and you get a buying level of 74.94. Table 17-9 shows the four stocks you should buy.

If you look at the price appreciation of the four stocks, it compares very favorably with the average price change of the whole list, which was only 73.2 percent.

Table 17-9

Stock	Price change 12-31-78 to 4-30-85 (%)
Allied Corporation	+ 136.3
Owens-Illinois	+ 146.9
United Technologies	+ 96.1
Woolworth	+ 123.2
Average price appreciation	+ 125.6

Table 17-10

Stock	Final score	Price change 5-31-84 to 5-31-85 (%)
Chemical N.Y.	78.05	+ 71.5
Citicorp	80.30	+ 65.8
Columbia Gas	69.28	− 3.5
Consolidated Edison NY	70.15	+ 43.4
Consolidated Natural Gas	70.57	+ 31.6
Duke Power	62.75	+ 44.6
Enserch	54.38	+ 18.7
Exxon	70.00	+ 35.4
First International Bank	77.88	+ 60.6
Florida Power & Light	57.72	+ 36.6
Mean score	69.11	
Standard deviation	8.65	
Buy level	77.76	
Average price change for all 10 stocks		+ 40.5

An Interesting High-Yield Illustration

For those who are interested primarily in stocks with a high yield, Table 17-10 provides an example taken from 1984. All of these stocks had a high yield and included utilities, banks, and oil companies.

For those who care to make the calculation, the mean (or average) score is 69.11. Add in the standard deviation of 8.65, and you get a buying level of 77.76. Table 17-11 shows the three stocks you should buy.

Table 17-11

Stock	Price change 5-31-84 to 5-31-85 (%)
Chemical New York	+ 71.5
Citicorp	+ 65.8
First International Bank	+ 60.6
Average price appreciation	+ 66.0

If you examine the price appreciation of the three stocks, it compares very favorably with the average price change of the whole list, which was only 40.5 percent.

How about Some Real Proof!

So far, I have shown you four illustrations taken from my notebooks. Next, in Table 17-12 I will show you every test I have conducted on this idea, many of them dating back to the mid-1970s.

Among the 30 tests, the system worked 27 times and failed only three times, as denoted by an asterisk. What's more, the average price appreciation of the system stocks beat the groups they came from by an astounding 87 percent (calculated by dividing 75.20 percent into 40.21 percent).

How to Use This System

Now that you understand how to grade stocks, the next problem is which stocks to grade. This is where your judgment comes into play. By now, you should have some idea which stocks seem attractive to you. Here are characteristics to look for. Try to find stocks that have most of these characteristics:

- A rising trend of earnings, dividends, and book value per share.
- A balance sheet with less debt than other companies in its particular industry.
- An S&P rating of A− or better.
- A P/E ratio no higher than average.
- A yield that you find acceptable.

Table 17-12

	Price action of system stocks (%)	Price action of group (%)
	+ 31.32	+ 11.88
	+ 8.30	+ 5.73
	+ 32.48	+ 28.43
	+ 125.63	+ 73.20
	+ 63.80	+ 38.68
	+ 65.97	+ 40.47
	+ 31.08	+ 34.54*
	+ 14.70	+ 43.07*
	+ 59.38	+ 39.10
	+ 43.96	+ 23.10
	+ 47.15	+ 18.00
	+ 78.67	+ 31.20
	+ 83.10	+ 68.10
	+ 40.50	+ 25.90
	+ 87.10	+ 68.70
	+ 37.60	+ 8.80
	+ 74.50	+ 38.50
	+ 205.07	+ 70.60
	− 6.45	− 13.40
	+ 92.65	+ 68.60
	+ 229.40	+ 113.00
	+ 71.82	+ 36.60
	+ 46.00	+ 62.30*
	+ 206.90	+ 50.60
	+ 97.25	+ 56.50
	+ 36.10	+ 22.58
	+ 5.47	+ 4.17
	+ 32.68	+ 16.97
Averages	+ 75.20	+ 40.21

*The time the system failed.

- No heavy selling by insiders.
- Below-average payout ratios.
- Low popularity with institutions.
- A history of earnings and dividends that is not pockmarked by erratic ups and downs.
- A return on equity of 15 percent or better.
- A ratio of price to cash flow per share that is reasonable when compared to other stocks in its industry.

18

How to Restructure a Growth Portfolio

Most people buy stocks one at a time, without any conscious effort to build a diversified, well-rounded portfolio. They quite often favor certain industries such as utilities, oils, or banks. Or, they may pick stocks because of their high yields or because they know someone on the board of directors.

Whatever the strategy—if, indeed, there is a strategy—they often wind up with a jumbled assortment of stocks—perhaps 50 shares, often 100 shares, sometimes 200 shares—that doesn't stand up to the standards that would satisfy a professional.

In order to demonstrate some ideas on how to restructure one of these random assortments, I picked 15 stocks by letting my fingers do the walking. I used the 250 stocks that are monitored in our monthly market letter, *The Hickory 250*, which is available to investors by writing to Hickory Investment Advisors (see address at end of Introduction).

The stocks in this service are arranged by sector, such as basic industries, financial, utilities, consumer growth, and so forth. To construct the hypothetical portfolio in Table 18-1, I methodically worked my way through the list, picking every twentieth stock, paying no heed to which sector it was in.

The first thing you must do when restructuring a portfolio is to determine the objective of the investor. Let's assume that this couple is looking for growth of capital. They are conservative and want to own stocks that are least average in quality (B+). They are willing to take some risk.

Table 18-1

The portfolio of a man and woman, ages 43 and 41, whose objective is primarily growth of capital, using good-quality stocks.

Shares owned	Stock	Price 10-31-93 ($)	S&P rating	Dividend yield (%)	P/E ratio	Institu- tional owners	Total value ($)
100	ALCOA	68.00	B−	2.4	NM	520	6,800
300	AMP	62.38	B+	2.6	22.1	574	18,712
100	American International Group	90.00	A+	0.4	15.3	861	9,000
100	American Home Products	62.50	A+	4.7	13.4	952	6,250
300	Centerior Energy	15.00	B	10.7	16.3	177	4,500
100	Consolidated Freight	21.75	B−	Nil	NM	171	2,175
200	Genuine Parts	37.88	A+	2.8	18.8	407	7,576
50	Hitachi	79.25	NR	1.1	39.6	60	3,962
200	International Paper	59.50	B+	2.8	NM	601	11,900
200	Kroger	19.62	B	Nil	12.7	258	3,925
100	SCEcorp	21.12	A	6.7	14.5	484	2,112
100	Stanley Works	43.12	A−	3.2	19.2	269	4,312
200	Syntex	18.12	A	5.7	13.9	436	3,625
100	Texas Instruments	65.62	B−	1.1	14.7	468	6,562
200	Union Carbide	19.75	NR	3.8	23.0	342	3,950
Total value of portfolio							95,361

NR = No rating.
NM = Not meaningful.

To get a better picture of this portfolio, it is necessary to show how these stocks fit into a matrix of the 12 sectors that I discussed in Chapter 5 on diversification and asset allocation. In Table 18-2, the stocks are listed in their respective sectors, along with the percentage of assets in each sector.

The first problem with this portfolio is the poor distribution of the stocks among the 12 sectors.

Table 18-2

A sector analysis.

Shares owned	Stock	Price 10-31-93 ($)	S&P rating	Dividend yield (%)	P/E ratio	Institutional owners	Total value ($)
			Basic Industries				
100	ALCOA	68.00	B−	2.4	NM	520	6,800
200	International Paper	59.50	B+	2.8	NM	601	11,900
200	Union Carbide	19.75	NR	3.8	23.0	342	3,950
Total sector value (23.8 percent of total)							22,650
			Consumer Cyclical				
200	Genuine Parts	37.88	A+	2.8	18.8	407	7,576
Total sector value (7.9 percent of total)							7,576
			Energy				
No stocks represented							
			Credit Cyclical				
100	Stanley Works	43.12	A−	3.2	19.2	269	4,312
Total sector value (4.5 percent of total)							4,312
			Consumer Staples				
200	Kroger	19.62	B	Nil	12.7	258	3,925
Total sector value (4.1 percent of total)							3,925
			Capital Goods–Technology				
300	AMP	62.38	B+	2.6	22.1	574	18,712
100	Texas Instruments	65.62	B−	1.1	14.7	468	6,562
Total sector value (26.5 percent of total)							25,274
			Consumer Growth				
100	American Home Products	62.50	A+	4.7	13.4	952	6,250
200	Syntex	18.12	A	5.7	13.9	436	3,625
Total sector value (10.4 percent of total)							9,875

Table 18-2 (*Continued*)
A sector analysis.

Shares owned	Stock	Price 10-31-93 ($)	S&P rating	Dividend yield (%)	P/E ratio	Institutional owners	Total value ($)
		Utilities					
300	Centerior Energy	15.00	B	10.7	16.3	177	4,500
100	SCEcorp	21.12	A	6.7	14.5	484	2,112
Total sector value (6.9 percent of total)							6,612
		Conglomerates					
No stocks represented							
		Transportation					
100	Consolidated Freight	21.75	B−	Nil	NM	171	2,175
Total sector value (2.3 percent of total)							2,175
		Capital Goods					
50	Hitachi	79.25	NR	1.1	39.6	60	3,962
Total sector value (4.2 percent of total)							3,962
		Financial					
100	American International Group	90.00	A+	0.4	15.3	861	9,000
Total sector value (9.4 percent of total)							9,000

Based on the investor's objectives, this portfolio has a number of deficiencies. When we begin managing the portfolio of a new client, we frequently encounter situations that need a lot of work, as this one does.

We Avoid Wholesale Eradication

However, we do not immediately correct every fault. Instead, we work at it gradually. You might wonder why. Well, for one thing, most investors have owned their stocks for a number of years and would not look kindly on their wholesale eradication. Second, we want to take our time so as to be sure we are making the right move. Finally, we are extremely careful not to sell stocks with large built-in capital gains. If at all possible, we try to offset these gains against losses from other stocks.

Our procedure is to review each portfolio regularly, normally every six weeks. At that time, we might make one or two changes, waiting until later before making another switch.

But to show you how the final portfolio shapes up, I will make all necessary changes at once.

One Glaring Weakness

One major shortcoming is uneven representation in the 12 sectors, which were discussed in the Chapter 5 on diversification. If you examine Table 18-2, it should be obvious that the investor failed to be represented in all sectors. For instance, there are no stocks in either energy or conglomerates. Certain other sectors have too great a concentration of assets; others have too little.

My rule of thumb is to have at least 4 percent of the portfolio in each sector but no more than 12 percent. Typically, this translates into having at least one stock in each sector but no more than three.

The clients also said they wanted quality stocks, and yet several are rated less than B+, which is average. My suggestion is to sell these stocks first (see Table 18-3), with the exception of Hitachi, which is not rated. (Most foreign stocks are not rated by the *Stock Guide*.)

Table 18-3

Stocks to be removed from portfolio.

Shares owned	Stock	Price 10-31-93 ($)	S&P rating	Dividend yield (%)	P/E ratio	Institu- tional owners	Total value ($)
100	ALCOA	68.00	B−	2.4	NM	520	6,800
200	Union Carbide	19.75	NR	3.8	23.0	342	3,950
200	Kroger	19.62	B	Nil	12.7	258	3,925
100	Texas Instruments	65.62	B−	1.1	14.7	468	6,562
300	Centerior Energy	15.00	B	10.7	16.3	177	4,500
100	Consolidated Freight	21.75	B−	Nil	NM	171	2,175
	Total value of stocks to be eliminated						27,912

Whittle Down Some of the Sectors

With this task accomplished, we will have proceeds that can be invested in sectors that are below the 4 percent level. But before doing that, it would be a good idea to whittle down some of the sectors that are still top-heavy—those with more than 12 percent representation.

The first stock to get the ax will be International Paper because it represents 12.5 percent of the portfolio. Let's sell

100	International Paper	$59.50	B+	2.8	NM	601	$5,950

The next one to get the knife will be AMP. Even though it is an excellent company, it represents 19.6 percent of the portfolio. Let's sell

200	AMP	$62.38	B+	2.6	22.1	574	$12,485

The final stock to be reduced in size is American International Group. Here again, it is a fine company, but it constitutes 9.4 percent of the total. I suggest we sell half:

50	American International Group	$90.00	A+	0.4	15.3	861	$4,500

If all of these moves are made, the proceeds will total $50,847, or just over one-half the portfolio. As stated earlier, this process will take place over many months, perhaps as long as one year. Seen in this light, it is not quite as drastic a transformation.

High Turnover Is Not Needed

By contrast, many mutual fund portfolio managers will turn over 100 percent of the portfolio in one year—and some may turn over 200 percent. It is my contention that such high turnover is not needed. It merely increases transaction costs and generates capital gains, which are passed on to the investor.

Selecting the Replacements

Now that we have $50,847 to work with, the next step is to select some replacements.

Table 18-4

A sector analysis.

Shares owned	Stock	Price 10-31-93 ($)	S&P rating	Dividend yield (%)	P/E ratio	Institu- tional owners	Total value ($)
			Basic Industries				
50	Great Lakes Ch	76.38	A−	0.5	20.7	494	3,819
50	International Paper	59.50	B+	2.8	NM	601	2,975
Total sector value (7.1 percent of total)							6,794
			Consumer Cyclical				
200	Genuine Parts	37.88	A+	2.8	18.8	407	7,576
Total sector value (7.9 percent of total)							7,576
			Energy				
200	Repsol	29.62	NR	2.1	14.2	NR	5,925
100	Elf Aquitaine	39.00	NR	2.2	17.6	87	3,900
Total sector value (10.3 percent of total)							9,825
			Credit Cyclical				
100	Stanley Works	43.12	A−	3.2	19.2	269	4,312
Total sector value (4.5 percent of total)							4,312
			Consumer Staples				
100	Procter & Gamble	54.25	A−	2.3	NM	833	5,425
200	Sara Lee	26.50	A+	2.2	18.5	635	5,000
Total sector value (11.2 percent of total)							10,725
			Capital Goods–Technology				
100	AMP	62.38	B+	2.6	22.1	574	6,238
200	EG&G	18.00	A	3.1	12.5	235	3,600
Total sector value (10.3 percent of total)							9,838
			Consumer Growth				
100	American Home Products	62.50	A+	4.7	13.4	952	6,250
200	Syntex	18.12	A	5.7	13.9	436	3,625
Total sector value (10.4 percent of total)							9,875

Table 18-4 (*Continued*)
A sector analysis.

Shares owned	Stock	Price 10-31-93 ($)	S&P rating	Dividend yield (%)	P/E ratio	Institu-tional owners	Total value ($)
			Utilities				
50	British Telecomm	69.75	NR	3.6	23.4	139	3,488
100	SCEcorp	21.12	A	6.7	14.5	484	2,112
Total sector value (5.9 percent of total)							5,600
			Conglomerates				
200	Alcatel	26.50	NR	1.4	13.6	74	5,300
50	Textron	55.88	A	2.2	13.7	384	2,794
Total sector value (8.5 percent of total)							8,094
			Transportation				
200	Hunt, J.B.	21.00	B+	1.0	21.6	82	4,200
Total sector value (4.4 percent of total)							4,200
			Capital Goods				
50	Hitachi	79.25	NR	1.1	39.6	60	3,962
50	General Electric	97.00	A+	2.6	16.5	1363	4,850
Total sector value (9.2 percent of total)							8,812
			Financial				
50	American International Group	90.00	A+	0.4	15.3	861	4,500
200	Banco Bilbao	25.75	NR	4.0	9.4	33	5,150
Total sector value (10.1 percent of total)							9,650

Because the client's objective is growth of capital, it will not be necessary to seek stocks with a high dividend yield. On the other hand, such stocks will not be ignored because they often perform quite well.

Still another deficiency that should be dealt with is the lack of foreign stocks. At Hickory Investment Advisors, we aim for 20 percent participation in companies based outside the United States.

The Restructured Portfolio

Table 18-4 shows the restructured portfolio.

If the moves in Table 18-4 are made, the total value of the portfolio would be $95,379, which is about the same as the original.

Here Are the Improvements

With these changes made, the portfolio has been enhanced in the following ways:

- The percentage of foreign stocks has grown to 30.2 percent, represented by Spain (Repsol, an oil company; and Banco Bilbao, a bank), France (Alcatel, a conglomerate; and Elf Aquitaine, an oil company), Great Britain (British Telecommunications), Japan (Hitachi, electric equipment and machinery maker), and Panama (Syntex, a drug company).

- In the restructured list, all 12 sectors are represented, ranging from a low of 4.5 percent (credit cyclicals) to a high of 11.2 percent (consumer staples).

- The number of stocks has been increased from 15 to 21.

- Quality has been improved, with no stock being ranked below B+. What's more, several stocks are rated A+ (General Electric, Sara Lee, Genuine Parts, American International Group, and American Home Products).

It remains to be seen, of course, whether this will prove to be a winner in the marketplace. Because all stocks are priced as of October 31, 1993, you can have the pleasure of finding out how successful I have been in my stock picking. You will, of course, want to compare the action of these stocks against the Dow Jones Industrial Average, which was 3680.59 at the end of October 1993.

19
How to Restructure an Income Portfolio

Now that you have seen how to restructure a growth portfolio, you will be able to understand the procedure involved in revamping a group of income stocks.

The client in this instance is a 68-year-old widow. Her husband never consulted her when he made stock transactions. Thus, lacking prior investment experience, she feels the need of professional help. The list has a value of $133,581.

Table 19-1 shows how the portfolio breaks down, according to sector.

What Needs to Be Done?

It doesn't take a chairman of the Federal Reserve Board to figure out that this portfolio is all out of kilter. For instance, too great a percentage of assets is concentrated in one stock: Conrail, 32.6 percent. In addition, there are some missing sectors. And, of course, some of these stocks have rather low yields.

The widow is in search of more income and asks if it's possible to increase the portfolio's yield. In order to achieve the widow's goal, we will have to sell the following stocks (see Table 19-2) because all have a yield below 2.7 percent, which is about average in today's market.

Table 19-1

A sector analysis.

Shares owned	Stock	Price 10-31-93 ($)	S&P rating	Dividend yield (%)	P/E ratio	Institutional owners	Total value ($)
			Basic Industries				
100	Ball Corp.	25.88	A−	4.8	21.4	225	2,588
200	Weyerhaeuser	39.62	B+	3.0	15.8	632	7,925
200	Worthington	18.50	A−	1.9	24.0	236	3,700
Total sector value (10.6 percent of total)							14,213
			Consumer Cyclical				
100	Goodyear Tire	44.75	B	1.3	13.6	500	4,475
Total sector value (3.4 percent of total)							4,475
			Energy				
50	Amoco	55.88	B	3.9	16.0	937	2,794
Total sector value (2.1 percent of total)							2,794
			Credit Cyclical				
No representation							
			Consumer Staples				
300	Philip Morris	53.75	A+	4.8	10.7	1275	16,125
Total sector value (12.1 percent of total)							16,125
			Capital Goods–Technology				
300	Boeing	37.50	A+	2.7	9.8	677	11,250
50	TRW	67.38	B+	2.8	20.2	377	3,369
300	Digital Equipment	35.62	C	Nil	NM	455	10,688
Total sector value (18.9 percent of total)							25,307
			Consumer Growth				
100	Bausch & Lomb	51.88	A	1.7	16.7	402	5,188
200	Times Mirror	44.88	B−	0.7	NM	303	8,975
Total sector value (10.6 percent of total)							14,163

Table 19-1 (*Continued*)

A sector analysis.

Shares owned	Stock	Price 10-31-93 ($)	S&P rating	Dividend yield (%)	P/E ratio	Institu-tional owners	Total value ($)
			Utilities				
75	Central & South West	32.62	A	5.0	16.3	465	2,447
150	Southern Company	44.88	A−	5.1	14.1	503	6,731
Total sector value (6.9 percent of total)							9,178
			Conglomerates				
No representation							
			Transportation				
700	Conrail	62.12	B−	2.1	24.3	439	43,488
Total sector value (32.6 percent of total)							43,488
			Capital Goods				
No representation							
			Financial				
100	Banc One	38.38	A+	3.2	12.2	661	3,838
Total sector value (2.9 percent of total)							3,838

Table 19-2

Stocks to be sold.

Shares owned	Stock	Price 10-31-93 ($)	S&P rating	Dividend yield (%)	P/E ratio	Institu-tional owners	Total value ($)
200	Worthington	18.50	A−	1.9	24.0	236	3,700
100	Bausch & Lomb	51.88	A	1.7	16.7	402	5,188
200	Times Mirror	44.88	B−	0.7	NM	303	8,975
700	Conrail	62.12	B−	2.1	24.3	439	43,488
100	Goodyear Tire	44.75	B	1.3	13.6	500	4,475
300	Digital Equipment	35.62	C	Nil	NM	455	10,688

Table 19-3

A restructured portfolio for income.

Shares owned	Stock	Price 10-31-93 ($)	S&P rating	Dividend yield (%)	P/E ratio	Institu- tional owners	Total value ($)
		Basic Industries					
100	*Ball Corporation	25.88	A−	4.8	21.4	225	2,588
100	*Weyerhaeuser	39.62	B+	3.0	15.8	632	3,962
100	PPG	69.75	A	3.1	24.0	498	6,975
Total sector value (10.1 percent of total)							13,525
		Consumer Cyclical					
100	Sears, Roebuck	57.38	B	2.8	NM	679	5,738
200	Woolworth	22.62	A	5.1	12.7	401	4,524
Total sector value (7.7 percent of total)							10,262
		Energy					
100	*Amoco	55.88	B	3.9	16.0	937	5,588
50	Royal Dutch	105.75	A	3.8	17.2	837	5,288
Total sector value (8.1 percent of total)							10,876
		Credit Cyclical					
100	Great Western Financial	19.12	B	4.8	NM	287	1,912
400	RPM	17.88	A+	2.9	21.0	135	7,152
Total sector value (6.8 percent of total)							9,064
		Consumer Staples					
100	*Philip Morris	53.75	A+	4.8	10.7	1275	5,375
100	CPC International	48.00	A	2.7	18.5	580	4,800
Total sector value (7.6 percent of total)							10,175
		Capital Goods-Technology					
100	*Boeing	37.50	A+	2.7	9.8	677	3,750
50	*TRW	67.38	B+	2.8	20.2	377	3,369
50	United Technologies	62.00	B	2.9	NM	508	3,100
Total sector value (7.7 percent of total)							10,219

Table 19-3 (*Continued*)
A restructured portfolio for income.

Shares owned	Stock	Price 10-31-93 ($)	S&P rating	Dividend yield (%)	P/E ratio	Institu- tional owners	Total value ($)
		Consumer Growth					
100	Dun & Bradstreet	67.00	A+	3.6	20.6	694	6,700
100	Bristol-Myers	58.88	A+	4.9	13.3	1124	5,888
100	Glaxo	20.25	NR	3.6	15.6	375	2,025
Total sector value (10.9 percent of total)							14,613
		Utilities					
200	*Central & South West	32.62	A	5.0	16.3	465	6,524
50	Bell Atlantic	63.62	A−	4.2	18.8	693	3,181
100	British Gas	53.50	NR	4.3	NM	66	5,350
Total sector value (11.3 percent of total)							15,055
		Conglomerates					
300	Hanson	20.12	NR	4.7	14.7	358	6,038
Total sector value (4.5 percent of total)							6,038
		Transportation					
100	Norfolk Southern	66.25	A−	2.9	17.9	578	6,625
Total sector value (5.0 percent of total)							6,625
		Capital Goods					
100	Hubbell A	54.00	A+	3.0	17.8	70	5,400
100	GATX	38.00	B+	3.7	13.6	158	3,800
300	Westinghouse	14.50	B+	2.8	NM	372	4,350
Total sector value (10.1 percent of total)							13,550
		Financial					
100	*Banc One	38.38	A+	3.2	12.2	661	3,838
100	Lincoln National	45.50	B+	3.3	11.3	354	4,550
200	Banco Bilbao	25.75	NR	4.0	9.4	33	5,150
Total sector value (10.1 percent of total)							13,538

*Stock from original portfolio that is still held.

If the stocks in Table 19-2 are sold, we will have $76,514 to reinvest. Additional capital will be raised when large positions are reduced. For instance, we will cut Philip Morris from 300 shares to 100. On the other hand, some positions will be increased. Table 19-3 shows the suggested final portfolio.

With these changes made, the portfolio is now worth $133,540, or about the same as when we began to manage it. It has been enhanced in the following ways:

- The foreign stocks percentage has been raised to 17.9 percent, represented by Spain (Banco Bilbao, a bank), Great Britain (Hanson PLC, a conglomerate; and Glaxo, a large drug company), and the Netherlands (Royal Dutch Petroleum).

- All 12 sectors are represented, ranging from a low of 4.5 percent (conglomerates) to a high of 11.3 percent (public utilities).

- The number of stocks has been increased from 15 to 28.

- Most important, the annual dividend payments have been increased from $3578.90 (providing a yield of 2.7 percent) to $4916 (giving the investor a yield of 3.7 percent).

These stocks were selected and priced as of October 31, 1993. By the time you read this book, at least a year will have elapsed. The chances are that some of my stock selections worked out. Unfortunately, there will be at least one or two that bombed. My hope is, of course, that the group as a whole will vindicate my stock-picking prowess. If so, I will expect you to call me at 216-781-5600, so that you can congratulate me. Please do *not* call if this portfolio proves to be an unmitigated disaster.

20

Some Maxims on How to Keep on the Straight and Narrow

I have heard of people who read the last chapter first. If it suits them, they flip back to page one to see how things develop. To satisfy such readers, I have packed a lot of wit and wisdom into this final chapter. It is done in the form of maxims, or if you prefer, do's and don'ts.

Assuming you pay heed to these little tidbits, you should become a more savvy investor. If not, call me at (216) 781-5600, and I will gladly listen to your tale of woe.

- *Don't* be too enamored of popular stocks. If everyone owns them, who is left to buy? These owners are potential sellers. Examine the number of institutional owners (in the *Standard & Poor's Stock Guide*). Avoid stocks that have more than 1000 institutional owners. Concentrate on those owned by fewer than 500 institutional owners (such as mutual funds, banks, insurance companies, and pension plans).

- *Do* your own investing, and *don't* think mutual funds are the safe-and-sane road to riches. The cost of investing in mutual funds is high, normally 1.47 percent of assets. (By contrast, an investment advisor charges only 1 percent.) Mutual funds as a group do *not* do well. Typically, they fail to do as well as the general market. One other pitfall: when you invest in a mutual fund, you inherit capital gains built up before your time. Even so, you will have to pay the tax when a capital gain is declared or paid out.

- *Do* own at least 10 different industries (out of the 80 that are available). At Hickory, we divide stocks into 12 sectors, such as financial, utilities, transportation, conglomerates, and consumer growth. We try to own one or more stocks in each of the 12 sectors. The key to investing is diversity.

Don't do anything in investing for "tax reasons." Tax shelters are poor investments. Tax loss selling is primarily a way for brokers to increase commissions. (One exception: making charitable gifts with low-cost stock can make sense if you were going to sell the stock anyway.)

SOURCE: Charles D. Ellis in *Investment Policy, How to Win the Loser's Game*, Second Edition, 1993, Business One Irwin.

- *Don't* try to predict what the market will do. Invariably, you will be wrong. And so is *everyone else*. Name one person who has consistently been right about the market. You can't because there aren't any.

- *Don't* overtrade. Every time you make a change, you must pay two commissions, and you may have to pay taxes. It is far better to buy stocks and hold them. To be sure, some will be disappointments. But the winners will more than make up for your losses.

- *Don't* sell your winners too soon. Investors tend to sell their winners and keep their losers. "When I break even, I will sell this dog," they say. It may be 10 years before this dog returns to your purchase price.

- *Don't* buy electric utilities with extraordinarily high yields. In recent years, these stocks have been disasters. More than 30 electric utilities have slashed their dividends, including Long Island Lighting, Niagara Mohawk, Centerior Energy, Ohio Edison, CMS Energy, New York State Electric & Gas, Philadelphia Electric, and Middle South Utilities—the list is almost endless.

- *Don't* hold on to a stock for sentimental reasons. This is particularly true for a large holding. We often come across investors whose portfolios are made up largely of just one stock. If it turns out to be a company like U.S. Surgical, which fell from $134 to the low $20s, you won't be too happy.

- *Do* beware of WRAP accounts. WRAP accounts, which provide advisory, reporting, investment, and other services for a single fee, now total $114.5 billion. In conventional WRAPs, the fee covers asset-allocation advice and performance reports, as well as transaction, custodial, and similar expenses. In mutual fund WRAPs, transaction, custodial, and administration expenses are passed on by the funds. Typically, brokerage houses charge you $2\frac{1}{2}$ to 3 percent for these services. This large expense is almost impossible to overcome. Outperforming the market is difficult enough. When you tack on $2\frac{1}{2}$ or 3 percent, it is close to impossible—at least on a consistent basis.

The idea of money management for the common man sells like ice cream on the Fourth of July. To date, investors have sunk about $20 billion into WRAP accounts, and the amount will hit $700 billion by the end of the decade, according to industry enthusiasts.

But there's a catch. You can't trust the performance numbers presented by the broker because the managers handling private accounts don't have to give this information to the public. And if they do make their numbers available, there's little to prevent them from exaggerating. In fact, the only thing federal law requires private managers to do is register with the Securities and Exchange Commission.

The trouble is, for all practical purposes, nobody oversees either these money managers or the numbers they report, says A. Michael Lipper, president of Lipper Analytical in New York City. "If I say to you that I'm up 100% for the quarter but forget to note the decimal point between the one and the first zero, I really don't have much to fear," Lipper says.

Numbers aside, there's also no way of knowing for sure that you're getting the broker's top-performing private money manager. Side deals often dictate selection. For example, many brokers require their private money managers to trade only through them. Of course, this means investors can't be assured of getting the best terms on transactions.

Source: Ronald Fink in *Financial World*, May 12, 1992.

Patience Is Needed

- *Don't* try to avoid risk by investing in CDs and other fixed-income instruments. Common stocks are the best way to make money—if history means anything. To be sure, common stocks fluctuate and

have occasional sinking spells. Even so, a properly diversified portfolio will provide you with riches—just be patient.

- *Don't* try to get rich by buying low-priced stocks. Investors think a
  $5 stock has an easier chance of doubling than one priced at $50,
  $75, or $100. Perhaps. But it's also easier to fall 50 percent because
  the $5 stock has to decline only $2\frac{1}{2}$ points to lose 50 percent of its
  value. In the October 26, 1993, issue of *Forbes*, Laszlo Birinyi Jr.
  reports on an interesting study done by his firm on this very idea.
  Here's what he says:

"We went through the *Standard & Poor's Stock Guide* for 1979 and
found 656 issues trading at $5 or less. Of that number, only 151 were
in business by the end of 1989, a decade later."

He goes on to say: "If you had bought 100 shares of every one of the
656 companies, it would have cost you $217,800. Ten years later? You
would have just over half of it left—$120,780 to be exact."

Birinyi contrasts this dismal experience with this statement: "Had
you instead invested the same amount in an index fund, based on the
Dow Jones industrials, you would have had close to $700,000—a gain
of 228 percent. And many Dow stocks paid dividends while you
owned them. The number of $5 stocks that mailed significant dividend
checks is probably somewhere between none and very few."

"Let's now move higher up the price scale. What happened if you
bought only stocks trading at $50 or over? We found 134 such in 1979 ....
In rough numbers, however, 100 shares of each of these, which would
have cost $812,000, were worth at least $2,170,000 at the end of the
decade."

Effort Is Needed

- *Do* spend some time on your portfolio. Read your annual and quarterly reports. You might also read the Standard & Poor's tear sheets
  or *Value Line Survey*. If you were going to buy a car, refrigerator, or
  house, you would make an effort. *Do* the same thing with your stocks.

Fretting and Stewing
Won't Help

- *Don't* fret every time one of your stocks drops a point or two. That's
  what stocks do. They go up, they go down. Over the long haul, they
  go up. But they don't do it every day. Quit being a nervous Nellie.

Table 20-1
Stocks ranked by the number of analysts following the company.

	Rate of return (%), twenty years ending 1987
Most observed (top 20 percent, or first quintile)	7.88
2nd quintile	10.39
3rd quintile	11.76
4th quintile	16.30
Least observed	19.93

- *Don't* plunk a large bundle of cash—your Aunt Mary just left you $200,000—into the market all at once. Because stocks fluctuate, invest the money over a period of months. This is called dollar cost averaging.

- *Don't* go crazy over utilities. We often see portfolios with eight or ten utilities—usually the worst ones, of course. Here is our formula for the utility segment: invest 3 percent of your common stocks in electric utilities, 3 percent in natural gas, 3 percent in telephone stocks, and 3 percent in water.

- *Don't* seek safety and comfort in stocks that are followed by every brokerage house on Wall Street. Statistics show that these stocks tend to be disappointing performers. In the 20 years ending 1987, for instance, the "most observed" stocks had an annual rate of return of 7.88 percent. By contrast, the "least observed" climbed an impressive 19.33 percent. Table 20-1, provided by Goldman Sachs, a large and prestigious Wall Street firm, shows stocks in terms of the number of analysts watching them.

If you have difficulty finding out how many analysts follow a particular stock, you can refer to the *Standard & Poor's Stock Guide* and check the number of institutional owners. A stock with many hundreds of institutional owners is certain to be one that is followed by dozens of analysts.

How to Deal with Your Broker

- *Don't* let your broker soak you for the full commission if you are a substantial investor. If the broker balks at giving you a discount, go somewhere else.

- *Don't* ever buy a new issue or a new underwriting. If the broker says there is no commission, don't buy. These products are for someone else. They rarely do well, and quite often they turn out to be disasters.

- *Do* buy stocks that have three characteristics: reasonably priced (based on yield or P/E); better than average growth of dividends, earnings, or book value; sound balance sheets—mostly equity, not debt.

Spice Up Your Portfolio with Foreign Stocks

- *Do* invest at least 20 percent of your common stock portfolio in foreign stocks. There are two reasons: U.S. stocks are presently quite high. Foreign markets fluctuate to a different drummer. Each market rises and falls, depending on local conditions. Thus, when the U.S. market is falling, several foreign markets are rising. Foreign stocks will make your portfolio less risky.

- *Do* make sure you examine the dividend payout ratio. This is calculated by dividing the annual earnings per share into the annual dividend. A low payout ratio indicates your company is interested in future growth. By retaining a large portion of earnings, the company can invest in new plants, research, and a strong sales force.

Another area to stay away from is that of complicated asset allocation strategies that claim they can tell you exactly when to flip from stocks to bonds or cash and then back again. Many are based on supposedly sophisticated computer formulas. With a high-powered computer and thousands of financial statistics to choose from, experts can find dozens of investment patterns that have moved in line with market changes in the past. Trouble is, history doesn't necessarily repeat. If there were formulas for successful investing, we'd all be rich.

Source: David Dreman in "The Contrarian" column, *Forbes*, August 15, 1993.

Even No-Load Funds
Aren't Free

- *Don't* become enamored with mutual funds. As a group, mutual funds underperform the market. One reason is cost. The average mutual fund charges 1.47 percent for expenses and management. That means that if the stocks in the portfolio are yielding 3 percent, you actually get only 1.53 percent. This applies to no-load mutual funds. Those that charge a commission may penalize you even more.

- *Don't* buy stock—or any other investment—over the telephone, unless you know the broker well. Disreputable brokers often call from faraway cities. Your name appears on their sucker list. The chances of their being honest are remote. No matter what they say, don't believe them. These "bucket shops" are constantly being prosecuted by the authorities. Frequently, you read about huge swindles. Sometimes the victims are intelligent, well-known people—in other words, successful people like you. After all, stupid people don't usually have the money to invest. What this means is this: even you can be hoodwinked. The best strategy is to hang up, particularly if they mispronounce your name.

You Can't Avoid Taxes
Forever

- Investors are often reluctant to take profits because they don't want to pay the tax. This reluctance can sometimes prove painful if the stock in question is vulnerable to a decline. The loss could be greater if you hold on to a stock that is destined to seek lower levels. Table 20-2 is a list of well-known stocks that plunged from their highs. In retrospect, it would have been a better strategy to sell them and pay the tax *before* the decline.

Low-Multiple Stocks Have
Winning Ways

- *Do* invest in stocks with low P/Es. One of the best strategies for investment success revolves around the price/earnings ratio (sometimes called the P/E or the multiple).

- Another proven strategy is to invest in the 10 stocks that have the highest yield in the Dow Jones Industrial Average. *Do* hold these stocks for one year and make appropriate changes so that you

Table 20-2
The penalty of not taking capital gains in time.

Stock	High ($)	Subsequent Low ($)
IBM	175.88	45.88
Merck	56.62	33.00
Pfizer	87.00	52.50
U.S. Surgical	134.50	25.38
Westinghouse Electric	39.38	9.38
Philip Morris	86.62	45.00
A.T. Cross	41.00	14.50
Columbia Gas	56.50	14.00
CMS Energy	39.62	14.88
Boeing	61.88	33.38
Tenneco	71.00	31.25
Jostens	38.62	16.50
Great Atlantic & Pacific	65.38	21.38

remain in the 10 stocks with the highest yield. You can find this list on page 3C of *The Wall Street Journal*.

- *Do* read at least one book on the stock market each year. This should be easy because there are a half dozen new ones published every month. You can read about them in an excellent publication called the *AAII Journal*, which is published by the American Association of Individual Investors. Speaking of good reading, don't forget the publications I discussed in Chapter 2: *Barron's, Forbes, Financial World, Fortune, The Wall Street Journal*, and *The New York Times*. The more you know, the fewer mistakes you'll make.

- *Don't* concentrate heavily in two or three industries, such as utilities, banks, and oil companies. A good rule of thumb is to invest no more than 10 percent in any single industry.

Characteristics to Look for When You Buy Stocks

- *Do* pick stocks with the following characteristics: a low P/E ratio, an above-average yield, a low dividend payout ratio, a sound balance sheet, a record of consistent dividend and earnings increases, ownership by insiders, a good sales force, and a management that thinks long term.

- *Do* pay attention to your stocks by reading annual and interim reports, if you are going to manage your own portfolio. Before you invest, compare the stock you want to acquire by reading about other companies in the same industry.

Companies Rarely Bite or Bark

- *Don't* be timid about calling the company if you want more information on a stock you are examining. The phone number can be found on the Standard & Poor's tear sheet. In most instances, the name of the investor contact is listed at the bottom of the second page. Have a list of questions ready, and fire away. You'll be surprised at how eager this person is to help you better understand the company.

Pitfalls of the Dividend Reinvestment Plan

- *Don't* be too quick to sign up for the dividend reinvestment program (DRIP). To be sure, this idea has merit because it permits you to reinvest your dividends at little or no cost. It also enables you to invest additional sums—sometimes up to several thousand dollars a year. On the other hand, the DRIP has some serious shortcomings. For one thing, there is usually a considerable delay in getting your money invested or liquidated because it has to be done by mail. In addition, the company may hold your investment until a specific date rather than investing it when it comes in. Meanwhile, the price could have changed by several points. Perhaps the biggest problem is taxes. When you sell your shares, you will have a horrendous job of calculating your cost basis. Each and every purchase—including every reinvested dividend—must be calculated separately.

- *Don't* get married to a stock. All stocks have times when they fall out of bed. Give serious thought to a disciplined sell strategy. Although it won't always prove correct, I believe that it makes sense to sell a stock when it drops 15 percent from its purchase price. Let's say you buy XYZ at $40. If it drops to $34, you should sell. What if it goes up, instead? If that occurs, move your sell price up. For instance, if the stock reaches $80, you would sell at $68 because 15 percent of $80 is $12. The advantage of this sell strategy is that it keeps you from suffering huge losses.

Avoiding the Perfect Stock

- *Don't* buy a stock that seems too perfect. It may have a clean balance sheet, excellent management, good products, and a long string of earnings increases. All too often, such stocks have low yields and high price/earnings ratios. They are typically overpriced. At the first sign of trouble, the stock price will come tumbling down.

Just how dependable are analysts' estimates?

The answer, I am afraid, is: They are utterly *undependable*.

In a previous *Forbes* article (December 9, 1991) I show that analysts missed their forecasts by an average of over 40% during the 1973–90 period. Adding to the insult, the estimates were made three months or less before the end of the quarter reported upon, and analysts could make changes up to two weeks before the end.... It was a comprehensive study. We used a sample of 67,375 analysts' quarterly estimates and included most of the large stocks on the New York and American stock exchanges between 1973 and 1990. A minimum of six analysts' estimates were required to avoid distortions caused by a few outlying forecasts; as many as 20 or more estimates were recorded for more widely followed companies.... Of what value are estimates that are seriously wrong two-thirds or three-quarters of the time? Not much.

Source: David Dreman in "The Contrarian" column, *Forbes*, October 11, 1993.

A Fond Farewell

A retired doctor called me from Florida this morning to ask me about a large French oil company, Elf Aquitaine. He informed me that he owned 30,000 shares of Elf. Because the stock sells for $35 a share, that works out to a million bucks. Either he's very rich, or he is a plunger. If there's one thing you should take away from *Straight Talk about Stock Investing*, it is this: diversify. I realize that doctors make quite a bit of money, but I can't believe they make enough to put $1 million into a single stock.

Even a veteran investor never knows ahead of time which stocks will be winners. Oftentimes, I'm quite surprised when a stock does better than I had originally expected. To illustrate: I paid $36 for ENDESA in 1993. It's a plain vanilla electric utility operating in Spain. This morning the stock was selling for $55 and had a yield of only 2.7 percent, or about one-half the yield provided by U.S. utilities. Never in my wildest dreams could I have predicted this would happen within a few short months.

So, when a well-meaning broker tells you his pet stock will go from $33 to $75, hang up the phone.

Predicting is impossible. I never do it.

By now, you should be well aware that I am a conservative investor who owns a gang of stocks because I like stocks and because I don't know exactly which ones are best.

You should also know that I pay attention to dividend yields, price/earnings ratios, balance sheets, dividend payout ratios, and institutional ownership. This is not exactly a complex idea—and certainly doesn't take a lot of time and research to implement.

Even if you are new to the game of investing, you should be able to fashion a portfolio that will lead to riches.

Oh, one thing more. Be patient. Rome was not built in a day. But the Roman Empire lasted 1000 years.

Which reminds me, my next book will be entitled *The Age of Caesar and Cicero*. If you buy a copy, I, too, will become rich—or, should I say "richer"?

Index

AAII Journal, 35, 259
Accelerated depreciation, 53
Account executive, 47
ADRs (*see* American depositary receipts)
Air Products, 229
Alcatel Alsthom (ALA), 5, 69, 74, 115,
    121–122, 244, 245
ALCOA, 95, 138, 175, 177, 179, 195, 238,
    239, 241
Allied Corporation, 232, 233
AlliedSignal, 84, 87, 90, 93–96, 138, 143,
    144, 165, 170, 175, 177, 179, 181, 184,
    185, 186, 187, 197
American Association of Individual
    Investors, 35
American Brands (AMB), 72, 74, 89, 90,
    140, 144, 167, 177, 183, 232
American Can, 84, 90, 94, 140, 177, 183,
    232
American depositary receipts (ADRs), 5,
    47, 112–123
American Express, 91–92, 96, 138, 139,
    141, 175, 179, 195, 197, 199
American Home Products, 238, 239, 243,
    245
American International Group, 238, 240,
    242, 244, 245
American Standard, 143
American Stock Exchange, 47
Ameritech, 163, 167, 229, 230
Amoco, 143, 144, 168, 247, 249
AMP, 238, 239, 242, 243
Anaconda, 177
Analyst, 48
Analysts' estimates, dependability of,
    261
Anheuser-Busch, 229
Annual reports, 48
Annual Report Service, Public Register, 11
Appreciation, 48
Asset, 48

Asset allocation, 3, 48, 64–65, 79–80, 161,
    216
    adjusting, 216–219
    and risk, 151
AT&T, 84, 87, 90, 91, 93, 96–97, 138, 140,
    143, 144, 165, 168, 176, 183, 195, 197,
    200, 232
A. T. Cross, 259

Back-testing, 8, 176
Balance sheet, 4, 48
Balanced mutual fund, 48
Ball Corporation, 228, 231, 247, 249
Baltimore Gas & Electric, 228, 231
Banc One, 248, 250
Banco Bilbao, 244, 250, 251
Bankers Trust, 229, 230
Bard, C. R., 229
Barnett Banks, 229
Barron's, 6, 35, 41, 42, 152
Basic industries, 69
Basic One, 228
Basic reports, 23
Basis point, 48
Bausch & Lomb, 229, 247, 248
Bay Tact Corporation, 11
Bear markets, 49, 89–93
Bell Atlantic, 163, 250
BellSouth, 144, 163
Belly-up, 49
Bemis, 108–110
    financial strength, 110
    growth, 109–110
    value, 109
    Value Line comments, 110
Beta coefficient, 148
Bethlehem Steel, 90, 94, 138, 140, 175, 177,
    179, 195
Big Board, 49
Birinyi, Laszlo, Jr., 261

Blue chip, 49
Boeing Corporation, 93, 138, 168, 175, 179, 195, 198, 200, 247, 249, 259
Bogle, John C., 58
Bogle on Mutual Funds (Bogle), 58
Bond, 49
Bond ratings, 49
Bonds, 3
Book value, 49
Bristol-Meyers Squibb (BMY), 68, 74, 228, 250
British Gas (BRG), 71, 74, 250
British Telecommunications (BTY), 5, 120–121, 244, 245
Brokers, 24, 256–257
Brown, Ferris, 228
Brown-Furman, 228, 231
Bruno's, 228
Bucket shops, 258
Building your portfolio, 9
Bull market, 49
Business Week, 6, 41
Buy and hold, 50

Call price, 50
Calls, 59
Capital Cities, 229, 230
Capital gain, 50
Capital goods companies, 69
Capital goods–technology, 70
Capital Holding, 229, 230
Capital-intensive, 50
Capitalization, 50
Carolina Power, 229, 230
Case histories, 9–10
Cash flow, 50, 149
Caterpillar, 138, 175, 179
Centerior Energy, 238, 240, 241
Central & South West, 248, 250
Certificates of deposit (CDs), 3, 18, 19, 51
Charming Shoppes, 228, 229
Chartered financial analyst (CFA), 51
Chemical New York, 233, 234
Chevron, 84, 87, 91–93, 95–97, 138, 141, 165, 175, 177, 183, 186, 195, 197, 199, 232
Chief executive officer (CEO), 51
Chief financial officer (CFO), 51
Chief operating officer (COO), 51

Chrysler Corporation, 177
Churning, 51
Citicorp, 143, 233, 234
Clean balance sheet, 51, 148–149
Clink, Mary, 42
Closed-end investment company, 51
CMS Energy, 259
Coastal Corporation, 229
Coca-Cola, 138, 152, 168, 175, 179, 181, 184, 185, 186, 187, 195, 198, 200, 229
Columbia Gas, 233, 259
Common stock fund, 52
Common stocks, 3, 4, 40–63, 155–156
    investment alternatives, 43
    losses in, 43–45
    stock market:
        beating, 45–46
        fear of, 42–43
Compound annual growth rate, 52
Conglomerates, 69
Conrail (CRR), 70, 74, 248
Consolidated Edison NY, 233
Consolidated Freight, 238, 240, 241
Consolidated Natural Gas, 233
Consolidated Papers, 100–101, 104, 105–107
    dividends, 105–106
    financial strength, 106–107
    insider purchases/sales, 101
    safety, 100–101
    timeliness, 100
Consolidated Rail Corporation (CRR), 74
Consumer cyclicals, 68–69
Consumer growth sector, 68
Consumer staples, 67, 70
Convertible bonds, 52
Cooper Industries, 228
Cooper Tire, 228, 229
CoreStates, 228, 231
Corning, 228
Coupon, 52
Coverage ratio, 52
CPC International, 143, 249
Crash of 1987, 18, 145
Credit cyclicals, 67, 68
CSX, 144, 170
Cumulative preferred stock, 52
Current assets, 52
Current liabilities, 53
Current ratio, 53
Cyclical industries, and risk, 151

Dayton Hudson, 229
Debenture, 53
Debt-to-equity ratio, 53
Deficit, 53
Deluxe, 230
Depreciation, 53
Detroit Edison, 143, 144, 167, 170, 229, 230
Digital Equipment, 247, 248
Dillards, 228
Dilution, 53
Discount rate, 34
Disney (*see* Walt Disney)
Diversification, 53, 64–81
     asset allocation, 3
     importance of, 3
     industries vs. sectors, 66–72, 253
     local stocks, 72–79
     and mutual funds, 2
     poor diversification, curing, 65–66
     and risk, 151
     rules to follow, 64–65
     ultimate portfolio, 72
Dividend Investor, The (Knowles/Petty), 82
Dividend payout ratio, 53
Dividend reinvestment plan (DRIP), 54,
     260–261
Dividend yield, 54, 101, 202–211
Dividends, 4, 54
Dollar cost averaging, 54, 146, 152–154
     forms of, 155
Dominion Resources, 228, 231
Dover Corporation (DOV), 71, 74, 228
Dow Jones, 228, 230
Dow Jones Averages, 54–55
Dow Jones Industrial Average, 2, 8, 18, 54,
     85, 89, 174
*Dow Jones–Irwin Guide to Using The Wall
     Street Journal* (Lehmann), 34
Dreman, David, 35, 44, 263, 267
DRIP (*see* Dividend reinvestment plan)
Duke Power, 148, 233
Dun & Bradstreet (DNB), 68, 74–75, 250
Du Pont, 84, 87, 91–93, 95–97, 138, 143,
     144, 168, 175, 177, 199, 232

Earnings, 55
Eastman Kodak, 84, 87, 91–92, 95–97, 138,
     141, 149–150, 151, 175, 177, 179, 183,
     187, 195, 197, 199, 232

Edleson, Michael E., 161
Effort, need for, 255
EG&G (EGG), 71, 75, 148–151, 243
Electric utilities, 253
Elf Aquitaine (ELF) [*see* Societe Nationale
     Elf Aquitaine (ELF)]
Eli Lilly, 44
Emergency reserve of living expenses, 20
Emerson Electric (EMR), 71, 75, 229, 230
ENDESA (ELE), 5, 116–118, 262, 268
Energy sector, 70
Enserch, 233
Equity capital, 50
Ericsson Telecomm, 5, 43, 59, 115
Esmark, 94, 177
Evensky, Harold, 20
Exchange rate mechanism (ERM), 55
Exit fees, 10
Exxon, 84, 90, 91–93, 95–97, 138, 140, 141,
     175, 177, 179, 183, 187, 195, 197, 228,
     230, 232, 233

Fabozzi, Frank J., 58
Fear of investing, 17–18, 42
Federal funds, 34
Federal funds rate, 55
Feldstein, Sylvan G., 58
Financial Analysts Journal, 24, 35–36, 42
Financial strength, 4, 106–107, 110, 147
     determining, 172
     measure of, 173–178
Financial World, 6
Financially weak stocks, buying, 4
Financials, 69
First International Bank, 233, 234
First Union, 228, 231
Fisher, Kenneth L., 35
Fixed-income securities, 55
Fixed-income trap, avoiding, 80
Fleetwood Enterprises (FLE), 68, 75
Fleming, 229
Florida Power & Light, 233
Forbes, 6, 35, 41, 57, 152
Foreign investing, 5, 112–123, 257
     Alcatel Alsthom (ALA), 121–122
     allocating percentage of portfolio to,
          112–113
     British Telecommunications (BTY),
          120–121

Foreign investing (*Cont.*):
  ENDESA (ELE), 116–118
  foreign currencies, fluctuations in,
    113–145
  Grand Metropolitan PLC (GRM), 119
  Hanson PLC, 116
  Hong Kong Telecommunications
    (HKT), 121
  reasons for buying, 113
  Repsol, S.A. (REP), 120
  and risk, 16
  Societe Nationale Elf Aquitaine (ELF),
    118–119
  taxes/dividends, 115–116
  Telefónica de España, S.A. (TEF), 122–123
  Vodafone Group PLC (VOD), 118
Four-factor stock selection method,
  220–236
  complexity of, 221–222
  development of, 222–223
  examples, 224–230
  historical performance, 231–233
  how to use, 234–236
  income, 230–231
  normalized P/E and payout ratios, 224
  payout ratio, 223
Fretting, uselessness of, 255–256
Front-end load mutual funds, 55
Fundamental analysis, 55

GATX, 144, 167, 170, 250
General Electric, 87, 138, 153, 168, 175,
  177, 179, 181, 183, 184, 185, 186, 187,
  195, 198, 200, 232, 244, 245
General Foods, 90, 94, 177, 232
General Mills, 144
General Motors, 84, 87, 90, 91, 93, 95–97,
  138, 140, 141, 143, 144, 152, 165, 175,
  177, 185, 186, 195, 197, 200, 232
Genuine Parts (GPC), 69, 75, 238, 239, 243,
  245
Glaxo, 250
Goal setting, 12–22
  retirement, 13–17
  selectivity, importance of, 19–22
  stock investments, 17–19
Goodyear Tire, 84, 94, 95, 96, 138, 140, 143,
  170, 175, 177, 179, 181, 185, 187, 195,
  232, 247, 248

Gould, Carole, 20
Graham, Benjamin, 42
Grainger, 229, 230
Grand Metropolitan PLC (GRM), 5, 72, 75,
  119
Great Atlantic & Pacific, 259
Great Lakes Chemical (GLK), 71, 75–76,
  243
Great Western Financial, 249
Greenmail, 55
Growth:
  characteristics of, determining, 150
  evaluating, 104
Growth portfolio, restructuring, 237–245

Hanson PLC (HAN), 69, 76, 116, 250, 251
Hemline theory, 55
Hewlett-Packard 12C, 104
  determining standard deviation with,
    86, 88
  how to use, 105
Hewlett-Packard Corporation, 168
Hickory 250, The, 237
Hickory Investment Advisors, 11, 151,
  237, 244, 253
  address, 11
High-payout ratios, 216
High-P/E stocks, 214
High yield, obsession with, 4–5
High-yield stocks, faltering of, 185–188
Hitachi Corporation, 238, 240, 244
Hong Kong Telecommunications (HKT),
  5, 115, 121
Houghton Mifflin, 44–45
Hubbell A, 250
Hubbell, Inc. (HUB.A), 71, 76
Hulbert, Mark, 35, 57

IBM, 87, 91–92, 97, 138, 141, 153, 168, 174,
  175, 179, 184, 185, 186, 187, 195, 197,
  199, 232, 259
  demise of, 134–135
INCO, 94, 167, 177
Income portfolio, restructuring, 246–251
Income statement, 56
Index fund, 56
Indicated yield, 56
Industries vs. sectors, 66–72, 253

Information sources, 6, 23–39
Inland Steel, 170
Insider buying/selling, 56
Institutional owners of stocks, number of,
     252
Intel (INTC), 59, 71, 76
Intelligent Investor (Graham), 43
International Harvester, 89, 90, 94, 177,
     183
International Paper, 84, 90, 138, 175, 177,
     179, 195, 238, 239, 242, 243
Interpublic Group of Companies, Inc.
     (IPG), 69, 76
Investment advisor, 56
Investment fears, 17–18, 42
Investment terminology, 6
Investor mistakes, 4–5
IPALCO Enterprises (IPL), 62, 71, 76

James River, 167
J.B. Hunt (JBHT), 59, 70, 76, 244
Jefferson-Pilot (JP), 70, 76
Johns-Manville, 89, 90, 94, 140, 177
Jostens, 259
J.P. Morgan, 92, 138, 139, 141, 175, 195, 199
Junk bonds, 56

Kimberly-Clark (KMB), 71, 77
Kink, Ronald, 254
Kmart Corporation (KM), 69, 77
Knowles, Harvey C. III, 82
Kroger, 238, 239, 241
KU Energy Corporation (KU), 71, 77

Lazarides, Steve, 59
Lehmann, Michael B., 34
Leverage, 56–57
Limit orders, 57
Limited partnerships, 57
Lincoln National (LNC), 70, 250
Lipper, A. Michael, 254
Lipper Analytical Services, 2, 254
Liquidity, 57
Local stocks, 72–79
Lone Star, 143
Low-cost producers, and risk, 152
Low-multiple stocks, 258–259

Lubrizol Corporation (LZ), 71, 77
Lynch, Peter, 61

Margin, 57
Marketing, as key to success, 152
Market letters, 57
Market timing, 57
Maturi, Richard J., 47
Maturity date, bonds, 49
McDonald's, 138, 175, 179, 181, 184, 185,
     186, 187, 195, 198, 200
McGee, Suzanne, 42
Merck, 138, 168, 174, 179, 181, 184, 185,
     186, 187, 195, 198, 200, 232, 259
Minnesota Mining & Manufacturing, 84,
     87, 91–92, 97, 138, 168, 175, 179, 184,
     195, 197, 200, 232
Mobil Corporation, 143, 144
Money-market funds, 3, 43, 58, 65, 155
Monsanto Corporation, 143, 144
Moody's Handbook of Common Stocks, 38
Morgan, J.P. (*see* J.P. Morgan)
Morningstar, 2
Morris, George, 35–36
Moving average, 58
Municipal Bond Handbook
     (Feldstein/Fabozzi/Pollack), 58
Municipal Bond Market (White), 58
Municipal bonds, 58
Mutual funds, 1–2, 58, 65, 252–253, 258

National City Corporation (NCC), 70, 77
Navistar, 89
Net worth, 58
New York Stock Exchange, 5, 27, 49, 58
New York Times, The, 24, 26
Niemiec, Dick, 27
No-load mutual funds, 2, 55, 58, 258
Nonconvertible bonds, 52
Norfolk Southern, 143, 144, 250
Northeast Utilities, 148
NYNEX, 163

Odd lot, 59
Options, 59
Over the counter (OTC), 59
Overtrading, 253

Owens-Illinois, 177, 232, 233

Pacific Telesis, 163
Packaged products, 24
Payout ratio, 59, 202–203, 216, 221–226
Penny stock, 59
P/E ratio [see Price/earnings (P/E) ratio]
Perfect stock, avoiding, 261
Pfizer, 168, 259
Philip Morris, 84, 87, 89, 93, 138, 174, 175,
      179, 181, 184, 185, 186, 187, 195, 198,
      199, 247, 249, 251, 259
Phillips, Don, 2
Picking stocks, systematic methods of, 5–6
Planning, 22
Point, 59
Poison pill, 59
Pollack, Irving M., 58
Popular stocks, 252, 256
Portfolio manager, 59–60
Portfolio restructuring, 9
PPG, 249
Predictions, personal, 253
Preferred stock, 60
Price/earnings (P/E) ratio, 60, 102,
      220–227, 264–265
Price range, 60
Price-to-book value, 103, 149
Price-to-cash-flow ratio, 103, 149
Price-to-revenues ratio, 102, 149
Prime rate, 34, 60
Primerica, 93, 165, 186
Procter & Gamble, 138, 152, 175, 177, 179,
      183, 195, 198, 200, 232, 243
Prospectus, 60
Public Register's Annual Report Service, 11
Public utilities, 55, 60, 69, 148, 256
   coverage ratio, 52
   and diversification, 66
   electric, 253
   rate base, 61
Publications, 24–25
Puts, 59

Quality, determining, 172–173

Random walk theory, 60–61

Rate base, 61
Raytheon, 167
Reports, Wall Street firms, 25
Repsol, S.A. (REP), 115, 120, 243
Research, 150–151
Retirement, 13–17
   forced, 13
   investing in your future, 14–15
   preparing for, 15–16
   Social Security, 14–16
Reuters (RTRSY), 59, 68, 77
Risk, reducing, 42, 146–156
   and asset allocation, 151
   clean balance sheet, 51, 148–149
   cyclical industries, 151
   and diversification, 151
   dollar cost averaging, 152–154
   financial strength, 147
   foreign investing, 16
   growth characteristics, determining,
      150, 152
   research, 150–151
   value, examining carefully, 149–150
   Value Line risk measures, 148
   yield, avoiding extremes in, 146–147
R.J. Reynolds, 143
Roadway Services (ROAD), 59, 70, 77–78
Round lot, 61
Royal Dutch Petroleum (RD), 5, 72, 78,
      249, 251
R.R. Donnelly, 228

Sara Lee, 243, 245
SCEcorp, 143, 144, 167, 170, 238, 240
Schlumberger, 168
Sears, Roebuck, 84, 87, 91–93, 95–97, 137,
      138, 139, 140, 141, 174, 175, 177, 179,
      181, 183, 184, 185, 186, 187, 195, 197,
      199, 232, 249
Sectors, 66–72, 253
Selectivity, importance of, 19–22
Selling stock, 213–219
Sherwin-Williams Company (SHW), 78
Shook, R. J., 47
Shook, R. L., 47
Short selling, 61
Skyline Corp. (SKY), 68
Slatter System, 6–9
Snap-On Tools (SNA), 68, 78

Social Security, 14–16
Societe Nationale Elf Aquitaine (ELF), 5,
    72, 75, 118–119, 243, 261
Southern Company, 248
Southwestern Bell, 163
Spin-offs, 174
Standard & Poor's:
    address, 36
    tear sheets, 38–39, 255
Standard & Poor's 500, 2
Standard & Poor's Midcap 400 Guide, 38
Standard & Poor's Stock and Bond Guide,
    36
Standard & Poor's Stock Guide, 24, 36–37,
    86, 147, 172, 202
Standard deviation, 61, 84–88, 173
Standard Oil California, 90, 94
Stanley Works, 238, 239, 243
Stock:
    buying:
        characteristics to look for, 259–260
        examining before, 6
        over the telephone, 258
    failure to examine before buying, 4
    institutional owners of, number of, 252
    and risk, 155–156
    sentimental attachment to, 5, 253
    when to sell, 213–219
Stock analysis, 99–111
    Bemis example, 108–109
    Consolidated Papers example, 100–101,
        104, 105–107
    growth, 104
    value, determining, 101–104
    Westvaco Corporation example,
        107–108
Stock dividend, 61
Stock investments, 17–19
Stock market:
    bear markets, 89–93
    beating, 45–46
    dealing with ups and downs of, 80–81
    favorites, avoiding, 83–84
    fear of, 42–43
    historical portfolio performance, 94–98
    playing, 83–98
    standard deviation, 84–88
Stock-picking systems, 5–6
    example of, 6–9
    fallibility of, 89

Stock splits, 61
Stock ticker symbols, 61–62
    memorizing, 33–34
Stone, Amey, 2
Straight-line depreciation, 53
Straight Talk about Mutual Funds, 58
Subsidiary, 61
Symbol, 61–62
Syntex, 238, 239, 243

Take-or-pay contract, 62
Taxes, 258
Tax-loss carry forwards, 62
Tear sheets, Standard & Poor's, 38–39
Tektronix, 148, 150–151
Telefónica de España, S.A. (TEF),
    122–123
Templeton, John, 42
Tenneco, 259
Texaco Inc. (TX), 72, 78, 84, 87, 90, 91–92,
    95–97, 138, 140, 141, 175, 177, 179, 183,
    184, 187, 195, 197, 199, 232
Texas Instruments, 238, 239, 241
Textron (TXT), 69, 244
Ticker symbols, 61–62
    memorizing, 33–34
Times Mirror, 247, 248
Timken, 167, 170
Transportation sector, 69
TRW, 144, 167, 170, 247, 249
12b-1 charges, 10
Turnover, 242

Unilever, N.V. (UN), 5, 67, 72, 78
Union Carbide, 84, 90, 91–93, 95–97, 137,
    138, 139, 140, 141, 143, 165, 174, 175,
    177, 179, 184, 186, 195, 197, 199, 232,
    238, 239, 241
United Technologies Corporation (UTX),
    71, 78–79, 87, 90, 91–93, 97, 139, 165,
    175, 177, 179, 195, 197, 199, 232, 233,
    249
USG, 143
U.S. Steel, 89, 90, 140
U.S. Surgical, 153, 259
US West, 163
USX, 84, 87, 93, 95, 96, 177
Utilities (*see* Public utilities)

Value, 101–111
  determining, 101–104
    dividend yield, 54, 101, 202–211
    price/earnings (P/E) ratio, 60, 102
    price-to-book value, 103
    price-to-cash-flow ratio, 103
    price-to-revenues ratio, 102
  and risk, 149–150
Value Line Survey, 24, 37–38, 110, 152, 219, 255
  company groupings, 38
  and company P/Es, 104
  compared to Standard & Poor's tear sheets, 38–39
  risk measures, 148
Vodafone Group PLC (VOD), 118
Vujovich, Dian, 58

Walgreen, 229
Wall Street Dictionary, The (Shook/Shook), 47
Wall Street Journal, The, 24, 26–34, 41, 70, 82, 152, 202
  annual dividend, 34
  most active stocks, 31–33
  new high list, 27–29, 34
  new low list, 27–31, 34
  ticker symbols, memorizing, 33–34
  volume of trading, 34
Wall Street Words (Maturi), 47
Wal-Mart, 229

Walt Disney, 138, 175, 179, 195, 228, 229
Westinghouse Electric, 87, 91–92, 94, 96, 97, 137, 139, 141, 167, 175, 177, 179, 181, 183, 184, 185, 186, 187, 195, 197, 199, 250, 259
Westvaco Corporation, 107–108
  distortion, warning against, 108
  growth, 108
  value evaluation, 107
Weyerhaeuser, 167, 170, 247, 249
White, Wilson, 58
White knight, 62
Wholesale eradication, avoiding, 240–241
Williamson, Gordon, 117
Winners, selling, 253
Wire house, 62
Wisconsin Energy, 143, 144, 167, 170
Woolworth, 90, 91–94, 97, 139, 141, 177, 178, 179, 184, 195, 197, 199, 232, 233, 249
Working capital, 62
Worthington, 247, 248
WRAP accounts, 254
Wrigley, 143

Yield, 54, 101, 202–211
  avoiding extremes in, 146–147
  high, obsession with, 4–5
Yield to maturity, 62

Zero coupon bonds, 63

About the Author

John Slatter has more than 30 years of stock market experience as a broker, security analyst, portfolio manager, and financial writer. Currently he is the senior portfolio strategist for the Cleveland-based Hickory Investment Advisors, Inc., which specializes in managing portfolios for investors. Best known for his famous Dow 10 stock-picking strategy, Mr. Slatter is frequently quoted by *The Wall Street Journal, The New York Times, The Christian Science Monitor, Money*, and scores of syndicated columns and advisory letters. He is the author of the book *Safe Investing* and numerous articles for *Barron's*.